The Road to
Little Dribbling

Also by Bill Bryson

The Last Continent

Mother Tongue

Neither Here Nor There

Made in America

Notes from a Small Island

A Walk in the Woods

I'm a Stranger Here Myself

In a Sunburned Country

Bryson's Dictionary of Troublesome Words

Bill Bryson's African Diary

A Short History of Nearly Everything

A Short History of Nearly Everything: Special Illustrated Edition

The Life and Times of the Thunderbolt Kid

Shakespeare: The World as Stage

Bryson's Dictionary for Writers and Editors

At Home: A Short History of Private Life

At Home: A Short History of Private Life: Illustrated Edition

One Summer

BILL BRYSON

The Road to

LITTLE

DRIBBLING

ADVENTURES OF AN AMERICAN IN BRITAIN

Doubleday

NEW YORK · LONDON · TORONTO · SYDNEY · AUCKLAND

Book design by Michael Collica
Jacket design by Roberto de Vicq de Cumptich and John Fontana
Jacket photographs: landscape © Brian Jannsen / Alamy Stock Photo; sheep © Jodie Nash /
Shutterstock; mailbox © Dostoevsky / Shutterstock; sky © Shutterstock

Library of Congress Cataloging-in-Publication Data
Names: Bryson, Bill, author.
Title: The road to Little Dribbling : adventures of an American in Britain /
by Bill Bryson.
Description: New York, NY : Doubleday, an Imprint of
Penguin Random House, [2016]
Identifiers: LCCN 2015027450   ISBN 9780385539289 (hardcover)
ISBN 9780385539296 (eBook)
Subjects: LCSH: Bryson, Bill—Travel—Great Britain.
Great Britain—Description and travel.   Great Britain—Civilization—21st century.
Classification: LCC DA632 .B79 2016   DDC 914.104/8612—dc23 LC record available
at http://lccn.loc.gov/2015027450

MANUFACTURED IN THE UNITED STATES OF AMERICA

1 3 5 7 9 10 8 6 4 2

First United States Edition

To James, Rosie, and Daphne. Welcome.

Contents

Prologue   1

  1. Bugger Bognor!   15

  2. Seven Sisters   31

  3. Dover   40

  4. London   50

  5. Motopia   66

  6. A Great Park   75

  7. Into the Forest   89

  8. Beside the Seaside   107

  9. Day Trips   121

 10. To the West   140

 11. Devon   153

 12. Cornwall   167

 13. Ancient Britain   186

 14. East Anglia   196

 15. Cambridge   214

 16. Oxford and About   224

 17. The Midlands   239

 18. It's So Bracing!   251

 19. The Peak District   264

 20. Wales   279

 21. The North   295

22. Lancashire   311
23. The Lakes   324
24. Yorkshire   339
25. Durham and the Northeast   348
26. To Cape Wrath (and Considerably Beyond)   361

Afterword and Acknowledgments   379

Cape Wrath
John o'Groats
Dunnet Head
Culloden
Ullapool
Inverness
Glenelg
Glencoe
North Berwick
Edinburgh
Newcastle
Durham
Barnard Castle
St. Bees
Leyburn
Sellafield
Barrow-in-Furness
Kirkby Lonsdale
Blackpool
Lytham
Grimsby
Liverpool
Manchester
Llandudno
Buxton
Skegness
Sheringham
Cromer
Alderley Edge
Ashbourne
Overstrand
Happisburgh
Dunwich
Ironbridge
Cambridge
Aberystwyth
Birmingham
Aldeburgh
Fishguard
Blenheim Palace
Sutton Hoo
Uffington
Oxford
LONDON
South Foreland
Windsor
Avebury
Virginia Water
Staines
Tintagel
Stonehenge
Dover
Lost Gardens of Heligan
Lyme Regis
Bournemouth
Eastleigh
Eastbourne
Penzance
Torquay
Christchurch
Bognor Regis
Brighton & Hove
Mousehole
Totnes
Dartmouth
Lyndhurst
Salcombe

IRISH SEA
NORTH SEA
The Bryson Line
N.G.

The Road to
Little Dribbling

Prologue

I

ONE OF THE THINGS that happens when you get older is that you discover lots of new ways to hurt yourself. Recently, in France, I was hit square on the head by an automatic parking barrier, something I don't think I could have managed in my younger, more alert years.

There are really only two ways to get hit on the head by a parking barrier. One is to stand underneath a raised barrier and purposely allow it to fall on you. That is the easy way, obviously. The other method—and this is where a little diminished mental capacity can go a long way—is to forget the barrier you have just seen rise, step into the space it has vacated and stand with lips pursed while considering your next move, and then be taken completely by surprise as it slams down on your head like a sledgehammer on a spike. That is the method I went for.

Let me say right now that this was a serious barrier—like a scaffolding pole with momentum—and it didn't so much fall as crash back into its cradle. The venue for this adventure in cranial trauma was an open-air parking lot in a pleasant coastal resort in Normandy called Etretat, not far from Deauville, where my wife and I had gone for a few days. I was alone at this point, however, trying to find my way to a cliff-top path at the far side of the parking lot, but the way was blocked by the barrier, which was too low

1

for a man of my dimensions to duck under and much too high to vault. As I stood hesitating, a car pulled up, the driver took a ticket, the barrier rose, and the driver drove on through. This was the moment that I chose to step forward and to stand considering my next move, little realizing that it would be mostly downward.

Well, I have never been hit so startlingly and hard. Suddenly I was both the most bewildered and relaxed person in France. My legs buckled and folded beneath me and my arms grew so independently lively that I managed to smack myself in the face with my elbows. For the next several minutes my walking was, for the most part, involuntarily sideways. A kindly lady helped me to a bench and gave me a square of chocolate, which I found I was still clutching the next morning. As I sat there, another car passed through and the barrier fell back into place with a reverberating clang. It seemed impossible that I could have survived such a violent blow. But then, because I am a little paranoid and given to private histrionics, I became convinced that I had in fact sustained grave internal injuries, which had not yet revealed themselves. Blood was pooling inside my head, like a slowly filling bath, and at some point soon my eyes would roll upward, I would issue a dull groan, and quietly tip over, never to rise again.

The positive side of thinking you are about to die is that it does make you glad of the little life that is left to you. I spent most of the following three days gazing appreciatively at Deauville, admiring its tidiness and wealth, going for long walks along its beach and promenade, or just sitting and watching the rolling sea and blue sky. Deauville is a very fine town. There are far worse places to tip over.

One afternoon as my wife and I sat on a bench facing the English Channel, I said to her, in my new reflective mood, "I bet whatever seaside town is directly opposite on the English side will be depressed and struggling, while Deauville remains well-off and lovely. Why is that, do you suppose?"

"No idea," my wife said. She was reading a novel and didn't accept that I was about to die.

"What *is* opposite us?" I asked.

"No idea," she said and turned a page.

"Weymouth?"

"No idea."

"Hove maybe?"

"Which part of 'no idea' are you struggling to get on top of?"

I looked on her smartphone. (I'm not allowed a smartphone of my own because I would lose it.) I don't know how accurate her maps are—they often urge us to go to Michigan or California when we are looking for some place in Worcestershire—but the name that came up on the screen was Bognor Regis.

I didn't think anything of this at the time, but soon it would come to seem almost prophetic.

II

I first came to England at the other end of my life, when I was still quite young, just twenty.

In those days, for a short but intensive period, a very high proportion of all in the world that was worth taking note of came out of Britain. The Beatles, James Bond, Mary Quant and miniskirts, Twiggy and Justin de Villeneuve, Richard Burton and Elizabeth Taylor's love life, Princess Margaret's love life, the Rolling Stones, the Kinks, suit jackets without collars, television series like *The Avengers* and *The Prisoner*, spy novels by John le Carré and Len Deighton, Marianne Faithfull, Petula Clark, Dusty Springfield, quirky movies starring David Hemmings and Terence Stamp that we didn't quite get in Iowa, Harold Pinter plays that we didn't get at all, Peter Cook and Dudley Moore, *That Was the Week That Was*, the Profumo scandal—practically everything really.

Advertisements in magazines like *The New Yorker* and *Esquire* were full of British products in a way they never would be again—Gilbey's and Tanqueray gin, Harris tweeds, BOAC airliners, Aquascutum suits and Viyella shirts, Keens felted hats, Alan Paine sweaters, Daks trousers, MG and Austin Healey sports cars, a hundred varieties of Scotch whisky. It was clear that if you wanted quality and suavity in your life, it was British goods that were in large part going to supply it. Not all of this made a great deal of sense even then, it must be said. A popular cologne of the day was called Pub. I am not at all sure what resonances that was supposed to evoke. I have been drinking in England for forty years and I can't say that I have ever encountered anything in a pub that I would want to rub on my face.

Because of all the attention we gave Britain, I thought I knew a fair amount about the place, but I quickly discovered upon arriving that I was very wrong. I couldn't even speak my own language there. In the first few days, I failed to distinguish between *collar* and *color, khaki* and *car key, letters* and *lettuce, bed* and *bared, karma* and *calmer.*

Needing a haircut, I ventured into a unisex hairdresser's in Oxford, where the proprietress, a large and vaguely forbidding woman, escorted me to a chair, and there informed me crisply: "Your hair will be cut by a vet today."

I was taken aback. "Like a person who treats sick animals?" I said, quietly horrified.

"No, her *name* is Yvette," she replied and with the briefest of gazes into my face made it clear that I was the most exhausting idiot that she had encountered in some time.

In a pub I asked what kind of sandwiches they had.

"Ham and cheese," the man said.

"Oh, yes please," I said.

"Yes please what?" he said.

"Yes please, ham and cheese," I said, but with less confidence.

"No, it's ham *or* cheese," he explained.

"You don't do them both together?"

"No."

"Oh," I said, surprised, then leaned toward him and in a friendly but confidential tone said: "Why not? Too flavorful?"

He stared at me.

"I'll have cheese then, please," I said contritely.

When the sandwich came, the cheese was extravagantly shredded—I had never seen a dairy product distressed before serving—and accompanied by what I now know was Branston pickle, but what looked to me then like what you find when you stick your hand into a clogged sump.

I nibbled it tentatively and was pleased to discover that it was delicious. Gradually it dawned on me that I had found a country that was wholly strange to me and yet somehow marvelous. It is a feeling that has never left me.

My time in Britain describes a kind of bell curve, starting at the bottom left-hand corner in the "Knows Almost Nothing at All" zone, and rising in a gradual arc to "Pretty Thorough Acquaintanceship" at the top. Having attained this summit, I assumed that I would remain there permanently, but recently I have begun to slide down the other side toward ignorance and bewilderment again as increasingly I find myself living in a country that I don't altogether recognize. It is a place full of celebrities whose names I don't know and talents I cannot discern, of acronyms (BFF, TMI, TOWIE) that have to be explained to me, of people who seem to be experiencing a different kind of reality from the one I know.

I am constantly at a loss in this new world. Recently I closed my door on a caller because I couldn't think what else to do with him. He was a meter reader. At first I was pleased to see him. We haven't had a meter reader at our house since Edward Heath was prime minister, so I let him in gladly and even fetched a stepladder so that he could climb up and get a clear reading. It was only when he departed and returned a minute later that I began to regret our deepening relationship.

"Sorry, I also need to read the meter in the men's room," he told me.

"I beg your pardon?"

"It says here there is a second meter in the men's room."

"Well, we don't have a men's room because this is a house, you see."

"It says here it's a school."

"Well, it's not. It's a house. You were just in it. Did you see roomfuls of young people?"

He thought hard for a minute.

"Do you mind if I have a look around?"

"I beg your pardon?"

"Just a little look. Won't take five minutes."

"You think you're going to find a men's room that we have somehow overlooked?"

"You never know!" he said brightly.

"I'm shutting the door now because I don't know what else to do," I said and shut the door. I could hear him making mild bleatings through the wood. "Besides, I have an important appointment," I called back through the wood. And it was true. I did have an important appointment—one, as it happens, that has everything to do with the book that follows. I was about to go to Eastleigh to take a British citizenship test.

The irony of this was not lost on me. Just as I was becoming thoroughly remystified by life in modern Britain, I was being summoned to demonstrate that I understood the place.

III

For a long time, there were two ways to become a British citizen. The first, the trickier but paradoxically much the more common method, was to find your way into a British womb and wait for nine months. The other way was to fill out some forms and swear an oath. Since 2005, however, people in the second category have additionally had to demonstrate proficiency in English and pass a knowledge test.

I was excused the language test because English is my native tongue, but no one is excused the knowledge test, and it's tough. No matter how well you think you know Britain, you don't know the things you need to know to pass the Life in Britain Knowledge Test. You need to know, for instance, who Sake Dean Mahomet was. (He was the man who introduced shampoo to Britain. Honestly.) You need to know by what other name the 1944 Education Act is known. (The Butler Act.) You need to know when life peerages were created (1958) and in what year the maximum length of a working day for women and children was reduced to ten hours (1847). You have to be able to identify Jenson Button, the racing car driver. (No point asking why.) You can be denied citizenship if you don't know the number of member states in the Commonwealth, who Britain's enemies in the Crimean War were, the percentages of people who describe themselves as Sikh, Muslim, Hindu, or Christian, and the actual name of the Big Ben tower. (It's the Elizabeth Tower.) You even have to know a few things that aren't in fact true. If, for instance, you are asked, "What are the two most distant points on the British mainland?" you have to say, "Land's End and John o'Groats" even though they are not. This is one tough test.

To prepare, I ordered the full set of study guides, consisting of a shiny paperback called *Life in the United Kingdom: A Guide for New Residents* and two auxiliary volumes: an *Official Study Guide,* which tells you how to use the first book (essentially, start at page one and move through the following pages one at a time, in order), and a volume of *Official Practice Questions and Answers*, containing seventeen practice tests. Naturally, I did a couple of these before reading a word of the study guides and was horrified at how poorly I did.

The study guide is an interesting book, nicely modest, a little vacuous at times, but with its heart in the right place. Britain, you learn, is a country that values courtesy and fair play, is rather good at art and literature, venerates democratic ideals, and has often shown itself to be commendably inventive, especially around things that run on steam. The people are a generally decent lot who garden, go for walks in the country, eat roast beef and Yorkshire pudding on Sundays (unless they are Scottish, in which case they may go for haggis). They holiday at the seaside, queue patiently, vote sensibly, respect the police, cherish the monarch, and practice moderation in all things. Occasionally they go to a public house (or "pub") to drink a responsibly modest amount of good English ale and to have a friendly chat or a game of skittles. (You sometimes feel that the people who wrote the guidebook should get out more.)

At times the book is so careful about being inoffensive that it doesn't actually say anything at all, as in this discussion, given here in full, of the contemporary music scene: "There are many different venues and musical events that take place across the UK." Thank you for that rich insight. (And I don't like to be a smart aleck, but venues don't take place. They just are.) Sometimes the book is simply wrong, as when it declares that Land's End and John o'Groats are maximally remote, and sometimes it is dubious and wrong. It cites the actor Anthony Hopkins as the kind of person Britons can be proud of without apparently pausing to reflect that Anthony Hopkins is now an American citizen living in California. It also misspells his first name. It calls the literary area of Westminster

Abbey "Poet's Corner," perhaps in the belief that they keep only one poet at a time there. Generally, I try not to be overfussy about these things, but if it is a requirement that people who take the test should have a full command of English, then perhaps it would be an idea to make certain that those responsible for the test demonstrate a similar proficiency.

And so, after a month's hard study, the day of my test arrived. My instructions were to present myself at the appointed hour at a place called Wessex House in Eastleigh, Hampshire, the nearest testing center to my home. Eastleigh is a satellite of Southampton and appears to have been bombed heavily during the Second World War, though perhaps not quite heavily enough. It is an interestingly unmemorable place—not numbingly ugly but not attractive either; not wretchedly poor but not prosperous; not completely dead in the center, but clearly not thriving. The bus station was just an outer wall of a Sainsbury's supermarket with a glass marquee over it, evidently to give pigeons a dry place to shit.

Like many British towns, Eastleigh has closed its factories and workshops, and instead is directing all its economic energies into the making and drinking of coffee. There were essentially two types of shop in the town: empty shops and coffee shops. Some of the empty shops, according to signs in their windows, were in the process of being converted into coffee shops, and many of the coffee shops, judging by their level of custom, looked as if they weren't far from becoming empty shops again. I am no economist, but I am guessing that that's what is known as a virtuous circle. One or two more adventurous entrepreneurs had opened discount stores or betting shops, and a few charities had taken over other abandoned premises, but on the whole Eastleigh seemed to be a place where you could either have a cup of coffee or sit and watch pigeons defecate. I had a cup of coffee, for the sake of the economy, watched a pigeon defecate across the way, then presented myself at Wessex House for my test.

Five of us were present for testing on this particular morning. We were shown to a roomful of desks, each with a computer screen and a mouse sitting on a plain mat, and seated so that we couldn't see anyone else's screen. Once settled, we were given a practice test of four questions to make sure we were comfortably in command of our mouse and mousepad. Because it was a practice test, the questions were encouragingly easy, along the lines of:

Manchester United is:

(a) a political party

(b) a dance band

(c) an English football team

It took about fifteen seconds for four of us to answer the practice questions, but one lady—pleasant, middle-aged, slightly plumpish, I am guessing from one of those Middle Eastern countries where they eat a lot of sticky sweets—took considerably longer. Twice the supervisor came to see if she was all right. I passed the time discreetly looking in my desk drawers—they were unlocked but empty—and seeing if there was any way to have fun moving a cursor around a blank screen. There isn't.

At length the woman announced that she had finished and the supervisor came to check her work. He bent to her screen and in a tone of quiet amazement said: "You've missed them all."

She beamed uncertainly, not sure if this was an achievement.

"Do you want to try them again?" the supervisor asked helpfully. "You're entitled to try again."

The woman gave every appearance of having no very clear idea of what was going on, but gamely elected to press on, and so the test began.

The first question was: "You've seen Eastleigh. Are you sure you want to stay in Britain?" Actually, I don't recall what the first question was or any of those that followed. We weren't allowed to bring anything to the desk, so I couldn't take notes or tap my teeth thoughtfully with a pencil. The test consisted of twenty-four multiple-choice questions and took only about three minutes. You either know the answers or you don't. I presented myself at the supervisor's desk upon completion, and we waited together while the computer checked my answers, a process that took about as long as the test itself, and at last he told me with a smile that I had passed, but he couldn't tell me exactly how I did. The computer only indicated pass or fail.

"I'll just print out your result," he said. This took another small age. I was hoping for a smart parchment-like certificate, like you get when you do a first aid course, but it was just a faintly printed letter confirming that I was certified as intellectually fit for life in modern Britain.

Beaming like the lady from the Middle East (who appeared to be hunting around for a keyboard when last I glimpsed her), I left the building feeling pleased, even a little exhilarated. The sun was shining. Across the way at the bus station, two young men were having a morning aperitif from matching cans of lager. A pigeon picked at a cigarette butt and squeezed out a little shit. Life in modern Britain, it seemed to me, was pretty good.

IV

A day or so later, I met my publisher, a kindly and much loved fellow named Larry Finlay, for lunch in London, to discuss a subject for my next book. Larry lives in quiet dread that I will suggest some ludicrously uncommercial topic—a biography of Mamie Eisenhower, perhaps, or something on Canada—and so always tries to head me off with an alternative suggestion.

"Do you know," he said, "it's twenty years since you wrote *Notes from a Small Island*?" (This was my first book about Britain. It did awfully well there.)

"Twenty years?" I replied, amazed at how much past one can accumulate without any effort at all.

"Ever thought about a sequel?"

I considered for a moment. "Actually there is a certain timeliness to that," I said. "I'm just about to take out British citizenship, you know."

"Really?" Larry said. In his eyes, I could see little glinting pound signs where his pupils normally were. "You're giving up your American citizenship?"

"No, I keep it. I'll have British and American both."

Larry was suddenly racing ahead. Marketing plans were forming in his head. Underground posters—not the really big ones, the much smaller kind—were springing to mind. "You can take stock of your new country," he said.

"I don't want to end up going back to all the same places and writing about all the same things," I said decisively.

"Then go to different places," Larry agreed. "Go to"—he searched for a name to nominate, somewhere no one's ever been— "Bognor Regis."

I looked at him with interest. "That's the second reference I have heard to Bognor Regis this week," I said.

"Think of it as a sign," Larry said.

Later that afternoon, at home, I pulled out my ancient and falling-apart *AA Complete Atlas of Britain* just to have a look. Apart from anything else I was curious to see what is the longest distance you can travel in Britain in a straight line. It is most assuredly not from Land's End to John o'Groats, despite what my official study guide had said. (What it said, for the record, is: "The longest distance on the mainland is from John o'Groats on the north coast of Scotland to Land's End in the southwest corner of England. It is about 870 miles.") For one thing, the northernmost outcrop of mainland is not John o'Groats but Dunnet Head, eight miles to the west, and at least six other nubbins of land along that same stretch of coastline are more northerly than John o'Groats. But the real issue is that a journey from Land's End to John o'Groats would require a series of zigzags to overcome Britain's irregular shape. If you allow zigzags, then you could carom about the country in any pattern you wished and thus make the distance effectively infinite. I wanted to know what was the farthest you could travel in a straight line without crossing salt water. Laying a ruler across the page, I discovered to my surprise that the ruler tilted away from Land's End and John o'Groats, like a deflected compass needle. The longest straight line actually started at the top left-hand side of the map at a lonely Scottish promontory called Cape Wrath. The bottom, even more interestingly, went straight through Bognor Regis.

Larry was right. It was a sign.

For the briefest of periods, I considered the possibility of traveling through Britain along my newly discovered line (the Bryson Line, as I would like it now to become generally known, since I was the one who discovered it), but I could see almost at once that that wouldn't be practical or even desirable. It would mean, if I took it literally, going through people's houses and yards, tramping across trackless fields, and fording rivers, which was clearly crazy; and if I just tried to stay close to it, it would mean endlessly picking my way through suburban streets in places like Macclesfield and Wolverhampton, which didn't sound terribly rewarding either. But I could certainly use the Bryson Line as a kind of beacon, to guide my way. I determined that I would begin and end at its terminal points, and visit it from time to time en route when I conveniently could and when I remembered to do so, but I wouldn't force myself to follow it religiously. It would be, rather, my *terminus ad quem*, whatever exactly that means. Along the way, I would, as far as possible, avoid the places I went on the first trip (too much danger of standing on a corner and harrumphing at how things had deteriorated since I was last there) and instead focus on places I had never been, in the hope I could see them with fresh, unbiased eyes.

I particularly liked the idea of Cape Wrath. I know nothing about it—it could be a caravan park, for all I know—but it sounded rugged and wave-battered and difficult to get to, a destination for a serious traveler. When people asked me where I was bound, I could gaze toward the northern horizon with a set expression and say: "Cape Wrath, God willing." I imagined my listeners giving a low whistle of admiration and replying, "Gosh, that's a long way." I would nod in grim acknowledgment. "Not even sure if there's a tearoom," I would add.

But before that distant adventure, I had hundreds of miles of historic towns and lovely countryside to get through, and a visit to the celebrated English seaside at Bognor.

Chapter 1

Bugger Bognor!

BEFORE I WENT THERE for the first time, about all I knew about Bognor Regis, beyond how to spell it, was that some British monarch, at some uncertain point in the past, in a moment of deathbed acerbity, called out the words "Bugger Bognor" just before expiring, though which monarch it was and why his parting wish on earth was to see a medium-sized English coastal resort sodomized are questions I could not answer.

The monarch, I have since learned, was King George V, and the story is that in 1929 he traveled to Bognor on the advice of his physician, Lord Dawson of Penn, who proposed that a spell of fresh sea air might help him recover from a serious lung complaint. That Dawson could think of no better treatment than a change of scene is perhaps a reflection of his most outstanding characteristic as a doctor: incompetence. Dawson was in fact so celebrated for medical ineptitude that a ditty was composed in his honor. It went:

Lord Dawson of Penn
Has killed lots of men.
So that's why we sing
God save the King.

The king chose Bognor not because he held any special affection for it, but because a rich chum of his named Sir Arthur du Cros had a mansion there called Craigweil House, which he offered to the king for his private use. Craigweil was by all accounts an ugly and uncomfortable retreat, and the king liked nothing about it, but the sea air did do him good and after a few months he was well enough to return to London. If he left with any fond memories of Bognor, he didn't relate them.

Six years later, when the king relapsed and now lay dying, Dawson blandly assured him that soon he would be well enough to return to Bognor for another holiday. "Bugger Bognor," the king reportedly said and thereupon died. The story is nearly always dismissed as fiction, but one of George V's biographers, Kenneth Rose, maintains that it could be true and that it certainly would not have been out of character.

Because of the king's short residency, Bognor petitioned to have the word "Regis" added to its title, and in 1929 this was granted, so that interestingly its supreme elevation and onset of terminal decline date from almost precisely the same moment.

Like so much of coastal Britain, Bognor has seen better days. Once everyone went to the seaside for holidays in Britain, but now hardly anyone does. It is cheaper to have a package holiday on the Mediterranean, where the weather is more reliably balmy, so many of the old resort towns wear a forlorn air. Bognor remained popular through the 1960s, but its real heyday was the twenties and thirties. It had a Theatre Royal, a grand Pavilion with what was said to be the finest dance floor in the south of England, and a much esteemed if not very accurately named Kursaal, where no one was cured of anything but patrons could roller skate to the music of a resident orchestra and afterward dine beneath giant palms. All that is distant history now.

The pier at Bognor survives, but barely. Seaside piers are a curious British phenomenon that I still don't entirely understand. Years ago, when I was still quite new to Britain, I went with my future wife to Brighton for the day and there I saw my first pier, jutting out into the sea like a runway to nowhere. I'm from Iowa. We don't have a lot of coastal infrastructure. I asked her what piers were for.

"Well, they let you walk out and see the sea," she explained as if I were a little simple.

"But we can see the sea from here," I pointed out.

"Yes, but you can see it better from a pier because it is *over* the sea."

"Can you see coral reefs and shipwrecks and things?" I asked hopefully.

"No, it's just murky water."

"Can you see France?"

"Of course not. You just see the sea." Her tone betrayed just a hint of exasperation. "You take the air. It's very bracing."

"And then what?"

"Then you go back to the promenade and stroll about and have some cockles or whelks and perhaps an ice cream, and then you get on a train and go home. It's lovely, especially if it doesn't rain."

"I see," I said, but really I was just being polite.

This introduction to the British seaside coincided almost exactly with the beginning of its long decline. The 1970s saw the rise of package holidays to the Mediterranean, which were cheaper than British holidays, even with air fares factored in, and allowed the British to experience a phenomenon they couldn't get at home: sunburn. So resorts like Bognor began to fade away.

The pier at Bognor perfectly encapsulates its decline. Once it was a thousand feet long, but various owners took to lopping lengths off it following fires or storm damage so that today it is just a stub three hundred feet long that doesn't quite reach the sea. For years Bognor had an annual birdman competition, in which competitors tried to get airborne from the pier end using various homemade contraptions—bicycles with rockets strapped to the sides and that sort of thing. Invariably the competitors would travel an amusingly short distance and splash into the water, to the delight of the watching crowds, but eventually the shortened pier meant that they were crash-landing on sand and gravel in a way that was more alarming than amusing. The competition was canceled in 2014 and appears now to have moved permanently a few miles down the coast to Worthing, where the prizes are bigger and the pier actually stands over water.

In an effort to reverse Bognor's long decline, in 2005 Arun District Council formed the Bognor Regis Regeneration Task Force with the goal of bringing £500 million of investment to the town. As it became clear that nothing on that scale would ever be forthcoming, the target was quietly reduced first to £100 million and then to £25 million. These also proved too ambitious. Eventually it was decided that a more realistic target was a sum of about zero. When it was realized that that goal had already been reached, the task force was wound up, its work completed. Now, as far as I could tell, all the authorities are doing for Bognor is just keeping it ticking over, like a patient on life support.

But for all that Bognor isn't such a bad place. It has a long beach with a curving concrete promenade, and a town center that is compact and tidy, if not actively thriving. Just inland from the sea is a sylvan retreat called Hotham Park, with winding paths, a boating pond, and a toy railway. But that, it must be said, is about it. If you do a web search for things to do in Bognor, Hotham Park is the first thing that comes up. The second suggested attraction is a shop selling mobility scooters.

I walked down to the seafront. A good number of people were ambling along, enjoying the sunshine. We were about to have a lovely summer and even now at ten thirty in the morning you could see that this day was going to be, by English standards, a scorcher.

My original plan was to stroll west along the front to Craigweil, to see where the king had stayed, but that hope was dashed when I learned that Craigweil was torn down in 1939 and that today the site is lost somewhere beneath a housing estate. So instead I walked east along the promenade toward Felpham because that was the direction that nearly all the other strollers were going and I assumed they knew what they were doing.

On one side stood the beach and a bright, glittering sea, and on the other was a line of smart modern homes, all with high walls to preserve their privacy from us on the promenade. The owners, however, had not solved the obvious problem that a wall designed to keep passersby from peering in also keeps those on the inside from seeing out. If the occupants of these smart houses wanted to look at the sea, they had to go upstairs and sit on a balcony, but that meant exposing themselves to our gaze, and nothing makes a Briton more miserable than sacrificing his privacy. We could see everything about them—whether they were tanned or pale, having a cold drink or a hot one, were tabloid readers or broadsheet readers. The people on the balconies pretended not to be bothered about this, but you could tell they were. It was a lot to ask after all. They had to pretend first of all that their balconies somehow made them invisible to us, and then additionally they had to pretend that we were in any case such an incidental part of the panorama that they had never actually noticed us down there looking up at them. That was a lot of pretending to have to do.

As a test, I tried to make eye contact with the people on the balconies. I smiled as if to say, "Hello there, I see you!" but they always looked quickly away or affected not to see me at all, but rather were absorbed by something far off on the horizon, in the general vicinity of Dieppe or possibly Deauville. Sometimes I think it must be a little exhausting to be English. At all events, it seemed obvious to me that we on the promenade had much the better deal since we could see the sea at all times without having to go to a higher elevation and we never had to pretend that no one could see us. Best of all, at the end of the day we could get in our cars and drive home to somewhere that wasn't Bognor Regis.

My plan, after Bognor, was to take a bus along the coast to Brighton, and I was quietly excited about this. I had never experienced this stretch of coastline and had great hopes for it. I had printed out a timetable and carefully selected the 12:19 as the best bus for my purposes, but as I ambled to the bus stop now, thinking I had minutes to spare, I watched in mild dismay as my bus departed just ahead of a cloud of black smoke. It took me a minute to work out that my watch was not right, that the battery was evidently dying. With a half hour to kill till the next bus, I went into a jeweler's shop, where a cheerless man looked at the watch and told me that a replacement battery would be £30.

"But I barely paid that for the watch," I sputtered.

"That may explain why it's not working," he said and handed it back with a look of majestic indifference.

I waited to see if he had anything more to say, if there existed within him the faintest flicker of interest in helping me to get the right time on my wrist and possibly in the process keep his business going. It appeared not.

"Well, I'll leave it for now," I said. "I can see you are very busy."

If he had any appreciation for my rich instinct for mirth, he failed to show it. He gave a shrug and that was the end of our relationship.

I was hungry, but now had only twenty minutes before the next bus, so I went into a McDonald's for the sake of haste. I should have known better. I have a little personal history with McDonald's, you see. Once a few years ago after a big family day out we stopped at a McDonald's in response to cries from a backseatful of grandchildren pleading for an unhealthy meal, and I was put in charge of placing the order. I carefully interviewed everyone in the party—about ten of us, from two cars—collated the order onto the back of an old envelope, and stepped to the counter.

"OK," I said decisively to the youthful attendant when my turn came, "I would like five Big Macs, four quarter-pound cheeseburgers, two chocolate milkshakes—"

At this point someone stepped up to tell me that one of the children wanted chicken nuggets instead of a Big Mac.

"Sorry," I said and then resumed. "Make that *four* Big Macs, four quarter-pound cheeseburgers, two chocolate milkshakes—"

At this point, some small person tugging on my sleeve informed me that he wanted a strawberry milkshake, not a chocolate one. "Right," I said, returning to the young attendant, "make that four Big Macs, four quarter-pound cheeseburgers, *one* chocolate milkshake, one *strawberry* milkshake, three chicken nuggets . . ."

And so it went as I worked my way through and from time to time adjusted the group's long and complicated order.

When the food came, the young man produced about eleven trays with thirty or forty bags of food on them.

"What's this?" I said.

"Your order," he replied and read my order back to me off the cash register: "Thirty-four Big Macs, twenty quarter-pound cheeseburgers, twelve chocolate shakes . . ." It turned out that instead of adjusting my order each time I restarted, he just added to it.

"I didn't ask for twenty quarter-pound cheeseburgers, I asked for four quarter-pound cheeseburgers five times."

"Same thing," he said.

"It's not the same thing at all. You can't be this stupid."

Two of the people waiting behind me in line sided with the young attendant.

"You did ask for all that stuff," one of them said.

The duty manager came over and looked at the cash register. "It says twenty quarter-pound cheeseburgers here," he said as if it were a gun with my fingerprints on it.

"I know what it says there, but that isn't what I asked for."

One of my grown children came over to find out what was going on. I explained to him what had happened and he weighed the matter judiciously and decided that, taken all in all, it was my fault.

"I can't believe you are all this stupid," I said to an audience that consisted now of about sixteen people, some of them newly arrived but already taking against me. Eventually my wife came over and led me away by the elbow, the way I used to watch her lead jabbering psychiatric patients off to a quiet room. She sorted the mess out amicably with the manager and attendant, brought two trays of food to the table in about thirty seconds, and informed me that I was never again to venture into a McDonald's whether alone or under supervision.

And now here I was in McDonald's again for the first time since my earlier fracas. I vowed to behave myself, but McDonald's is just too much for me. I ordered a chicken sandwich and a Diet Coke.

"Do you want fries with that?" the young man serving me asked.

I hesitated for a moment, and in a pained but patient tone said: "No. That's why I didn't ask for fries, you see."

"We're just told to ask like," he said.

"When I want fries, generally I say something like, 'I would like some fries, too, please.' That's the system I use."

"We're just told to ask like," he repeated.

"Do you need to know the other things I don't want? It is quite a long list. In fact, it is everything you serve except for the two things I asked for."

"We're just told to ask like," he repeated yet again, but in a darker voice, and deposited my two items on a tray and urged me, without the least hint of sincerity, to have a nice day.

I realized that I probably wasn't quite ready for McDonald's yet.

The bus service from Bognor Regis to Brighton via Littlehampton is advertised as the Coastliner 700, which makes it sound sleek and stylish, possibly turbocharged. I imagined myself sitting high above the ground in air-conditioned comfort in a plush velveteen seat, enjoying views over bright sea and rolling countryside through softly tinted glass, the kind so subtly colored that you feel like turning to the person sitting beside you and saying, "Is this glass lightly tinted or is Littlehampton ever so slightly blue?"

In fact, the bus when it wheezed in had none of these features. It was a cramped and airless single-decker filled with hard metal edges and molded plastic seats. It was the sort of vehicle you would expect to be put on if you were being transferred between prisons. But on the plus side it was cheap—£4.40 for the journey to Hove, which was less than I had spent on a pint of lager in London the night before.

I was still cautiously excited for I was about to travel through a succession of small and, I hoped, charming resorts: Littlehampton, Goring-by-Sea, Angmering, Worthing, Shoreham. I imagined them as the sort of happy villages that you would find in a children's picture book from the 1950s—high streets with pleasant tearooms and shops with bright striped awnings selling pinwheels and beach balls, and people walking along holding cones with globes of yellow ice cream. But for the longest time—a good hour or more—we never went near the sea or even any identifiable communities. Instead we rolled through an endless clutter of suburbia on bypasses and divided highways, passing nothing but box stores, gas stations, car dealerships, and all the other vital ugliness of our age. An earlier passenger had discarded a pair of glossy magazines in the seat pocket beside mine and I lifted one out now in a moment of bored curiosity. It was one of those magazines with a strangely emphatic title—*Hello!, OK!, Now!, What Now! Not Now!*—and the cover lines all seemed to be about female celebrities who had gained a lot of weight recently, though none that I saw looked exactly sleek to begin with. I had no idea who any of them were, but their lives made fascinating reading. My favorite article—it may be my favorite thing in print ever—concerned an actress who took revenge on her feckless partner by charging a £7,500 vaginal makeover to him. Now that is what I call revenge. But what, pray, do you get with a vaginal makeover? Wi-fi? Sauna? Regrettably, the article failed to specify.

I was hooked. I found myself absorbed in the sumptuously mismanaged lives of minor celebrities whose common denominators appeared to be tiny brains, giant boobs, and a knack for entering into regrettable relationships. A little further on in the same issue I found the arresting headline "Don't Kill Your Baby for Fame!" This turned out to be a piece of advice from Katie Price, a former topless model with a pneumatic chest who has refashioned herself as a thinker and magazine columnist, to a rising star of similar pulchritude named Josie. Ms. Price is not a writer to mince words. "Listen up, Josie," she wrote, "I think you're absolutely disgusting. Having boobs and getting an abortion doesn't make you famous!" Though intellectually and emotionally I was inclined to agree with Katie on this point, it did rather seem from the article that Josie was living proof of the contrary.

The photographs of Josie depicted a young woman with breasts like party balloons and lips that brought to mind those floating booms they use to contain oil slicks. According to the article, she was expecting "her third son in two months," which I think we can agree is quite a rate of reproduction. The article went on to say that Josie was so disappointed at having another boy and not the girl she had longed for that she had taken up smoking and drinking again as a signal of displeasure to her reproductive system. She was even considering having an abortion, which is why Ms. Price had leapt so emotionally into the fray. The article noted in passing that young Josie was considering book deals from two publishers. If it turns out that my own publisher is one of them, I will personally burn down their offices.

I hate to sound like an old man, but why are these people famous? What qualities do they possess that endear them to the wider world? We may at once eliminate talent, intelligence, attractiveness, and charm from the equation, so what does that leave? Dainty feet? Fresh, minty breath? I am at a loss to say. Anatomically, many of them don't even seem quite human. Many have names that suggest they have reached us from a distant galaxy: Ri-Ri, Tulisa, Naya, Jai, K-Pez, Chlamydia, Mo-Ron. (I may be imagining some of these.) As I read the magazine, I kept hearing a voice in my head, like the voice from a 1950s B-movie trailer, saying: "They came from Planet Imbecile!"

From wherever they spring, they exist in droves now. As if to illustrate my point, just beyond Littlehampton a young man with baggy pants and an insouciant slouch boarded the bus and took a seat across from me. He was wearing a baseball cap several sizes too large for his head. Only his outsized ears kept it from falling over his eyes. The bill of the cap was steamrollered flat and still had its shiny, hologram-like price sticker attached. Across the brow in large capitals was the word "OBEY." Earphones were sending booming sound waves through the magnificent interstellar void of his cranium, on a journey to find the distant, arid mote that was his brain. It must have been a little like the hunt for the Higgs boson. If you took all the young men in southern England with those caps and that slouch and collected them all together in one room, you still wouldn't have enough IQ points to make a halfwit.

I turned to the second magazine, *Shut the Fuck Up!* In this one, I learned that Katie Price was not perhaps the paragon of wise counsel that I had to this point assumed. Here we were given a guided tour of Ms. Price's dazzlingly commodious love life. This included three marriages, two broken engagements, several children, and seven other earnest but short-lived commitments—and this was just the most recent fragment of her busy existence. All of Ms. Price's relationships were stupendously unsatisfactory, none more so than the latest. She had married a fellow named Kieran, whose chief talent, I believe, was an ability to make his hair stand up in interesting ways. Not long after they moved into Katie's 1,100-room mansion, Katie discovered that Kieran had been romping with her very best (now presumably formerly very best) friend. As if this were not enough (and in Ms. Price's world very little ever is), she discovered that *another* of her very best friends was also road-testing Kieran. Ms. Price was understandably furious. I think we could be looking at the Buckingham Palace of vaginal makeovers here.

Turning the page, I found a heartwarming profile of a couple named Sam and Joey, whose talents I was genuinely unable to identify. I would be interested to know if anyone could. Sam and Joey were evidently very successful, for they were looking for a large property in Essex—"ideally a castle," a friend reported. It was at this point that I realized that my brain was dripping onto the pages, so I put the magazine down, and instead watched the passing suburban scene outside my window.

Gradually, helplessly, and with many fitful jerks of the head, I lapsed into the deepest of slumbers.

I awoke with a start and found myself in some uncertain place. The bus had stopped beside a town park, large, rectangular and green, and busy with people. It was bounded on three sides by small hotels and apartment buildings, and was open to the sea on the fourth. It was very fetching. Immediately outside my window and running away from the park was a pedestrian lane that looked appealing, too. Perhaps this was Hove. I had heard that Hove was very nice. I stumbled hastily off the bus and wandered about a bit, wondering how I could find out where I was. I couldn't bring myself to approach anyone and say, "Excuse me, where am I?" so I just wandered until I came to an information board that informed me I was in Worthing.

I explored the pedestrian lane, called Warwick Street, and had a cup of tea, then strolled down to the seafront, which was dominated by a sensationally ugly multistory parking lot. You do wonder what planning officials think. "Hey, I've got an idea. Instead of having attractive hotels and apartment blocks beside the sea, let's put up a giant windowless car park. That'll bring the crowds in!" I thought about walking the rest of the way to Brighton, but then I realized that what I could see in the hazy, uttermost distance was Brighton itself and it was clearly a long way away—more than eight miles, according to my trusty Ordnance Survey map, and that was considerably farther than I cared to go on foot just at the moment.

So I got on another bus, all but identical to the first one, and resumed my journey by road. The trip began promisingly enough, but soon the coast road became a long string of scrapyards, building supply outlets, car repair shops, and finally a giant power station, as we made our way into Shoreham. We got caught in a long tailback because of roadworks and I fell asleep again.

I awoke in Hove, exactly where I wished to be, and exited the bus with my usual stumbling haste. I had recently by chance read about George Everest, the man for whom Mount Everest was named, and learned that he was buried in St. Andrew's churchyard in Hove, and I thought I might look in on his grave. Until I read about old

George, I had never paused to wonder how the mountain got its name. It turns out that it should never have been named for him. For one thing, he never saw it. Mountains, in India or elsewhere, hardly played a part in his life at all.

Everest was born in 1790 in either Greenwich or Wales (depending on which sources you credit), the son of a lawyer, and educated at military schools in Marlow and Woolwich before being packed off to the Far East, where he became a surveyor. In 1817, he was sent to Hyderabad, in India, to serve as chief assistant on an enterprise known as the Great Trigonometrical Survey. The aim of the project was to survey an arc of longitude across India as a way of determining the circumference of the Earth. It was the life's work of an interestingly obscure fellow named William Lambton. Nearly everything about Lambton is uncertain. The *Oxford Dictionary of National Biography* says he was born sometime in the period 1753 to 1769—an arrestingly broad range of possibility. Where he grew up is quite unknown, as are all the other details of his early life and education. All that can be said is that in 1781 he joined the army, went to Canada to survey its boundary with the new United States, and then was dispatched to India. There he got the idea of surveying his arc. He worked on it exhaustively for some twenty years before dying abruptly in northern India in 1823—though exactly where, when, and what of are not known. George Everest merely completed the project. It was important work, but it went nowhere near the Himalayas.

Photos of Everest from late in life show a cheerless face almost perfectly encircled by white hair and beard. Life in India didn't much agree with him. He spent twenty years there more or less constantly unwell, suffering from typhus and chronic bouts of Yellapurum fever and diarrhea. He spent extended periods at home on sick leave. He returned permanently to England in 1843, long before the mountain was named. It is almost the only mountain in Asia to have an English name. British cartographers were generally fairly scrupulous about preserving native designations, but Mount Everest was known locally by a range of names—Deodhunga, Devadhunga, Bairavathan, Bhairavlangur, Gnalthamthangla, Chomolungma, and several more—so there wasn't one to fix on. The British most commonly called it Peak XV. No one at the time had any idea that it was the tallest mountain in the world, and therefore deserving of special attention, so when someone put Everest's name on the map it wasn't intended as a momentous gesture. In the end the trigonometrical survey was found to be largely inaccurate anyway, so Lambton and Everest died having achieved very little.

George Everest, incidentally, didn't pronounce his name Ev-er-rest, as everyone says it today, but as *Eve*-rest—just two syllables—so that the mountain is not only misnamed but mispronounced. Everest died aged seventy-six in Hyde Park Gardens, London, but was carted off to Hove for burial. No one knows why. He had no known connection to the town or to any part of Sussex. I was greatly taken with the idea of the most famous mountain in the world being named for a man who had no connection to it and whose name we don't even pronounce correctly. I think that's rather splendid.

St. Andrews is a striking church, large and gray, with a dark, square tower. By the gate stood a large sign saying *The Church of St. Andrew Welcomes You,* but the spaces for the vicar's name, the times of services, and the phone number for the churchwarden were blank. Three groups of vagrants occupied the churchyard, drinking and enjoying the sunshine. Two guys in the nearest group were arguing heatedly over something, but I couldn't tell what. I hunted around among the gravestones, but most inscriptions were weathered to the point of illegibility. Everest's grave has been exposed to the salty air of Hove for almost 150 years, so it seemed unlikely it would survive in identifiable form. One of the two arguing fellows stood up and had a pee against the boundary wall. As he did so, he took a simultaneous interest in me, and shouted questions at me over his shoulder in a vaguely hostile manner, asking me what I was looking for.

I told him I was looking for the grave of a man named George Everest. He astounded me by saying, in quite a cultivated voice, "Oh, just over there," and nodded at some gravestones a few feet from me. "They named Mount Everest after him, but he never actually saw it, you know."

"So I've read."

"Stupid fucker," he said, a touch ambiguously, and hefted his organ back into his pants with an air of satisfaction.

And so ended my first day as a tourist in Britain. I presumed that at least some of the following ones would be better.

Chapter 2

Seven Sisters

Some woman I have never met regularly sends me e-mail alerts telling me how to recognize if I am having a stroke.

"If you feel a tingling in your fingers," one will say, "you could be having *A STROKE*. Seek medical attention *AT ONCE*." (The alerts come with lots of italics and abrupt capitalizations, presumably to underline how serious a matter this is.) Another will say: "If you sometimes can't remember where you parked your car in a big parking lot, you are probably *HAVING A STROKE*. Go to an emergency room *IMMEDIATELY*."

The uncanny thing about these messages is how accurately they apply to me. I have every one of the symptoms, and there are hundreds of them. Every couple of days I learn of a new one.

"If you think you might be producing more ear wax than usual . . ."

"If you sometimes sneeze unexpectedly . . ."

"If you have had toast at any time in the last six months . . ."

"If you celebrate your birthday on the same date every year . . ."

"If you feel anxious about strokes after reading stroke warnings . . ."

"If you have any of these symptoms—or *ANY OTHER* symptoms—find a doctor at once. An embolism *THE SIZE OF A DUCK EGG* is heading straight for your *CEREBRAL CORTEX*!!"

Taken together, the alerts make clear that the best indicator of a stroke is whatever you were doing just before you had a stroke. Lately the warnings have been accompanied by alarming accounts of people who failed to heed the signals. "When Doreen's husband, Harold, noticed that his ears were red after he got out of the shower," one might begin, "they didn't think anything of it. How they wish they had. Soon afterward, Doreen found Harold, her husband of forty-seven years, slumped face-first in a bowl of Rice Krispies. *HE WAS HAVING A STROKE!* Harold was rushed to the hospital but critical minutes had been lost, and now he is a *VEGETABLE* who spends his afternoons watching Judge Judy. Don't let this happen to you!!"

I don't actually need memos to know that things are not going well with my body. All I have to do is stand before a mirror, tilt my head back, and look up my nostrils. This isn't something I do a great deal, you'll understand, but what I used to find was two small, dark caves. Now I am confronted with a kind of private rainforest. My nostrils are packed with fibrous material—you can't even really call it hair—of the sort you would find in a thick coir doormat. Indeed if you were to carefully pick apart a coir doormat until all you had was a pile of undifferentiated fibers, and shoved 40 percent of the pile up one nostril and 40 percent up the other, and took the rest and put that in your ears so that a little was tumbling out of each, then you would be me.

Somebody needs to explain to me why it is that the one thing your body can suddenly do well when you get old is grow hair in your nose and ears. It's like God is playing a terrible, cruel joke on you, as if he is saying, "Well, Bill, the bad news is that from now on you are going to be barely continent, lose your faculties one by one, and have sex about once every lunar eclipse, but the good news is that you can braid your nostrils."

The other thing you can do incredibly well when you are old is grow toenails. I have no idea why. Mine are harder than iron now.

When I cut my toenails, I see sparks. I could use them as body armor if I could just get my enemies to shoot at my feet.

The worst part about aging is the realization that all your future is downhill. Bad as I am today, I am pretty much tiptop compared with what I am going to be next week or the week after. I recently realized with dismay that I am even too old now for early onset dementia. Any dementia I get will be right on time. The outlook generally is for infirmity, liver spots, baldness, senility, bladder dribble, purple blotches on the hands and head as if my wife has been beating me with a wooden spoon (always a possibility), and the conviction that no one in the world speaks loud enough. And that's the best-case scenario. That's if everything goes absolutely swimmingly. There are other scenarios that involve catheters, beds with side railings, plastic tubing with my blood in it, nursing homes, being lifted on and off toilets, and having to guess what season it is outside—and those are all still near the best-case end of the spectrum.

Unnerved by my dossier of stroke warnings, I did some research and it appears that there are two fundamental ways to avoid having a stroke. One is to die of something else first. The other is to get some exercise. I decided, in the interests of survival, to introduce a little walking into my life. And so it was, the day after my trip from Bognor to Hove, that I was to be found fifteen or so miles to the east wheezing my way up a steep hill to a breezy top called Haven Brow, the first in a series of celebrated eminences gracing the Sussex coast and known as the Seven Sisters.

The Seven Sisters is one of the great walks of England. From the top of Haven Brow the view is just sensational. Ahead of you stretches a hazy infinity of rolling hills, each ending at the seaward side in a sudden plunge of limestone cliffs. On a sunny day like this one, it is a world of simple, bright elements: green land, brilliant white cliffs, deep blue sea, matching sky.

Nothing—and I mean really, absolutely nothing—is more

extraordinary in Britain than the beauty of the countryside. Nowhere in the world is there a landscape that has been more intensively utilized—more mined, farmed, quarried, covered with cities and clanging factories, threaded with motorways and railroad tracks—and yet remains so comprehensively and reliably lovely over most of its extent. It is the happiest accident in history. In terms of natural wonders, you know, Britain is a pretty unspectacular place. It has no alpine peaks or broad rift valleys, no mighty gorges or thundering cataracts. It is built to really quite a modest scale. And yet with a few unassuming natural endowments, a great deal of time, and an unfailing instinct for improvement, the makers of Britain created the most superlatively park-like landscapes, the most orderly cities, the handsomest provincial towns, the jauntiest seaside resorts, the stateliest homes, the most dreamily-spired, cathedral-rich, castle-strewn, abbey-bedecked, folly-scattered, green-wooded, winding-laned, sheep-dotted, plumply-hedgerowed, well-tended, sublimely decorated 50,318 square miles the world has ever known—almost none of it undertaken with aesthetics in mind, but all of it adding up to something that is, quite often, perfect. What an achievement that is.

And what a joy it is to walk in it. England and Wales have 130,000 miles of public footpaths, about 2.2 miles of path for every square mile of area. People in Britain don't realize how extraordinary that is. If you told someone in the Midwest of America, where I come from, that you intended to spend the weekend walking across farmland, they would look at you as if you were out of your mind. You couldn't do it anyway. Every field you crossed would end in a barrier of barbed wire. You would find no helpful stiles, no kissing gates, no beckoning wooden footpath posts to guide you on your way. All you would get would be a farmer with a shotgun (or in Iowa a glass of lemonade and a slice of pie) wondering what the hell you were doing blundering around in his alfalfa.

So if there is one thing I enjoy and admire in Britain, it is the pleasure of being on foot and at large in the open air. I was on the South Downs Way, which runs for a hundred miles from Winchester to Eastbourne along the rolling chalk downs of the south coast. I have done most of the trail in chunks over the years, but this is my favorite stretch. To my left were bosomy hills of green and gold, to the right a spangled plane of bright blue sea. Dividing the two were cliffs of brilliant white. You can, if you dare, creep right up to the cliff edge and look over. Generally you find a straight drop down two hundred feet to a rocky beach. But almost no one ever does this. It's too unnerving and way too dangerous. These cliff edges are crumbly, so everyone keeps well back. Even frolicking dogs brake and retreat when they see the fall. All along this stretch of coast the path is a grassy lawn, cropped by sheep, sometimes hundreds of yards wide, so even the most absentminded walker—the sort of person who can't be trusted around automated parking barriers, say—can amble along in a state of blissful unawareness and remain safe.

The South Downs Way is not only lovely but getting better. At Birling Gap, roughly halfway between the start of the Seven Sisters and Eastbourne, there used to be a fairly horrible café, but the National Trust has absorbed it into its tasteful care and converted it into a paradise for people who look as if they have just stepped out of a Patagonia catalog. Now there is a smart cafeteria full of scrubbed wooden tables and lovely sea views, clean restrooms, a gift shop for people who think that £10 is not too much to pay for six ginger cookies so long as they come in a nice tin, and a small but interesting museum. I went to the museum first and appreciated its intelligence and thoughtfulness. It tells you a great deal about the geology of the Sussex coast, including that it is eroding by a foot or so a year on average, though Birling Gap itself is tumbling into the sea at nearly twice that rate. Across the way from the National Trust café there used to stand a row of cliff-top houses.

Now just four houses remain, and house number four looked like it might soon be called Beach Cottage.

I was also interested to discover that the Seven Sisters—which are, namely, Haven Brow, Short Brow, Rough Brow, Brass Point, Flat Hill, Bailey's Hill, and Went Hill—don't include Belle Tout or Beachy Head, two of the mightiest eminences of all along this stretch of coast, which meant that I was in the process of climbing nine hills, not seven. No wonder I was tired. Sobered by this thought, I fortified myself with a posh sandwich and bottle of organic soda pop at the National Trust café, then returned to the long, lonesome trail.

Not long after Birling Gap, the path arrives at a sweeping prospect across the downs that strikes nearly every British visitor as familiar whether they have ever walked this way or not. It is a view that was immortalized in a Second World War poster by an artist named Frank Newbould. The poster shows a shepherd guiding a flock of sheep across the downs. Below, in the middle distance, is an attractive farmhouse. At the top of a facing hill is the iconic Belle Tout lighthouse. The sea is just visible as a line across a distant valley. The caption says: "Your Britain—fight for it now." I have always thought it interesting that of all the possible things worth dying for in 1939, it was the countryside that was selected. I wonder how many people would feel that way now. Newbould took a few small liberties in the work—he improved the shape of the hills, tidied up the farmstead, altered the course of the path slightly—but not so much as to render the view fictitious. It is a testament to the British nation that more than seventy years after Newbould painted this expansive prospect, it is as fine now as it was then.

Taking the English countryside for granted, assuming that it will always be like this, is almost certainly its greatest threat. The sad irony is that the things that make the landscape of Britain comely and distinctive are almost entirely no longer needed. Hedgerows, country churches, stone barns, verges full of nodding wildflowers and birdsong, sheep roaming over windswept fells, village shops and post offices, and much more can only rarely now be justified on economic grounds, and for most people in power those are the only grounds that matter. Looked at economically, we don't even need farmers. Farming accounts for just 0.7 percent of GDP, so if all farming in Britain ceased tomorrow the economy would barely notice. Successive governments have done almost nothing to preserve most of these things. There is a strange, blind, foolish inclination to suppose that the features that make the British countryside are somehow infinitely self-sustaining, that they will always be there, adding grace and beauty. Don't count on it.

Belle Tout lighthouse itself nearly didn't survive. It was decommissioned in the early 1900s and became derelict. Canadian soldiers used it for target practice during the Second World War, though mercifully failed to destroy it. After the war it was restored, but by the late twentieth century it was in danger of falling into the sea, so some good soul paid a fortune to have it mounted on rails and moved a safe distance back from the cliff edge. So now it is safe for another few decades until the crumbling cliffs sneak up on it again.

After Belle Tout comes a long descent almost to sea level, then a steady climb toward the summit of Beachy Head. It's a long haul up a broad grassy strip, rather like walking on a golf fairway, but worth it for the payoff at the top where you get the most sensational views of the famous Beachy Head lighthouse with its jaunty red and white stripes, standing in the sea at the base of the cliffs.

At the top of the hill, where it flattens out, is a parking area where busloads of schoolchildren can get off and scatter a little litter around—it's a tradition, I guess; school groups come from all over to put their potato chip bags and candy bar wrappers in the gorse and bracken, bless their sweet, undersupervised little hearts—but I am pleased to say that this was the only place along the entire walk that I encountered litter.

After the summit at Beachy Head, there comes a broad, parklike expanse of land with a selection of paths plunging downhill to the old resort town of Eastbourne. The views over the town's sweeping seafront with its golden beach and scallops of advancing waves are very fine, too, though marred by a single high-rise apartment house called South Cliff Tower, which stands distractingly in the foreground. It's a charmless building that should never have been allowed, but there you are. The world is full of shitty things that should never have happened. Look at Sean Hannity.

In nearly all other respects, however, Eastbourne is a good place. The promenade is well kept, with big houses and smart hotels on one side and broad beaches on the other—all leading to a good old-fashioned pier, one of the few truly classic piers still standing. Just after my visit, the pier was badly damaged in a fire—seaside piers in England seem to be amazingly combustible; I don't know why—but according to press reports it will be lovingly restored. I most emphatically hope so. It would be a tragedy to see it go.

The charm of Eastbourne is that it is so comfortably old-fashioned, and nowhere is that better encapsulated than in a café where I always stop called Favo'loso. It is the most wonderful establishment. It is like stepping into a 1950s movie called *Summer Milkshake* or *Ice Cream Holiday* or something. Favo'loso is spotless and polished and shiny; it basks in a retro gleam. The food is decent, the servers efficient and friendly, the prices reasonable. What more could you ask? It is my favorite place in East Sussex, if not on the entire south coast. Two days before I left on this trip, I googled "Favo'loso Cafe" to check the address and was led, all but inevitably, to TripAdvisor, where I was appalled to discover that most people didn't view it very favorably at all. One recent visitor pronounced himself "Dissapointted" with the experience. Well, here is a new rule: If you are too stupid to spell "disappointed" even approximately correctly, you are not allowed to take part in public discourse at any level.

Trawling through the reviews, I found that hardly anybody spoke warmly of Favo'loso's carefully preserved atmosphere. In fact, most were critical of the decor, calling it old-fashioned and in need of an update. I do despair. We live in a world that has practically no appreciation for quality, tradition, or classiness, and in which people who can't spell even common words get to decide what survives. That can't be right, surely. I was, as a TripAdvisor correspondent might put it, deply trubbled.

Chapter 3

Dover

N OW HERE IS A question that is harder to answer than you might think: Is Britain a big country or a little one?

Looked at one way, it is self-evidently small, a modest chunk of land floating in chilly waters off the northwestern edge of Europe. Of the total surface area of Earth, Great Britain occupies just 0.0174069 percent. (I should note that I can't absolutely vouch for that number. It was calculated for me by my son some years ago for a newspaper article I was writing. He was only about thirteen years old at the time, but he had a calculator with over 200 buttons on it and he seemed to know what he was doing.)

By other measures, however, Britain is incontestably substantial. Amazingly, it is the thirteenth-largest land mass on the planet and that includes four continents—Australia, Antarctica, America, and Eurasia-Africa (which geographers, being anally retentive and unimaginative, classify as a single mass). Only eight islands on Earth are bigger: Greenland, New Guinea, Borneo, Madagascar, Baffin, Sumatra, Honshu, and Vancouver. By population, Britain is the fourth largest island state, behind only Indonesia, Japan, and the Philippines. By wealth, it is second. Measured by decent music, old stony buildings, variety of boiled sweets, and reasons for not going to work because of the weather, it is number one by a very large margin. Yet it is only seven hundred miles from top to bottom and so slender in profile that no one in the country is ever more than seventy miles from one of its edges.

Taken all in all, it has long seemed to me that Britain is just about the perfect size for a country—small enough to be cozy and embraceable, but large enough to maintain a lively and independent culture. If the rest of the world vanished tomorrow and all that was left was the United Kingdom, there would still be good books and theater and standup comedy and universities and competent surgeons and so on. (Plus England would get to win the World Cup every time and Scotland would always qualify.) This cannot be said of many other nations. If Canada were the only country to survive, the world would be a nicer, politer place, but there would be way too much ice hockey. If it were Switzerland you would have glorious scenery, precision watches, reliable trains, and, well, that's it.

Interestingly, the thing that made me realize that Britain is an optimal size was the rarely discussed subject of cow attacks. This is a topic that we don't pay as much attention to as perhaps we ought. I first heard about cow attacks some years ago while walking on the South Downs Way with a reporter from a walking magazine. I had just become president of the Campaign to Protect Rural England, a venerable conservation organization, and he was interviewing me about the countryside. At some point—we were crossing a field in the vicinity of the Devil's Dyke, near Brighton, if I recall correctly—he mentioned that we should proceed cautiously because there was a bull in our field.

"You're kidding," I squeaked, but sure enough, watching us lugubriously from about fifty feet away, was a great rectangular block of beef.

"Just walk normally," my companion instructed in a taut whisper, "or you'll attract his attention."

"But we're on a national footpath," I protested, my sense of unfairness momentarily outweighing my instinct to flee. "Surely a farmer can't put a bull in a field with a footpath through it," I added. I turned to see what my companion had to say about this and discovered that he was now about seventy yards ahead of me and running like hell. I waddled briskly behind him, casting whimpering glances over my shoulder, but the bull stayed rooted to his spot.

When we were both safely on the other side of the field wall, I repeated my complaint that surely it was not legal to put bulls in fields with public trails through them.

"Actually it is," my companion told me. "The rule is that bulls can be placed in fields with footpaths as long as they are with beef cows and not dairy cows."

I was of course bewildered by this. "Why one and not the other?" I asked.

"No idea. But the real danger," he went on, "is cows. Cows kill a lot more people than bulls."

Whatever is the next level beyond pained incredulity is the level I reached now. For years I had been striding boldly through herds of cows in the belief that they were the one group of animals larger than a chicken that I could intimidate with the shake of a stick, and now this was being taken away from me.

"You're kidding," I said again.

"Afraid not," he responded in the solemn tone of someone with experience in the matter. "Cows attack a *lot*."

The next day I did the one thing you should obviously never do. I looked for more information on the Internet. My informant was right. Walkers in Britain, it seems, are killed by cows all the time. Four people were fatally trampled in one eight-week period in 2009 alone. One of these unfortunates was a veterinarian out walking her dogs on the Pennine Way, another long-distance trail, in Yorkshire. This was a woman who understood animals and liked them, probably had treats for cows in her pocket—and they still trampled her. More recently, a retired university lecturer named Mike Porter was trampled to death by an angry herd—yes, angry—in a field near the Kennet and Avon Canal in Wiltshire, a place where I had been walking only the year before. "It looked like they wanted to kill him," one eyewitness breathlessly told the *Daily Telegraph*. It was the fourth serious attack on walkers in five years just by this one herd.

Now what, you may reasonably wonder, does this have to do with Britain being the right size for a country? Well, stick with me, please. A couple of weeks later I was in Colorado, visiting my son Sam who works in Vail, when I happened to read an article in the *Denver Post* about a man named Dexter Lewis who had been convicted of going into a bar called Fero's just before closing time, ordering the bartender and four remaining customers to lie down, and then killing them in cold blood as part of a robbery. Now if anyone did anything like that in England, it would be front-page news across the nation. But in America a gruesome murder in Denver is not guaranteed to be news in Memphis or Detroit or anywhere outside Colorado. Those places have murders of their own to be preoccupied with. It wasn't a particularly big article even in the *Denver Post*.

This is when it occurred to me that the issue here is not how often bad things happen, but how often they are reported, which is quite a different matter, of course. In America, a cow trampling would never make the national news other than in highly exceptional circumstances. If, let's say, Dick Cheney was trampled to death by cows (and we can always dream), that would be national news. But if it was just some guy walking his dog in Sodom, Indiana, no one outside Indiana—probably no one outside Sodom County—would hear about it. There could be a national epidemic of cow tramplings and no one would know it because the news wouldn't travel far enough for trends to become apparent. But in Britain if a single cow tramples a walker anywhere in the country, it will almost certainly make headlines. The story of the veterinarian killed in Yorkshire was reported in all the national newspapers except the *Daily Star,* and I am guessing that that was only because the people at the *Star* couldn't spell "veterinarian."

I like being in a country where when cows attack, word of it gets around. That's what I mean when I say Britain is cozy. It is a nice quality for a country to have. The only downside to this is that it means Britons are frightened of things that are never going to happen to them. Cow attacks are actually quite rare. That's what makes them news when they happen. But because people read about cow attacks at regular intervals, they *perceive* them as being common.

As an experiment, I asked several British friends this question: "What are the chances if you are walking in a field with cows that the cows will attack you?" Every one of them grew instantly animated, and said something along the lines of "Actually, surprisingly good. I read about it in the papers. It happens far more often than you'd expect."

Ask the same question of an American and he would say: "Why would I be in a field with cows?"

We'll return to this issue in due course, but first let's pay a visit to Dover.

I know I said at the outset that I was going to avoid the places I went in *Notes from a Small Island,* but I felt I just had to look in on Dover when I was so close by already. I have a peculiar fondness for the place—or if not fondness exactly, a kind of abiding concern—that I can't entirely explain. Partly, I suppose, it is because Dover was where I first set foot on English soil, so in a very literal sense it is the place I have known the longest. I spent my first forty-eight hours in Britain there and I quite liked Dover. Of course, I knew nothing else of Britain at that point, but in those days Dover wasn't at all a bad place. It had cinemas and pubs and restaurants and a busy high street. The endless bustle of the ferry port clearly brought people and commerce to the town. But on every subsequent visit I have made to Dover it has visibly deteriorated. I keep hoping to find the buzzing, prosperous little place I first saw, and instead I am greeted by a sad air of ghostliness and decline.

In *Notes from a Small Island*, I wrote about arriving late and looking longingly into the windows of a ritzy hotel on the seafront, where people were dining in an atmosphere of elegance far beyond anything I could afford. That hotel was the Churchill. About seven or eight years ago, arriving in Dover on the car ferry from Calais, on an impulse I decided to stop at the Churchill for lunch—to treat myself to a little of the high life that I couldn't afford all those years ago. Well, it was a strange experience. The hotel still strived for an air of elegance, but it was based much more on memory than merit. I had the dining room more or less to myself. The menu, instead of being a hefty leatherette book, was just a laminated sheet, and it was full of misspellings. I ordered a Caesar salad. When it arrived there was nothing to eat it with.

The waitress saw my look of puzzlement. "Do you want a knife and fork with that?" she said.

"Well, yes," I answered. "It's a salad."

"I didn't know if you had your own," she said grumpily, as if this were mostly my fault, and flumped off to get some.

The salad was a kind of lettuce soup with some shredded chicken afloat on it. It was a small consolation to know that however long I live and however many other disappointing salads are placed before me, I would never receive a worse one than this. With respect to Caesar salads, life could only get better. I assumed from this experience that I would not venture into the Churchill again, but now on this latest visit I found myself approaching it once more, as if drawn by some masochistic magnetism, hoping against hope that I would find it improved since my last visit. Alas, the Churchill was no longer there. Dover's last outpost of stateliness is gone. The window I had once gazed into was soaped over. A man walking past with a little dog told me that the Churchill had closed about five years earlier, though another hotel now occupied part of the old premises. I looked around the corner and he was right. The central part of the old hotel was now called the Dover Marina Hotel. It looked awfully quiet. Most things in Dover look quiet these days.

Time appears to be leaving Dover behind. Cheap flights to European destinations and the Channel Tunnel are between them slowly killing the ferry business. Hovercraft services to the continent ceased in 2000, and the number of passengers on conventional ferries fell by a third in the following decade, though they seem to have recovered very slightly since then. The loss of business has clearly been a blow to the town, but Dover seems to be doing a pretty good job of its own of running itself down. Not long before my visit, the council installed new benches on the seafront that were designed not to be comfortable. When asked by the local paper why they had chosen uncomfortable benches, a councillor replied somewhat bewilderingly: "If they were too comfortable, we would have the gentlemen and ladies of the day lounging on them." And that is perhaps all you need to know to understand why Dover is dying.

I walked to the old South Foreland lighthouse, which was decommissioned some years ago and is now in the care of the National Trust. For a long time this was the highest lighthouse light in England, though it was the lofty cliff rather than the building itself that made it so. As lighthouses go, this one is pretty squat. South Foreland was the site of an important but forgotten piece of history. It was there that the first electric light in the world was put to use, way back in 1858, long before Thomas Edison brought us the modern lightbulb. The light at South Foreland was an arc lamp, invented by yet another man about whom almost nothing is known, Frederick Hale Holmes. Holmes's light was too bright for domestic use but perfect for a lighthouse. The equipment was temperamental and expensive, however, and eventually it was given up as too much bother, but for a decade or so this was the one place in the world where you could see an electric light in operation. About a quarter of a century later, South Foreland made history again when Guglielmo Marconi transmitted the first international radio signal from there to a receiver at Wimereux, near Boulogne, in France.

I first heard of Frederick Holmes and South Foreland when I was researching another book about five years ago, and visited it then. On that occasion, I was one of a party of three or four people who were shown around by a keen National Trust volunteer. The volunteer didn't know much about Holmes or Marconi, but he was a fount of knowledge with respect to the mechanical operation of the light. It took one hundred and ten turns of a crank to give two and a half hours of rotation to the light, he told us, and it took forty seconds for the light to make one complete rotation. We also learned that no two lighthouses within a hundred miles of each other had the same light sequences.

"Goodness," we said appreciatively.

The man showed us banks of batteries and cogs and things like that. The illumination from the lighthouse was one million candlepower, he said. I was so impressed with the equipment that I took a photograph.

He held up a hand like a bodyguard dealing with paparazzi. "Photography is not permitted," he said.

"Why not?" I asked, bewildered.

"National Trust policy."

"But it's a lighthouse," I pointed out. "It's not the Bayeux tapestry."

"Trust policy," he said again, more crisply this time, in the tone of a man who would stab his wife in the eye with an ice pick if the head office told him it was policy.

I was about to explain to him that this is why I get so frustrated with the National Trust, because of its irksome sense of its own perfection, but I imagined my wife pinching me by the elbow and leading me toward fresh air and the distraction of a sea view, so I said nothing more. My wife has spent so many years pinching my elbow and leading me away from officious idiots—many of them in the employ of the National Trust, it must be said—that I no longer need her there. It's become a kind of Pavlovian response.

So I stepped outside, back into a beautiful clear day, and instantly felt much better. France, 20.6 miles off, was clearly—startlingly—visible. You could practically wave to people in Calais. Many of the older English visitors around me eyed the French coast grimly, not at all pleased to realize it was that close. Most watched it warily, as if they thought it might be secretly inching closer, stealing English water.

On this latest visit, however, I arrived to find that the lighthouse was closed for the day, which was probably just as well, all things considered. So I just stood and enjoyed the views. France, I was pleased to note, seemed to be exactly where I had last left it.

From up here, I could see the shallow smudge of brown that marked the treacherous Goodwin Sands. You wouldn't think it on such a tranquil day, but this is one of the most historically lethal places on the planet, the site of the greatest concentration of ship-wrecks anywhere. More than a thousand wrecks are recorded on the Goodwin Sands. The worst incident was on November 27, 1703, when the biggest storm anyone had ever seen drove fifty ships onto the sandbanks, where they were tipped on their sides and reduced to splinters. More than two thousand men died. The Royal Navy lost 20 percent of its men that night.

Along the coast in Devon, Henry Winstanley, designer and builder of the celebrated Eddystone Lighthouse—probably the most famous lighthouse in the whole of England at that time—was by chance in the lighthouse that night. He had long expressed a desire to be in it during a really big storm. He got his wish that night but his belief in its impregnability proved to be a little misplaced. When the weather cleared and a crew rowed out to rescue Winstanley, they found the lighthouse had been completely swept away. Winstanley and the five men who were with him were never seen again. And on that sobering note, let's move on to London.

Chapter 4

London

GREEN PARK

O NE OF THE MYSTERIES of the London Underground these days is whatever became of the trains on the Circle Line. They used to come along every few minutes, but now generally you wait ages. On this particular morning, when our story resumes, a great many of us had been standing on a platform at Gloucester Road station for about twenty-five minutes without any sign of action on the line at all.

"I remember when trains used to go by here," I said brightly to a man standing beside me.

"Don't the trains go by here?" he asked in sudden alarm.

He was a fellow American and was evidently new to London and possibly to humor.

"I was just joking," I said gently and indicated the many people standing on the platform with us. "We wouldn't all be standing here if there weren't really any trains."

"But we are all standing here and there aren't any trains."

I couldn't think of an answer to this, so I just nodded and grew silent. My new American friend was studying a fully unfolded Underground map. He seemed to be giving up on the Circle Line.

"Where do I go to get the Piccadilly Line?" he asked at length.

"Oh, Piccadilly Line trains aren't stopping here just now."

He looked at me narrowly, wondering if this was another of my quips.

"They're replacing the elevators, so Piccadilly Line trains aren't stopping at this station for the next six months."

"It's taking them six months to replace the elevators?" he said in undisguised wonder.

"Well, there are two of them," I answered in a spirit of fairness. I watched him studying his map. "You may also want to know that the Circle Line doesn't go in a circle," I added helpfully.

He looked up with real interest.

"The trains used to go around in endless circles, but now they all stop at Edgware Road and everybody has to get off one train and get on another."

"Why?" he asked.

"No one knows," I answered.

"This sure is a screwy country," he said.

"Yes, it is," I agreed happily.

Just then a train pulled in and everyone moved forward to board.

"Well, I hope you have a good trip," I said to my new friend.

He got on, but didn't say thanks or good-bye or anything. I kind of hope he got lost, actually.

I do like the London Underground. Putting the Circle Line trains to one side (which is evidently what London Underground does with them these days), nearly everything else about it is splendid. People forget how bad the Underground was once upon a time. When I first came to Britain, it was dirty, poorly managed, and crime-ridden in places. Several stations—Camden Town, Stockwell, and Tooting Bec to name but three—were positively dangerous at night. By 1982, fewer than 500 million people a year, a decline of 50 percent from the early 1950s, ventured into the Underground. A devastating fire at the King's Cross Underground station in 1987, when thirty-one people died after a discarded cigarette started a blaze in uncleared rubbish beneath a wooden escalator, showed how lamentably undermanaged the Underground had become.

Well, look at it now. The platforms are the cleanest places in London. The service is smooth and reliable. The staff, as far as I can tell, are unfailingly helpful and courteous. Passenger numbers have risen to an astounding 1.2 billion a year, which is more than all the aboveground rail journeys in the country combined. According to *Time Out* magazine, at any given moment six hundred thousand people are on the Underground, making it both a larger and more interesting place than Oslo. I read in the *Evening Standard* that the average speed of Underground trains is just twenty-one miles an hour, which doesn't seem very much (unless you travel regularly by train between Liss station and Waterloo, in which case it's like being on a rocket ship), but it all feels pretty brisk, and to convey such a massive number of people over such an enormous and aged system with rarely a hitch is an extraordinary achievement.

But then that's the thing about London. It does a lot of things supremely well and gets hardly any credit for it. So let me say right here, I think London is the best city in the whole world. I know it doesn't have New York's electricity and edgy dynamism or Sydney's harbor and sandy beaches or Paris's boulevards, but it has more of almost everything else that makes a city great—greenery, for one thing. Nobody realizes it, but London is one of the least crowded cities on earth. New York has ninety-three people per hectare, Paris eighty-three, but London just forty-three. If London were as densely populated as Paris, it would have a population of 35 million. Instead what it has is parks—142 of them—and more than six hundred leafy squares. Almost 40 percent of London is green space. You can have all the overwhelming noise and bustle of a metropolis, then turn a corner and hear birdsong. Perfect.

London is arguably the biggest city in the world. Not in terms of sprawl—though goodness knows there is plenty enough of that—or number of inhabitants, but in terms of density and complexity and depth of history. London is not just vast horizontally but vast across time. History has left it sumptuously jumbled. It's not even one city but two—Westminster and the City of London—plus a more or less infinite number of subsumed villages, boroughs, districts, wards, parishes, and geographical landmarks that cover the map with quaint and appealing names: Parsons Green, Seven Dials, Swiss Cottage, Barking, Tooting Bec, Chalk Farm, the mysteriously gallic Theydon Bois. Most of its best-known districts—the West End, Bloomsbury, Whitechapel, Mayfair—have no official existence or formal boundaries. They just are. Politically, London is a loose affiliation of 32 borough councils and the Corporation of the City of London, its responsibilities divided among a Greater London Authority, a London Assembly, 73 parliamentary constituencies, and 624 political wards. It is, in short, a great mess. At the head of it all is Mayor Boris Johnson, a man whose bumbling manner, whose very hair, is a monument to disorder. And yet somehow it works. It is a truly great city.

And it is just packed with stuff. London has 50,000 listed buildings, 150 scheduled ancient monuments, 900 conservation areas, 550 archaeological sites, and four World Heritage sites. It has forty-three universities, more than any other place else in the world. It has nearly three hundred museums. It has a garden museum, a cricket museum, a museum of typefaces and fonts. There are museums devoted to magic, canals, Freemasons, to Sigmund Freud. There is a museum in North Finchley devoted to the history of Belarus. (No idea.) Wimbledon has a terrific lawn tennis museum. The Royal London Hospital has a museum containing the magnificently deformed skeleton of Joseph Merrick, the celebrated Elephant Man, and an exhibition on Jack the Ripper (he committed his murders in the district), among much else. You can never run out of things to look at in London.

I had two weeks at my disposal, at least notionally. Both of my daughters had contrived to get pregnant simultaneously (though in separate buildings) and were scheduled to give birth at roughly the same time in different London hospitals, and I was under strict instructions to be nearby in order to—well, I don't know what. Boil water perhaps. Stand around in a willing but useless manner. Who knows? But in the meantime I had two weeks that I could fill in any way I wished so long as I stayed sober enough to drive and didn't stray too far.

I decided, impulsively, to start with a trip to Leighton House, home of the Victorian artist Frederic Leighton, on Holland Park Road in west Kensington, and now preserved as a museum. I didn't know a thing about Leighton, and I wasn't at all sure if that was my fault or his. It turns out he was the most famous artist of his age. Who'd have thought? I had walked past the house several times and always thought it looked intriguing—it's big and has an air of solemn importance, as if this is a house and a person you really ought to know about—so I had put it on my Things to Get Around to Eventually (But Probably Won't) list. It isn't often I knock something off this list, so I was rather pleased with myself just for thinking to go there. Besides, it was a rainy day: a good day for a museum.

I liked Leighton House immediately, not least because my ticket price was reduced from £10 to £6 on account of my great age. The house is gloomy and grand, but interestingly eccentric; it has, for instance, just one bedroom. In terms of decor it feels a little like a cross between a pasha's den and a New Orleans bordello. It is full of Arabic tiles, silk wallpapers, colorful ceramics, and lots of art, much of it involving bare-breasted young women, which I am always up for.

Leighton isn't terribly well remembered now, in part because many of his pictures ended up in odd places like the Baroda Museum in Gujarat, India, and Agnes Scott College in Decatur, Georgia, where not many of us go to look at pictures, and in part because his paintings are in any case a little overwrought for modern tastes. Most involve a lot of upstretched arms and pleading faces, and have titles like *And the Sea Gave Up the Dead Which Were in It* and *Perseus, on Pegasus, Hastening to the Rescue of Andromeda*.

But Leighton was hugely esteemed in his own lifetime. He was elected president of the Royal Academy in 1878, and in the New Year's honors list of 1896 he became the first—and so far still only—artist to be ennobled. He didn't get to enjoy the privilege long. He died less than a month later, and was interred in St. Paul's Cathedral as a national treasure, with great pomp. The *Oxford Dictionary of National Biography*, always eager to be at least fifty years out of touch, gives him eighty-two hundred words, a thousand more than it gives almost any of his better-remembered contemporaries.

Leighton lived alone in Leighton House for thirty years. His sexuality was always something of a mystery to those who were interested enough to think about it. After decades of apparent celibacy, he seems to have stirred to frisky life after he discovered a young beauty from the East End named Ada Pullen (who subsequently, for reasons unknown to me, changed her name to Dorothy Dene). Leighton scrubbed her up, bought her a fine wardrobe, schooled her in elocution and other cultural refinements, and introduced her into high society. If all that brings to mind Prof. Henry Higgins and Eliza Doolittle, it is no accident. George Bernard Shaw is said to have modeled *Pygmalion* on their relationship. Whether Leighton knew Ms. Dene in the full, biblical sense isn't known, but he certainly enjoyed painting her without clothes on, as the Leighton House collection enthusiastically attests.

Leighton's possessions were auctioned off straight after his death and the house itself was knocked about by subsequent owners and then wrecked by a German bomb during the war, so almost nothing worth seeing was left by the early postwar years, but little by little over a period of decades the house was restored to just as it was in Leighton's day, and it is now quite splendid. I can't say that a great deal of the artwork was entirely to my taste, but I did enjoy the experience very much and when I stepped outside the rain had stopped, the sun was shining, and London looked awfully fine, its streets glistening and cleansed (sort of).

And so passed a couple of happy weeks. Each day, without a great deal of thought beforehand, I did things that I had never done at all or hadn't done in years. I strolled through Battersea Park and then along the river to the Tate Modern, one of London's best new museums. I went to the top of Primrose Hill to take in the view across the city. I explored the quiet streets of Pimlico and the lost world of Westminster around Vincent Square. I went to the National Portrait Gallery and had tea in the crypt of St. Martin-in-the-Fields Church in Trafalgar Square. I walked through all the Inns of Court and visited the museum of the Royal College of Surgeons just because I happened to pass it. These are all wonderful things. You should do them, too.

I went to Southall one day to go to lunch with my friend Aosaf Afzal, who grew up near there and offered to show me around. Southall is the most overwhelmingly Asian place in Britain. For a long time, it even had a Punjabi pub, the Glass Junction, where you could pay for drinks in pounds or rupees, but that closed in 2012.

"A lot of Asians don't have a great pub-going culture," Aosaf explained.

It was certainly the liveliest and most colorful place I had ever seen in Britain, with shops stacked to the ceilings and spilling out onto the pavements with the most extraordinary range of wares— buckets, mops, saris, tiffin containers, brooms, sweets, you name it. Every shop seemed to sell exactly the same crazy range of items. Each appeared to be doing good business, but all that activity masks considerable deprivation. Hounslow, the borough in which Southall resides, is the second most rapidly degentrifying community in Britain, however exactly that is measured, Aosaf told me. "Hounslow has a population of two hundred fifty thousand but no bookshop and no cinema," he added cheerfully.

"Then why do you live here?" I asked.

"Because it is my home," he said simply. "It's where I am from, where my family is. And I like it."

It struck me that when I think of London and Aosaf thinks of London we think of two quite different cities, but this comes back to my earlier point. London isn't a place at all. It's a million little places.

Sometimes during this happy fortnight I just went about my business. I was walking down Kensington High Street one day when I remembered that my wife had instructed me to get some grocery items, so I popped into a Marks and Spencer store. It had evidently undergone a refurbishment since I was last there. In the middle of the main floor, where there used to be an escalator, there was now a staircase, which I thought slightly odd, but the really big surprise was when I went down to the basement and discovered that the food hall—the grocery department—was gone. Marks and Spencer stores always have a grocery section; I had been in this one a hundred times at least. I walked all over, but now there was nothing for sale in the basement but clothes.

I went up to a young sales assistant who was folding T-shirts and asked him where the food hall was, thinking they must have moved it to another floor.

"Don't have a food hall," he said without looking up.

"You got rid of the food hall?" I said in astonishment.

"Never had one."

Now I have to say right here that I didn't like this young man already because he had a vaguely insolent air. Also, he had a lot of gel in his hair. My family tell me that you can't dislike people just because they have gel in their hair, but I think it is as good a reason as any.

"That's nonsense," I said. "There's always been a food hall here."

"Never been one here," he responded blandly. "There's no food halls in any of our stores."

"Well, pardon me for saying so, but you're an idiot," I said matter-of-factly. "I have been coming here since the early 1970s, and there's always been a food hall here. Every Marks and Spencer's in the country has a food hall."

He looked at me for the first time, with a kind of unfolding interest. "This isn't a Marks and Spencer's," he said with something like real pleasure. "This is H&M."

I stared at him for a long moment as I adjusted to this new intelligence.

"Marks and Spencer's is next door," he added.

I was quiet for about fifteen seconds. "Well, you're still an idiot," I said quietly and turned on my heel, but I don't think it had the devastating effect I was hoping for.

After that, I resumed long days of walking, on account of it involves little contact with strangers. One afternoon, taking a shortcut between Euston Road and Tottenham Court Road, I chanced upon Fitzroy Square, a large open space enclosed by cream-colored

houses, nearly every one of which had a blue plaque on it announcing the identity of someone famous who had once lived there. Some
nine hundred of these plaques can be found on buildings all over
London. Fitzroy Square is particularly well endowed. It has plaques
to George Bernard Shaw, Virginia Woolf, James McNeill Whistler,
Duncan Grant, Roger Fry, Ford Madox Brown, and August Wil-
helm Von Hofmann, a German-born chemist who did novel and
transformative things with isomeric orthotoluidines and triphenyl
derivatives. That may not mean anything to you or me, but there
are chemists reading this page right now who are having orgasms.
In one corner of the square was an Indian YMCA—a YMCA just for
people from India; how splendid!—and opposite it was a statue to
Francisco de Miranda, liberator of Venezuela, who also lived here.
A later resident, it appears, was L. Ron Hubbard, beloved father of
Scientology. Goodness me, what a city.

Just beyond Fitzroy Square was a quiet, anonymous-looking
road called Cleveland Street. I couldn't think why the name was
familiar until I looked it up afterward and then it all came back.
Cleveland Street was the scene of one of the great scandals of the
nineteenth century. In the summer of 1889, a policeman stopped a
telegraph boy and found that he had a suspiciously large amount
of money in his pocket. The boy confessed that he had earned it
working in a homosexual brothel at 19 Cleveland Street. The police
investigated and found it full of men of superior rank, including
the sons of two dukes. But what made the story particularly juicy
was the widespread belief, hinted at in all the papers, that one of
the other Cleveland Street regulars was Prince Albert Victor, son
of the Prince of Wales and second in line to the throne. Later, this
same Albert would be proposed (on scanty evidence, it must be
said) as a possible Jack the Ripper, which must set some kind of
record for least salubrious royal personage. At all events, with
telling swiftness the prince was dispatched on a lengthy tour of
the empire, and on his return was summarily betrothed, whether

he wished it or not, to Princess Victoria Mary of Teck. Just over a month after the engagement was announced, however, the hapless prince caught pneumonia and, to the relief of nearly everyone, died. Amazingly—well, amazingly to me—Princess Victoria Mary thereupon married his brother, who went on to become King George V, our old friend of "bugger Bognor" fame. And all that, I think, may go some way to explaining why the royal family is occasionally just a trifle strange and emotionally challenged.

Now I am not saying that London is the world's best city because it had a homosexual brothel scandal or because Virginia Woolf and L. Ron Hubbard lived around the corner, or anything like that. I am just saying that London is layered with history and full of secret corners in a way that no other city can touch. And it has pubs and lots of trees and is often quite lovely. You can't beat that.

My two dear, pregnant daughters live in separate parts of London—Putney and Thames Ditton—about ten miles apart, and I decided one day to walk from one to the other after I realized that you can do so almost entirely through parkland. West London is extraordinarily well endowed with open spaces. Putney Heath and Wimbledon Common cover 1,430 acres between them. Richmond Park has 2,500 acres more, Bushy Park 1,100 acres, Hampton Court Park 750 acres, Ham Common 120 acres, Kew Gardens 300 more. Looked at from above, west London isn't so much a city as a forest with buildings.

I had never been on Putney Heath or Wimbledon Common— they run seamlessly together—and they were splendid. They were not at all like the manicured parks I had grown used to in London, but were untended and rather wild, and all the more agreeable for that. I walked for some time over heath and through woods, never very sure where I was despite having an Ordnance Survey map. The farther I walked, the more isolated things felt.

At one point it occurred to me that I hadn't seen anybody for about half an hour, couldn't hear traffic, had no idea where I would be when I next saw civilization. I had set off with the vague thought of walking past the site of Dwight D. Eisenhower's home during the Second World War, which I had by chance recently discovered lay more or less along the route I was taking today. I had read at the library about Eisenhower's domestic arrangements during the war. He could have had a stately home like Syon House or Cliveden, but instead he chose to live alone without servants in a simple dwelling called Telegraph Cottage on the edge of Wimbledon Common. The house was up a long driveway, the entrance guarded by a single soldier standing beside a pole barrier. That was all the security the Supreme Allied Commander enjoyed. German assassins could have parachuted onto Wimbledon Common, entered Eisenhower's property from the rear, and killed him in his bed. I think that's rather wonderful—not that Germans could have done that, of course, but that they didn't.

Although the Germans missed their chance to assassinate Eisenhower, they might easily have bombed him. Unbeknownst to Eisenhower or evidently anyone else on the Allied side, it seems, civil defense forces had erected a dummy anti-aircraft gun in a clearing just the other side of a hedge from Eisenhower's cottage. Dummy guns were put up all around London in an effort to fool German reconnaissance and trick their planes into wasting bombs. Fortunately for Eisenhower, the Luftwaffe seem to have overlooked this one.

Bearing in mind that I was largely lost, you may imagine my delight when I emerged from the common through the grounds of a rugby club, and discovered that I had more or less blundered onto the site of Eisenhower's cottage, though there is no telling the exact spot anymore. Telegraph Cottage burned down some years ago, and today the site is covered with houses, but I had a good stroll around and continued on to Thames Ditton satisfied that I had more or less hit my target, which is more than the Germans managed to do, thank goodness.

Buoyed up by my discovery, I carried on to Thames Ditton by way of Richmond Park and a long walk along the Thames. It was a very nice day. I had two weeks of very nice days and got to pretend it was work. That's why I do this for a living.

Of course not everything is ideal in London. About twenty years ago, my wife and I bought a small flat in South Kensington. At the time it seemed the wildest extravagance, but now after two decades of property price inflation we look like financial geniuses. But the neighborhood has changed. The gutters are permanently adrift in litter, some of it dragged there by foxes that scavenge through garbage left out overnight, most of it left by people who have neither brains nor pride (nor any fear of punishment). Workmen for some years have been quietly painting the street white one bucket at a time. The most dismaying loss, I think, is of front gardens. People seem strangely intent on getting their cars as close to their living rooms as possible, and to that end have been ripping out their little front yards and replacing them with paved service areas so that there is always a place for their cars and garbage bins. I don't quite understand why they are permitted to do this since nothing more obviously ruins a street. Not far from us is a street called Hurlingham Gardens, which should really be called Hurlingham Bin Storage Areas since nearly every owner has removed any trace of attractiveness from in front of their houses. The absence of any feeling of aesthetic obligation to one's own street is perhaps the saddest change in Britain in my time there.

On the larger scale, however, things have improved enormously in London. In the space of twenty years or so, London has acquired a memorable skyline, for one thing. It isn't that it has a huge number of tall buildings, but that the tall buildings it has are spread over a wide area. They don't jostle for attention, as in most cities, but stand alone so that you can admire them in isolation, like giant pieces of sculpture. It's a brilliant stroke. Now you get interesting views from all kinds of places—from Putney Bridge, from the Round Pond at Kensington Gardens, from platform 12 at Clapham Junction station—where there never used to be views at all. Scattered skyscrapers also have the incidental benefit of spreading prosperity. A new skyscraper in central London just adds more bodies to crowded streets and Underground stations, but a big new building in a more outlying area like Southwark or Lambeth or Nine Elms gives a jolt of economic input that can lift whole neighborhoods, creating demand for bars and restaurants, and making faded districts more desirable places to live or visit.

None of this was precisely intended. It is the by-product of something called the London Plan, which decrees that tall buildings may not impinge on protected views. One such view is from a certain oak tree on Hampstead Heath. (Well, why not?) No one can build anything that interrupts the view from the tree to St. Paul's Cathedral or the Houses of Parliament. There is a similar view from Richmond Park, miles from the city—so far out that I didn't even know you could see any of central London from there. London is crisscrossed by protected sightlines, which effectively requires tall buildings to be spaced out. It is a happy accident. But then that is London. It is centuries of happy accidents.

What is perhaps most extraordinary is how very nearly so much of it was lost. In the 1950s, Britain became obsessed with the idea that it needed to modernize, and that the way to do so was to tear down most of what the Germans hadn't bombed and cover what remained under steel and concrete.

One after another through the 1950s and '60s, grand plans were unveiled to bulldoze and rebuild great chunks of London. Piccadilly Circus, Covent Garden, Oxford Street, the Strand, Whitehall, and much of Soho all were proposed for redevelopment. Sloane

Square was to be replaced with a shopping center and high-rise apartment building. The area from Westminster Abbey to Trafalgar Square would become a new government district, "a British Stalingrad of concrete and glass slabs," in the words of one commentator. Four hundred miles of new motorways were to sweep through London and a thousand miles of existing roads, including Tottenham Court Road and the Strand, were to be widened and made faster—essentially turned into urban expressways—to tear through the heart of the city. Throughout central London pedestrians wishing to cross busy roads would be directed into tunnels or up onto metal or concrete footbridges. Walking through London would be like endlessly changing platforms at a mainline train station.

It all seems a kind of madness now, but there was remarkably little opposition. Colin Buchanan, Britain's most influential planner, promised that sweeping away the accumulated clutter of centuries and building gleaming new cities of concrete and steel would "touch a chord of pride in the British people and help to give them that economic and spiritual lift of which they stand in need." When a developer named Jack Cotton proposed to clear out most of Piccadilly Circus and build a 172-foot-high tower that looked like a cross between a transistor radio and a workman's toolbox, the proposal received the blessing of the Royal Fine Art Commission and was passed without dissent at a secret meeting of the Westminster Council Planning Department. Under Cotton's plan, the famous statue of Eros was to be raised up to a new pedestrian platform and integrated with a network of walkways and footbridges to keep people safely segregated from the speeding traffic below.

In 1973, the year I first settled in Britain, the most sweeping plan of all was unveiled: the Greater London Development Plan. This elaborated on all the earlier proposals and called for building a series of four orbital motorways, which would encircle the city like ripples on a pond, with twelve radial freeways bringing all the capital's motorways (the British equivalent of US interstate highways) into the very heart of the city. Freeways, mostly elevated, would slice through practically every district of London—through Hammersmith, Fulham, Chelsea, Earls Court, Battersea, Barnes, Chiswick, Clapham, Lambeth, Islington, Camden Town, Hampstead, Belsize Park, Poplar, Hackney, Deptford, Wimbledon, Blackheath, Greenwich, and more. A hundred thousand people would lose their homes. Almost nowhere would be spared the roar of speeding traffic. Remarkably, many people couldn't wait for this to happen. A writer for the *Illustrated London News* insisted that people "enjoyed being close to busy traffic" and cited the new Spaghetti Junction interchange in Birmingham as a place made lively and colorful by its infusion of speeding vehicles. He noted also the propensity of British people to picnic in lay-bys (small rest areas beside busy highways), which he interpreted as a fondness for "noise and bustle," rather than the fact that they were just insane.

The Greater London Development Plan would have cost a then-colossal £2 billion, making it the biggest public investment ever made in Britain. That was its salvation. Britain couldn't afford it. In the end, the visionaries were undone by the unmanageable scale of their own ambitions.

It is a mercy, of course, that none of these grand schemes ever saw life. But tucked in among them was one proposal that was quite different from all the others and might actually have been worth trying. It was called Motopia, and that is where I was headed next.

Chapter 5

Motopia

I TOOK THE 8:28 from Waterloo to Wraysbury via many stations. It was the morning rush hour, but all the rushing was in the opposite direction. My train was pleasingly empty. British train interiors used to be heavy and gloomy in a way that perfectly suited the dull, cheerless, stolid business of commuting. Now trains are full of bright oranges and reds. This one was rather annoyingly festive, like a children's fairground ride. I felt as if I should have had a toy steering wheel and little bell by my seat.

I was the only person to alight at Wraysbury station, which was unmanned and rather spookily deserted. The station stood a mile or so from the village, but it was a pleasant walk along a shady lane. Wraysbury is a strange, cut-off place. It is on the Thames opposite Runnymede and only a couple of miles from Windsor Castle as the crow flies, but it might as well be in Caithness for all its accessibility. It is separated from the outside world by an almost ludicrous number of barriers—two motorways, a railroad, acres of old gravel pits, an unbridged stretch of the Thames, three enormous reservoirs buttressed by hill-sized grassy banks and bounded by miles of high-security fences, and, finally, the great, impenetrable sprawl of Heathrow Airport and its service areas. The road approaches to Wraysbury are through zones largely filled with light industry, cement works, pumping stations, and other realms of heavy lorries and "Keep Out" signs. No one arrives in Wraysbury by accident and not many go there on purpose, but those who manage to pick their way through the surrounding dust and clutter find themselves in a sudden oasis of attractive tranquillity—or at least tranquil up to a height of about five hundred feet, for airplanes crowd the skies nearby as they begin and end their voyages at Heathrow.

But for those who can adjust to the noise above, Wraysbury is a sweet and agreeable place. The village has a church and a broad green with a cricket pavilion, a couple of good pubs, and a cluster of useful shops. The surrounding gravel pits have been filled with water to make recreational lakes, which are now the homes of many sailing and windsurfing clubs. Many of the houses are large and attractive, particularly where they overlook water. My wife grew up just across the Thames in Egham. From her side of the river, Wraysbury's rooftops are visible among the trees. This much I had seen a thousand times, but I had never been there, never had a reason to go.

"You'll like it," my wife promised.

She would know, for her father came from Wraysbury. He grew up in a small, dark, decrepit cottage with his poor widowed mother and elder sister at the end of a quiet, wooded lane a quarter of a mile or so from the village center. The cottage had no electricity or running water. The toilet was a privy at the bottom of the garden. My father-in-law used to tell us stories of how he would walk seven miles to Staines and back on a Saturday evening to buy a bag of stale buns for their supper, for that was all they could afford. It was a different world.

My wife had told me where the cottage was, and I found my way there now—or at least I found my way to where it had once been, for the cottage itself is long gone. It was blown to smithereens by a German bomb in 1943. Wraysbury offered nothing in the way of targets, so the bomber was either lost or perhaps just emptying out his bomb bay before turning for home. In any case, his tumbling bomb scored a direct, obliterating hit on my father-in-law's house. Luckily, no one was in at the time, so no one was injured, but the family lost everything and had to be rehoused. Thanks to his changed circumstances my father-in-law met a girl whom he would not otherwise have met, and in the fullness of time they married and produced two children, one of whom grew up and married me. So the direction of my life, not to mention the very existence of my children and grandchildren and whoever else follows, is directly consequent upon a German bomb that fell randomly on Wraysbury on a summer's evening long ago. I suppose all our lives must be at the end of a long chain of improbable coincidences, but it did seem fairly extraordinary to me, as I stood looking at the site of a long-vanished cottage, to think that if that bomb had fallen a hundred yards to either side or where the Germans had intended it to go, then my wife would never have existed and I wouldn't be in Wraysbury now. It further occurred to me that every bomb that fell in the war, on both sides of the Channel, must have changed lives in that way.

And with that considerable thought to chew upon, I turned and set off for the forgotten site of Motopia.

Had Motopia been built, everyone would know Wraysbury today. Motopia was a proposed model community based on the uniquely unexpected idea of banishing cars. It was the dream of a visionary named Geoffrey Jellicoe, who wasn't a town planner at all. He was a landscape architect, which doubtless explains why he gave cars a low priority. (No one seems to have noticed that Motopia was an odd name for a place that was designed to be essentially car-free.) Jellicoe's singular idea was to put the community's roads on rooftops, five stories up. Motopia was essentially to be a single giant building, built around a network of courtyards and standing in an eden of lakes and parkland. The lakes were to be fashioned out of the old gravel pits, which itself was quite an original notion. So Jellicoe had two big ideas that were radically out of step with the period—finding new uses for old industrial infrastructure and banishing cars from the daily landscape. Nobody thought like this then.

Altogether Motopia was to provide housing, shopping, offices, libraries, schools, and recreational space for a population of thirty thousand. Jellicoe envisioned people getting from place to place on moving sidewalks or in taxi boats along lakes and a small network of canals. He called his rooftop roads "motorways in the sky," which was more than a little absurd because the whole town was only about ten blocks across, the roads were narrow, and there were roundabouts every thirty or forty yards, so there was hardly scope for expressway-style acceleration, but his heart clearly was in the right place. The whole proposal was treated seriously enough that a site was chosen for it at Wraysbury and detailed plans were drawn up. It would have been lovely, if a little impractical. It certainly would have been worth trying. People would have come from all over the world to see it, so I was curious myself to see now this thing that never was.

Much of the proposed site for Motopia now lies under the M25 motorway and the neighboring Wraysbury Reservoir, built in 1967, but a good chunk of it remains undeveloped on Staines Moor, to the east of the village. It was an unexpectedly lovely walk down a green lane, with large, well-tended homes on one side and a broad, restored gravel pit, dotted with boats and sailboards, on the other. At length I came to a metal gate and an information board put up by the local council inviting me to follow a muddy track to Staines Moor. The track led to a footbridge over railroad tracks and thence to an underpass beneath the busy Staines bypass.

It was mostly wasteland and didn't look at all promising. I might well have turned back, but I saw that the underpass had a mural painted on it and out of politeness I went to inspect it. It depicted the animals to be found on the moor beyond and was lovingly done by an artist with real talent, who clearly felt some passion for this unknown piece of land. Intrigued, I walked to the end of the tunnel and stepped out into an astonishing sight—a sweep of green and golden countryside, a meadowland of trees and water, leading away to low green hills (which in actuality were the slopes of the surrounding reservoirs). It was as if someone had taken a square mile or so of the best Suffolk countryside and dropped it into the space between the motorway and bypass. Just before me the little River Colne broadened into a kind of marshy pond. A heron eyed me with undisguised loathing and with a few lazy flaps of wing departed to a spot a hundred yards away. In the middle distance planes took off from Heathrow, their noise a low grumble. The roar of traffic was reduced to a tolerable hum by the acres of waving grass.

Only gradually did I remember that I was standing in what would have been the heart of Motopia, and I suddenly realized that it would have been a tragedy if they had sacrificed this forgotten moor to build a town here. For the twenty thousand people of Staines, this was the only patch of accessible countryside for miles, but it was much more than that. An information board beside the pond informed me that this land had not changed in a thousand years. One hundred and thirty species of birds and three hundred species of plants had been recorded here.

I came upon a guy with a thousand tattoos walking a vicious-looking dog, but he said hello in a friendly manner.

"It's gorgeous here," I said.

"Yeah," he agreed. "Shame if they build on it."

"Is it under threat?" I asked in sincere alarm.

"They wanna put a runway here, mate."

"Here?" Heathrow seemed miles away—way beyond anything that could be reasonably considered contiguous.

He nodded. "You might be dodging jumbo jets next time you come here," he said and pleased himself with that.

Later I looked up Heathrow's proposals and he was right.

Staines Moor is the site of what is known as the South West Option for a third Heathrow runway. Under the proposal, Staines Moor would vanish completely. The new runway would extend Heathrow a mile to the south and a mile to the west, taking the airport to the very edge of Wraysbury. All the lovely homes I had lately walked past, as well as the lake beside them, would vanish. So would half of Wraysbury Reservoir. People in Wraysbury would be so close to the end of the runway that passing planes would all but blow their hats off their heads. The noise would surely be unbearable. Staines Moor would cease to exist at all.

The no-man's-land clinging to the edges of the Staines bypass and M25 is not a world built for pedestrians. It exists for the benefit of motorists and for people who need to get rid of large numbers of tires, old mattresses, and the remnants of demolished kitchens. Eventually amid puddles and detritus I came unexpectedly upon a footpath sign pointing the way toward Egham via a bridge over the Thames. This consisted of a path that ran exactly alongside, but about twenty-five feet below, the M25. It was surprisingly peaceful and rather lovely. The noise of traffic passed straight overhead, audible but strangely distant. I was in a calm world of greenery—a little tunnel through woodland. Butterflies flitted between stalks of wild buddleia. Swarms of tiny insects shone in the sunlight. After about half a mile the path sloped upward and abruptly emerged right beside the motorway at a bridge, where both roadway and path crossed the river together, divided by a waist-high barrier. I walked onto the bridge and into a most remarkable experience. On my left-hand side was a roar of speeding traffic of almost painful intensity on a road ten lanes across. This is the busiest stretch of road in the whole of Europe. But on my right was a scene of utter serenity—a Thames tableau caught in a moment of summery perfection. In front of me, about a hundred yards away, was a lock and pretty weir. A motorboat was in the lock, its owners doing things with ropes and cranks. Beside the lock was a hotel with a terrace where people were sitting having lunch in the sun. On the opposite bank were some attractive cottages and moored boats. If you were standing at a rack of postcards, this is the view you would select. Yet behind me, near enough to make my jacket flap, was the ceaseless flight of traffic. I was on the boundary between two worlds yards apart but wholly unaware of each other. It was surreal.

I don't think anyone ever crosses this bridge on foot. Ahead of me, the path was so overgrown as to be obliterated. I pushed through lush sprays of lacy flowers and nodding daisies. Wildflowers of purple and yellow and the most delicate pale blue sprouted everywhere. This was a garden growing on concrete. That is the most extraordinary fact about Britain. It wants to be a garden. Flowers bloom in the unlikeliest places—on railway sidings and waste ground where there is nothing beneath them but rubble and grit. You even see clumps of flowery life growing on the sides of abandoned warehouses and old viaducts. If all the humans in the UK vanished tomorrow, Britain would still be in flower. This is in complete contrast to America, where nature is wild and raw. You need flamethrowers to keep the weeds in check where I come from. Here it is just miles of accidental loveliness. It is really quite splendid.

At the bottom of the slope, I stepped out of this little wilderness onto the other side of the Thames and was confronted with one of my favorite views—the grassy, unspoiled flatness of Runnymede meadow, site of the signing of the Magna Carta, running up to the bottle-green majesty of Cooper's Hill, the most prominent eminence in this part of Surrey. I have known this area for years, but had never approached it from this angle or crossed Runnymede on foot, and was pleased to do so now. It is just a great empty field, now maintained by the National Trust, but it is ineffably glorious, particularly on a fine day such as I had now. At the top of Cooper's Hill is one of the country's great little-known shrines, the Air Forces Memorial, where beautifully inscribed in stone are the names of 20,456 airmen who died in the Second World War but have no grave. It is serenely beautiful and moving—I can't recommend it too highly—but it is at the top of a long, steep hill and was too distant for me to reach on this day. I headed instead across the field to the Magna Carta memorial, a little open-air rotunda erected in 1957 by the American Bar Association and memorable today as the only decent thing ever done by lawyers. It commemorates, of course, the signing of the Magna Carta somewhere in the vicinity. (No one knows exactly where. It was a long time ago.) I had it all to myself, as I expect any visitor would on most days.

Beyond, and of more particular interest to me, was the Kennedy Memorial, erected in memory of JFK shortly after his assassination. You reach it by going up a steepish path through the woods. The designer, I was delighted to discover, was none other than our old friend Geoffrey Jellicoe.

Jellicoe didn't have a huge budget or much time—the memorial was thrown up in the immediate aftermath of Kennedy's death—but he made the most of what he had. The path is made from sixty thousand small granite blocks, joined together to make steps, and it meanders up the hill in a pleasingly sinuous fashion. At the top is a large block of granite, cracked in places and showing obvious signs of repair here and there, inscribed with part of Kennedy's inauguration speech. Beside it was a bench and a hawthorn tree. I felt like I was the first person in years to go there.

At the bottom of the hill I met two slightly plumpish young women who were peering up the shrubby slope as if they thought there might be bears up there. They both wore outfits of khaki shorts, T-shirts, and sneakers. Each carried a little knapsack.

"Have you just come from the memorial?" one asked me.

"No, I was having a dump in the bushes," I wanted to say, but of course I didn't. "Yes I have," I said. Her accent was American, so I tried to sound American, too. "It's pretty neat," I said. It was the first time I had said "neat" since seventh grade, and I quite enjoyed it.

"Is it very far?"

"Not very. But there are steps."

A slight look of panic. "How many?"

"I don't know—maybe fifty or sixty."

They had a conference. One decided to retire to the nearby tea-room; the other more bravely elected to go for it and set off up the hill. Within a few steps, she was making the sort of grunts female tennis players make at Wimbledon when serving for an important point. I listened to her progress for a few moments, then turned to bid farewell to her companion, but she had already dismissed me, and was wholly preoccupied with the challenge of getting across five hundred feet of open ground before she could enjoy the relief of a chair and a soft drink. I didn't have the heart to tell her that the soft drink would almost certainly be small and served more or less at room temperature.

Runnymede, incidentally, is another British treasure that nearly didn't survive. In 1918 plans were unveiled to cover the meadow with houses. Urban Broughton, a Briton who had made a fortune in America, bought it from its potential developer to save it. When Broughton died, his widow, an American, gave it to the nation. So one of Britain's most historic sites remains pristine today because of the generosity of an American lady.

And with that patriotic thought in mind, I adjusted my pack and headed to Windsor.

Chapter 6

A Great Park

I N 1971, A SMALL, improbable chain of events was set in motion when the Department of Health in Britain sent posters to American institutions of higher learning that read: "Would you like to train to be a psychiatric nurse in England?"

Since the answer to that question was "Obviously no," the posters didn't attract much attention. Most, I suspect, were discarded upon receipt. But one somehow made it onto a crowded bulletin board in a dormitory at the University of Iowa, where two friends of mine from Des Moines, Elsbeth "Buff" Walton and Rhea Tegerstrom, saw it and, remarkably, very possibly uniquely, decided to respond. And so a few weeks later they were, rather startlingly, three thousand miles from home and proudly dressed in the sky blue uniforms and starched white caps of student nurses at Holloway Sanatorium in Virginia Water, Surrey.

Large parts of my life are the result of decisive actions taken by others, but I have never been more indebted to anyone than to Buff and Rhea for their bold leap across the ocean, for it changed my life completely, too. If not for them, I would never have settled in England or met my wife and this book would probably be called *My Forty Years in Peoria*. God bless them both.

I was drawn into Buff and Rhea's happy, eccentric orbit the following year when I stopped to see them at the end of a summer of hitchhiking around Europe. I was supposed to be on my way home to Des Moines, but during the course of an outstandingly convivial evening in the Barley Mow pub in Englefield Green, on the eastern edge of Windsor Great Park, they suggested that I should get a job at the hospital, too. Mental hospitals were always desperate for staff, they assured me. So the next day, I impetuously applied and to my mild astonishment was immediately accepted. It was rather like joining the army. I was sent to a basement storeroom where I was given two charcoal-gray suits, one thin black tie, two white shirts, three neatly folded white lab coats, some sheets and pillowcases, a set of keys, and enough other items to form a stack in my arms that I could not see over. I was assigned a room in the male staff quarters and told to report to Tuke Ward. I was now an employee of the National Health Service, a resident of England, a sort of grownup, and a full-time foreigner—four things I hadn't expected to be just twenty-four hours before. Not long after that I met a jolly decent student nurse named Cynthia, and found myself falling for her and falling for England simultaneously. Forty years later, I am still with them both.

So this was the part of the world where my English life began. I hadn't been back to the area for some years, and was eager to spend a day strolling through my former life. So, early on yet another bright summery morning—the weather was being most un-Englishly kind—I set off from my hotel in Windsor and found my way through the still-quiet streets of the town to the broad, processional way known as the Long Walk, leading from the town into Windsor Great Park and to the world of my past just beyond.

Windsor Great Park is a remnant of the ancient Windsor Forest and part of the royal estate. It is a little land of enchantment, like the set of a fairy tale, a rolling, timeless realm of woods and farms and the picturesque cottages of estate workers, charmingly threaded with wandering lanes that are largely free of traffic. (Only those with business on the estate are allowed to use them.) It has a lake, enormous lawns for polo, scattered statues and other ornaments, herds of grazing deer, and occasional walled enclosures beyond which are royal retreats, like the Royal Lodge, where the Queen lived as a girl. It is forty square miles of arcadian glory on the very edge of London, yet relatively few people visit it and hardly any plunge into its bosky interior.

The Long Walk ends with a slow climb to the summit of Snow Hill, where there is a giant equestrian statue of King George III and panoramic views of Windsor Castle and all the countryside around. Henry VIII, it is often said, rode up to this point to listen for the canons of London announcing the execution of Anne Boleyn. Everything was lovely except the sky. Planes wheeled just overhead, dragging shadows over the earth, as they prepared to land at Heathrow, five miles off to the east. They were low enough that I could read the serial numbers on their undersides, and very loud—louder even than at Wraysbury because Windsor is directly on a flight path. Goodness knows what it will be like for the people west of London if Heathrow gets a third runway. Already nearly half a million flights a year come and go at Heathrow. A third runway would increase that to 740,000. At what point do people decide that enough is enough?

I think we are there already. I am forever booking flights from London to distant places, and I can't remember ever not having lots of choices of every type—of airlines, times of departure, times of return. Does anyone really need 50 percent more of plenty? The argument is that if Heathrow doesn't expand, other European airports will steal its business. Charles de Gaulle airport, it is pointed out, handles ten million fewer passengers a year than Heathrow, but has four runways to Heathrow's two. Amsterdam has 20 million fewer passengers but six runways. If Heathrow doesn't build new runways, the argument goes, it will stop being able to compete. The question that occurs to me is then why hasn't that happened already?

I'll tell you what people will actually get with another runway. They will get more takeoffs and landings, but in smaller planes. There used to be five or six flights a day between Chicago and the other main cities of the Midwest. Now you may get a dozen flights a day, perhaps even more, but in tiny regional jets seating thirty people with their knees jammed up against their faces. So you have more choice but a much poorer service. With small planes, for one thing, it is much easier to cancel undersold flights and put everyone on the next plane.

Do you know, incidentally, why Heathrow was built where it is? After the war the task of choosing a location for a new London airport was given to Alfred Critchley, a Canadian-born business-man who had made a fortune first by promoting greyhound racing and then by getting into cement in a big way, so to speak. He consolidated a whole bunch of small cement makers into the mighty enterprise known as Blue Circle and became hugely wealthy in the process. During the war, Critchley helped to set up training programs for fliers, and because he knew a little about aviation and a great deal about the pouring of cement he was given the job after the war of deciding where to build a new airport to replace the old aerodrome at Croydon. I had always assumed that Heathrow was selected for some important practical reason—the porosity of the subsoil or depth of the water table or something—but in fact Critchley chose it because it was halfway between his house in Sunningdale and his office in London.

Critchley died in 1963 before Heathrow became the colossus it is now, so he had no idea what he was inflicting on the world. The Heathrow he last saw was still a place of pleasure and excitement. I happen to own three packets of Viewmaster discs of Heathrow from that period and they are a marvel to behold for they show that Heathrow in those days had about sixteen airplanes and a few dozen well-dressed customers. One man with an excellent mustache seemed to run the control tower all by himself. The terminals were sleek, modern, and practically empty. Everyone involved in the check-in process was immensely happy. Aboard the planes, everyone was happier still. The stewardesses not only served you a large tray of food, but stood smilingly by your seat and watched you eat it.

What a wonderful world that was, and how remote it seems now. It is a challenge to believe that there was ever a time that airline food was exciting, when stewardesses were happy to see you, when flying was such an occasion that you wore your finest clothes. I grew up in a world in which everything was like that: shopping malls, TV dinners, TV itself, supermarkets, freeways, air conditioning, drive-in movies, 3D movies, transistor radios, backyard barbecues, air travel as a commonplace—all were brand-new and marvelously exciting. It is amazing we didn't choke to death on all the novelty and wonder in our lives. I remember once my father brought home a device that you plugged in and, with an enormous amount of noise and energy, it turned ice cubes into shaved ice, and we got excited about that. We were idiots really, but awfully happy, too.

I had an enjoyable amble across the park and exited at a spot called Bishop's Gate, where I joined a network of wooded back lanes leading to Englefield Green. The broad green for which the village is named is by far its finest feature. It is, I suppose, three or four acres in size, and lined on every side with big houses. At its southern end stands the Barley Mow pub, smaller than I remembered but still handsome. It occurred to me with a shiver that it must be nearly forty years since I was last in it. It was too early for it to be open, but I peered through the windows and was glad to see that it hadn't changed in any alarming way. Across the green, visible above a fringe of billowy hedges, was a large house that Buff's boyfriend Ben pointed out to me once as the home of Leslie Charteris, creator of the Saint detective stories. This impressed me deeply. In Iowa, we were not used to seeing the houses of well-known people on account of there were no well-known people in Iowa.

I can't say I was a fan of Leslie Charteris myself or even knew a single thing about him, but each month my mother bought a *Saint* magazine for twenty-five cents at the supermarket and read the stories avidly, which was recommendation enough for me. This man was not only a famous author, he was a *magazine*. Whenever I passed the house after that, I always dawdled in the hope of glimpsing the elusive Charteris, but I never did. I imagined him to be a suave Englishman, like the Simon Templar character he created for his stories. In fact, I later learned, he was half Chinese, born Leslie Yin in Singapore in 1909. So even if I had seen him, I would probably have thought he was Charteris's herbalist or something. I had no way of knowing it at the time, but Charteris was a recluse and a bigot. Though he was at the height of his fame thanks to a television series starring Roger Moore, he had long since given up writing his own books, but left it to ghostwriters.

Away from the green, Englefield Green village was never very pretty and now seems to have given up trying. It used to have banks and butchers and greengrocers, but those are mostly gone now and instead there are coffee shops and little restaurants and an inordinate number of garbage bins outside every property. Goodness knows what they get up to there, but it sure generates a lot of waste.

Beyond the village, standing along the busy A30 at the top of Egham Hill, is the campus of Royal Holloway College, an outpost of the University of London. The college began as a single vast building, a kind of English Versailles set down on a hilltop in the outermost suburbs of London, and was the philanthropic gift of a patent medicine manufacturer named Thomas Holloway. Holloway College was one of the grandest buildings built anywhere on the planet in the nineteenth century and it still staggers on first sight. It is five hundred feet long across the front, a third of a mile around. It contains 858 rooms and embraces two spacious courtyards. But where Versailles was made for kings, Holloway College more nobly was built as a women's college, at a time when women's colleges were a rarity. Why Thomas Holloway and his wife, Jane, decided to sink much of their wealth into a college for women isn't known, any more than it is known why they decided to fund a companion building, Holloway Sanatorium, to house well-off deranged people, two and a half miles away in the village of Virginia Water.

Both were designed by an architect named William Henry Crossland, who produced these two colossal buildings, and then fell into a curious professional inertia. Though he lived another twenty-two years, Crossland never did another thing. Instead he took up with an actress eighteen years his junior named Eliza Ruth Hatt, and with her produced a second family while still remaining attached to the first, living some of the time with his wife and daughter in one house and some of the time with Hatt and the children she bore him in another. The effort of it all exhausted his body and his resources, and ultimately the patience of both his wife and mistress, for he died alone and destitute in cheap lodgings in London in 1908.

Which surely proves something.

I strolled on to Virginia Water along Bakeham Lane, which in the whimsical fashion of English roads changes its name to Callow Hill about halfway along. The road was rather busier than it had once been, and a good deal more littered around the edges, but otherwise was still leafy and pleasant. It is amazing how much you absorb and evidently hold on to forever on a route you have commonly walked, for I felt I remembered nearly everything—the curve of driveways, the pitch of house roofs, the knockers on front doors. It was extraordinary to recall so vividly things I hadn't thought about in decades, particularly when you consider that I can't remember what I had for breakfast or the names of anyone I haven't spent at least an hour with in the last two weeks.

At length I came to Christchurch Road, the straight and stately avenue leading into the village of Virginia Water. Once this was the loveliest road I could imagine, lined on both sides for a mile or so with dark and jaunty houses in a rambling arts and crafts style, each one a happy jumble of gables, porches, and jostling chimney pots, each standing in its own paradise of billowy shrubs and tumbling roses. It was, as I said in *Notes from a Small Island,* like stepping into the pages of a 1937 copy of *House Beautiful* magazine. Those houses are nearly all gone now, bought for a fortune only to be torn down and replaced by much larger homes in a style that might be called Russian Gangster.

The village center is much changed, too. Nearly all that I remember fondly is gone. The Tudor Rose, the world's most endearingly terrible restaurant, where all the food was black or dark brown, except the peas, which were a pale gray, has long since departed and is much missed by me, if no one else. The fishmongers, travel agents, and greengrocers are all gone, too. One of them—I don't remember which—had a royal warrant from the Queen Mother, which always impressed me. Barclays, the only bank in the village, had just permanently closed. A sign on the door invited us to go to Chertsey for our banking needs. Even more tragically vanished was the bookshop owned by the writer, actor, and film director Bryan Forbes. It was the ideal bookshop. I spent hours in there; read whole books in there. Every once in a while you would see Forbes himself, and that was always a thrilling moment for me, a boy from Iowa. Once I saw him talking to Frank Muir, a television personality known for his wit and erudition, and almost fainted from the excitement.

The bookshop was also the scene of my most outstanding

moment of manliness in life. I happened to be browsing there one day when a patient from the sanatorium whom I'll call Arthur came in. Arthur was middle-aged and unexpectedly distinguished-looking. Like many of the patients at the sanatorium, he came from a privileged background (the hospital had been private until the late 1940s) and he dressed quite well in the tweedy style of a country gentleman. You would never have taken him for a madman. But he had one quirk that kept him permanently institutionalized. He could not abide being spoken to by strangers. If someone merely smiled and said good day, Arthur would explode in froth and fury and pour forth a tumult of startlingly original insults. Everyone in the village knew this, so no one disturbed him on his daily rounds. It happened, however, that on this day the bookshop was in the care of a sweet, newly employed young woman who had no idea of Arthur's peculiarities, and asked him if she could help him find anything.

Arthur turned on her more in amazement than anger. It had been years since anyone had addressed him in a public place.

"How dare you speak to me, you sluttish bitch," he hissed, swiftly warming to the task. "Don't you come anywhere near me, you pustulant, spread-eagled daughter of Satan." Arthur was nothing if not expressive when roused. The young woman stared at him with a look I had only ever seen on a female face in horror movies in the moment between a shower curtain being yanked open and a dagger coming down.

I stepped up and in a sharp tone said: "Arthur, put the book down and leave at once."

That was all you had to do with Arthur—just speak to him firmly. Meekly, he returned the book to its shelf and wordlessly left the shop.

The young woman looked at me with simple, heartfelt amazement. "Thank you," she breathed.

I gave her a winning but bashful smile as I had seen Gary Cooper do in the movies. "Glad to be of help," I said. If I'd had a cowboy hat I would have touched the brim.

The door opened and Arthur put his head in. "Will I be allowed pudding tonight?" he asked anxiously.

"I haven't decided yet," I said, my tone curt once more. "We'll have to see how you behave."

Arthur made to depart again, but I called him back.

"And, Arthur, you must never trouble this young lady again," I added. "Do you understand?"

He muttered some pathetic acknowledgment and slunk off. I gave the woman another Gary Cooper smile. She was now regarding me with a look of frankest adoration. It's funny, but sometimes life throws these moments at you that have the capacity to change everything in an instant. In other circumstances, who knows where this encounter might have led? Unfortunately she was only about four feet tall and nearly spherical, so I simply shook her hand and wished her a good day.

Virginia Water has always been an outpost of great wealth, with private roads lined with giant houses curling around the exclusive Wentworth golf course. But around the fringes of the village are some neighborhoods of more modest homes, and it was in one of these, a prewar brick duplex with an unusually big garden, that my wife and I passed half a dozen happy years when my children were small and I was a young journalist on *The Times*. The area in which we lived was called Trumps Green, and I was very pleased, when I strode up there now, to find that it hadn't changed much. Our old road had lots more cars parked along it than formerly but otherwise was much the same. Around the corner from our house was a parade of shops that provided for more or less all our daily needs—a butcher's, a post office and newsagent, a small grocery store, and the world's most astonishingly well-stocked hardware store, presided over by a kindly man named Mr. Morley.

I loved Mr. Morley's shop. You were never disappointed there. Whatever was on your shopping list—linseed oil, two-inch masonry nails, coal scuttle, small can of Brasso metal polish—Mr. Morley had it. I am sure if you said to him, "I need 125 yards of razor wire, a ship's anchor, and a dominatrix outfit in a size eight," he would find them for you after rooting around for a few minutes among bird feeders and bags of bone meal.

Mr. Morley was always cheerful and upbeat. Business was always "not bad, could be worse." Mr. Morley seemed to me the last bastion of a vanishing world. So I can't tell you how pleased I was to see the shop sign *Morley Hardware* still in place and the windows still crowded with tools and useful items. When civilization finally collapses, when the dead rise up and walk again and the North Sea floods British shores, Mr. Morley will still be there, selling mothballs, flyswatters, seed packets, and galvanized wheelbarrows. As Britain sinks beneath the waves, it will be Mr. Morley, standing on the tallest of his many stepladders, who will be the last to go.

I pushed through the door, eager to see him. Mr. Morley always remembers me. I expect he remembers all his old customers. To my surprise there was another man behind the counter. I had never not seen Mr. Morley in there. I swear if you'd gone to the shop at midnight, you'd have found Mr. Morley standing at the counter in the dark, just waiting for it to be time to open.

"Is Mr. Morley on holiday?" I said.

"Oh, he's gone," said the man in a quiet, grave tone.

"Gone?"

"Dead, I'm afraid. Massive heart attack. About four years ago."

I was temporarily speechless. "Poor man," I said at last, but I was really thinking of myself. Mr. Morley and I were about the same age. "What a shame."

"Yes."

"What a terrible thing. Poor man."

"Yes."

I couldn't think of another thing to say. It occurred to me that I didn't have the faintest idea of whether Mr. Morley had a family or where he lived or anything at all about him. But then how would I ever have found out such a thing? "Good afternoon, Mr. Morley. Could I have a bag of mothballs and are you in a happy, stable relationship, heterosexual or otherwise?" He had no existence that I knew of outside his shop. So I just said thank you and in somber mood departed.

I strolled back into the village proper, to the boundary of the old sanatorium, now an elegant gated compound called Virginia Park. The sanatorium closed in 1980 and the building was converted into apartments. The grounds, where once there were gardens and a cricket pitch, are now filled solid with executive homes. For £895,000, according to a glossy brochure, you can buy a "magnificent townhouse in this Grade I–listed restored mansion." Well, let's be quite clear about this. It is not a restored mansion at all. It was a building full of gloriously demented people, some of them from Britain's finest families. Where you lay your head tonight could very well be where Lady Boynton routinely peed in the corner.

But what a wonderful retreat it was in its day. People have never had a more beautiful place to be lost and addled. Of William Henry Crossland's two great creations for Thomas Holloway, the sanatorium is to my mind much the finer. It, too, has an enormous frontage, but it is broken up with a great central tower and gables that make it more interesting and less forbidding. I remember one June evening when I was new there looking out a window from high up in the building onto the grounds and thinking it was the finest view I had ever seen. A cricket match between the Holloway staff and the staff of some other hospital was moving toward a stately conclusion below me. Long, end-of-day shadows lay across the lawn. The gardening detail—a ragtag army of patients lethally but trustingly armed with scythes and hoes and shears—was marching in broken ranks back from the vegetable garden. Britain in that moment really seemed a perfect place.

It's all long gone now, I'm afraid. When the sanatorium shut, the patients were moved to a new unit within a general hospital at Chertsey. In the beginning they were allowed to roam freely, as they always had, but that had to be brought to an end because the patients, robbed of all that was familiar, wandered into places they shouldn't go and disturbed people in the waiting areas by asking them for fags or calling them pustulant whores or any number of other things that weren't compatible with an efficient, modern general hospital. So they had to be locked away, and in no time at all most of them had sunk into a permanent torpor from which none of them ever stirred and no one had time to rouse them.

But it was great while it lasted. Looking back now, I really do think Britain had attained something approaching perfection just around the time of my arrival. It's a funny thing because Britain was in a terrible state in those days. It limped from crisis to crisis. It was known as the Sick Man of Europe. It was in every way poorer than now. Yet there were flower beds in roundabouts, libraries and post offices in every village, cottage hospitals in abundance, council housing for all who needed it. It was a country so comfortable and enlightened that hospitals maintained cricket pitches for their staff and mental patients lived in Victorian palaces. If we could afford it then, why not now? Someone needs to explain to me how it is that the richer Britain gets, the poorer it thinks itself.

All of the long-term patients at Holloway were quite mad—that is why they were long-term mental patients, after all—but sufficiently institutionalized on the whole that they could go to the village each day to buy tobacco or a newspaper or have a cup of tea in the Tudor Rose. To any outsider it must have seemed extraordinary, a village filled with normal citizens going about their daily business, but also liberally scattered with people who were clearly not right in the head, who conversed in an animated fashion with empty space or stood at the back of the village bakery with their nose pressed to the wall. You can't have a more civilized community than one in which hospital staff play cricket at the end of a summer's day and lunatics can wander and mingle without exciting comment or alarm. It was wonderful, possibly unsurpassable. It really was.

That was the Britain I came to. I wish it could be that place again.

Chapter 7

Into the Forest

I

ONCE OR TWICE A year I go walking with my old friends Daniel Wiles and Andrew Orme, and sometimes we are joined by another friend from California, John Flinn, as we were this year. We have walked the ancient tracks of England, from Offa's Dyke to the Ridgeway, traipsed through the steep hills and green meadows of the Peak District and Yorkshire Dales, followed the Thames from source to sea, clambered to the tops of Dorset's highest hills, and met many other challenges and adventures. Once we were chased from a Thames path by a very angry swan—you'd have fled, too, believe me—but otherwise our adventures have been pretty largely marked by hardiness, fortitude, and courage in the face of cows, with just tiny amounts of bitching here and there.

This year for various reasons we could only get together for three days, so we decided to meet at a hotel in Lyndhurst, in the heart of the New Forest, which pleased me very much. I lived for two years on the edge of the New Forest near Christchurch when I worked in Bournemouth as a young man, and have spent many a happy Saturday tramping around there. It's a lovely area. If you are from another country, you may need to be told that the New Forest isn't in fact new and not even altogether a forest. It hasn't been new since the time of the Norman Conquest and, though much of it is wooded, a great deal of it is open heathland and nothing like a forest as we normally think of it. "Forest" originally signified any area set aside for hunting. It could be wooded but didn't have to be. Nearly all of Britain's once-great forests—Sherwood Forest, Charnwood, Shakespeare's Forest of Arden—have gone altogether or are much reduced. Only the New Forest retains something of its ancient dimensions.

Throughout much of its history, the New Forest has been famous for its wild ponies, which graze wherever they like and wander picturesquely through the villages. Nowadays it is also celebrated for its traffic at Lyndhurst, the unofficial capital of the forest. People come from all over Britain to experience Lyndhurst's famous traffic jams, often without intending to. Perhaps no other town in Britain has been more comprehensively overwhelmed by the motorcar over a longer period with less imaginative attempts at amelioration. On a typical summer's day, some fourteen thousand vehicles are funneled through a constricted T-junction on Lyndhurst's high street, governed by a single set of traffic lights.

Unfortunately, out of all the people in the world to whom the authorities might have turned to solve the problem, they chose highway engineers. In my experience, the last people you want trying to solve any problem, but especially those involving roads, are highway engineers. They operate from the principle that while no traffic problem can ever truly be solved, it can be spread over a much larger area. At Lyndhurst some years ago they introduced an astoundingly circuitous one-way system, which appears to have been designed to take vehicles through as many formerly peaceful residential districts as could be packed into a single visit. The system ensures that anyone getting in the wrong lane, which is almost inevitable for newcomers, will have to go around twice more— once to discover that, oops, we're still in the wrong lane, and once to get into the right one. It has occurred to me that Lyndhurst may not receive fourteen thousand different vehicles a day, but just a couple of thousand going round and round again.

It used to be that people who knew the area would turn off onto back roads before reaching Lyndhurst and detour around the town altogether, thus getting to their destination sooner and helpfully removing themselves from the town's congestion. That is what I tried to do now. At a place called Pikes Hill, I shot down a side lane toward Emery Down, but discovered at once that the highway engineers, cunning souls, had narrowed the back roads to a single lane with occasional passing places to discourage freelance orienteering, with the result that traffic jams back there were as bad as any in Lyndhurst. I am serious when I say that this is how these halfwits operate—by endeavoring to make everywhere as bad as the part that caused the original problem. It took me an hour and a quarter to get the last mile and a half to my hotel on the high street.

My hiking companions were similarly inconvenienced in different places. By the time we managed to rendezvous it was nearly one o'clock and we were to a man famished, so our first piece of business was to find a place to eat. On the edge of Lyndhurst is a famous beauty spot called Swan Green, where a clutch of thatched cottages overlook the aforesaid green. It is a view that has featured on many a box of fudge. Opposite is the Swan Inn, to which we now repaired, happy to be in each other's company and looking forward to something to eat after our drives. We studied the bill of fare keenly, then presented ourselves at the bar to place our order.

"Oh, we're not taking food orders just now," the young bar attendant told us. "There's been a run on the kitchen," he added by way of explanation.

We looked around. It wasn't that busy.

"How long will it be?" we asked.

He considered the tranquil scene around him. "Hard to say. Three quarters of an hour maybe."

This was all the more confusing because the Swan Inn is one of those pubs that would like you to regard it as a restaurant, with chalkboards of specials all over the place and menus and silverware on the tables.

"Can I just check I have got this right?" I asked. "On a Sunday afternoon at the height of the tourist season, a number of people have turned up here wanting lunch, and this has taken you by surprise?"

"Well, we're short of staff because it's Sunday."

"But isn't Sunday one of your busiest days?"

He nodded emphatically. "I'll say."

"Yet it is everyone's day off?"

"Well, it's Sunday, you see," he said again as if I hadn't quite got it the first time.

Andrew was already leading me gently away by the elbow. He must have seen my wife do it at some point. We walked back into Lyndhurst and found a café that was able to serve us lunch without throwing the kitchen into a panic, and afterward, feeling much refreshed, we went for a good healthy tramp through dark woods and sunny heath.

What a joy walking is. All the cares of life, all the hopeless, inept fuckwits that God has strewn along the Bill Bryson Highway of Life, suddenly seem far away and harmless, and the world becomes tranquil and welcoming and good. And to walk with old friends multiplies the pleasure a hundredfold. Lyndhurst was heaving with people, particularly around a beauty spot on the edge of town called Bolton's Bench, which has a famous yew tree but, more particularly, a nearby parking lot. I read once that the furthest distance the average American will walk without getting into a car is six hundred feet, and I fear the modern British have become much the same, except that on the way back to the car the British will drop some litter and get a tattoo.

But as soon as we headed into the wooded enclosures beyond Bolton's Bench, we had the forest largely to ourselves, and what a treat it was. It was a perfect day for a walk. The sun was shining, the air was warm. We saw many grazing wild ponies. Wildflowers filled the sunny glades and nodded at the pathside. Andrew, our natural history expert, recited their names for us—ladies' bedsore, yellow cowpox, tickle-me-knickers, sneezle, old man's crack. I didn't have my notebook with me, so I may not have all the names exactly right, but that was the drift of it.

Allow me to introduce my companions:

Daniel Wiles is a retired maker of television documentaries. I met him twenty years ago when we made a program together and we have been friends ever since. He likes naps and an ice cream in the afternoon.

Andrew Orme is an old friend of Daniel's—indeed a very old friend, for they met at a boarding school when they were small, pale, skinny, frightened boys. They talk about those days a lot. Andrew is by far the smartest of us—he went to Oxford University, as we always boast proudly to landladies—so we let him carry the map and make all the important decisions.

John Flinn was for a long time the travel editor of the *San Francisco Chronicle,* but he is now retired. He does a lot of travel writing still, and passes through England from time to time and is thus able to join us pretty regularly. He loves baseball and shares with me an abiding admiration for the fashion model Cheryl Tiegs as she was forty years ago and, in our memories, will always be.

We tend not to see each other in between our semiannual walks, and so always have a lot of catching up to do. Daniel and Andrew walked along chattering about public school things—flagellation and steamed puddings, I suppose. They can go on for hours like that when they first get together. John and I talked about baseball and American politics. Because he is from California, John always has good stories about people doing strange things. This time he told me about how a person not far from his home had recently been Tasered, almost fatally, by a park warden for not having his dog on a leash.

"He was Tasered for not having his dog on a leash?" I asked. California stories always take a little getting your head around.

"Not intentionally exactly. The warden was trying to stop him from leaving the scene and Tasered him, and he had a heart condition and nearly died."

"Do the authorities often Taser people in your public parks?"

"There's a campaign to keep dogs on a leash. They're having a crackdown."

"An armed crackdown?"

"Well, they don't usually Taser people. It's just that the warden asked him to wait while she checked his identity—"

"Park wardens can do background checks?"

"Apparently. But for some reason it took a while and the man got tired of waiting and said to her, 'Look, either cite me or let me go.' But she wouldn't do either, so eventually, after several minutes more, he said, 'This is a waste of my time and I've got things to do and I don't think you actually have the authority to detain me because you are just a park warden, so I am going to go now.' And he started to leave."

"So she Tasered him?"

"Right between the shoulder blades, I expect."

We thought about this for a while and then talked about Cheryl Tiegs.

Because of our late start, we didn't go very far—a little over three miles to a place called Balmer Lawn, near Brockenhurst. It was intensely pretty in the late afternoon sunshine. We stood looking appreciatively at it for a minute, then turned and headed back to Lyndhurst. It was a modest start, but a good one.

—

Back at the hotel, I showered, then sat on the edge of my bed watching TV, waiting for it to be time for a drink, and wondering how many tens of thousands of days have passed since BBC One last showed a program that anyone not on medication would want to watch. I flicked through the channels to see what else was on and the very best option available was a program called *Great British Rail Journeys* in which a former politician named Michael Portillo with a taste for annoyingly colorful suits rides trains around the country for half an hour. Occasionally he would get off the train and spend approximately forty seconds with a local historian who would explain to him why something that used to be there is no longer there.

"So this used to be the site of the biggest prosthetics mill in Lancashire?" Michael would say.

"That's right. Fourteen thousand girls worked here in its heyday."

"Gosh. And now it's this giant supermarket?"

"That's right."

"Gosh. That's progress for you. Well, I'm off to Oldham to see where they used to make sheep dip. Ta-ta."

And this really was the best thing on.

At dinner I brought the subject up. "I like Michael Portillo," Daniel said, but then Daniel likes everybody. He told us that shows on some satellite stations have more people working in the studio than are watching at home.

I mentioned my observation that the world seems to be filling up with imbeciles. They explained to me that this is simply an affliction of age. The older you get the more it seems the world belongs to other people. Daniel, it turned out, had it much worse than I did. He had a whole list of demands for putting the world back to the way it ought to be. I can't remember exactly what they were, but I believe they included leaving the European Union, returning to the gold standard, bringing back capital punishment and the British Empire, restoring home deliveries of milk, and banning immigration.

"I'm an immigrant," I pointed out.

He nodded grimly. "You can stay," he allowed at last, "but you must understand you are permanently on probation." I assured him that I had never considered myself anything else.

The rest of the evening was mostly filled with drinking too much and recounting our afflictions, but as my afflictions are principally to do with memory loss I don't recall the details.

II

Years ago I lived next door to Ringo Starr and for about six months didn't know it. This was during a comparatively short period in my life when my wife and I lived in a row of old workmen's cottages in Sunningdale, in Berkshire, and when I say "next door" I mean that our back fence backed onto Ringo's estate. Ringo's house was hundreds of yards away up a grassy slope and hidden from view by trees, but it was still in the strict sense next door. I learned that Ringo was the owner of the estate from our neighbor Dougie, who lived, in the more traditional sense, next door.

"I'm surprised you haven't seen him around," Dougie said. "He's often in the Nag's Head. Nice chap."

I went home and said to my wife: "Guess who lives in the big house on the hill."

"Ringo Starr," she said.

"You knew?"

"Of course. We see him all the time around here. I stood behind him in the ironmonger's the other day. He was buying a hammer. Nice man. He said hi."

"Ringo Starr said hi to you? A Beatle said hi to you?"

"He's not really a Beatle anymore."

I ignored this, of course.

"The Beatle Ringo Starr bought a hammer in our local hardware store and said hi to you and you didn't think to tell me."

"It was just a hammer," she said.

This is the problem with the British. They all have stories like this. In fact, they all have better stories than this. I have no idea how we got onto the subject of the Beatles, but the next day as we were walking along a forestry track in dense woods, I mentioned my Ringo Starr story. My companions nodded appreciatively. Daniel allowed a suitable pause, out of politeness, and then said: "When I was at university I spent an afternoon with John Lennon."

I could see at once that this was going to out-trump me by about a thousand percent.

"Really?" I said. "How?"

"I did an interview with him. I believe it has become known as 'the lost interview.'"

Make that 10,000 percent.

"You conducted the 'lost interview' with John Lennon?"

"Yes, I suppose so."

"How?"

"Well, it was the winter of 1968. The Beatles had just done the Sergeant Pepper album. I was at Keele University. Another student, named Maurice Hindle, and I wrote to Lennon asking for an interview for the student magazine, not seriously expecting a reply, never mind an interview, and he said, 'Sure, come to my house at Weybridge.' So we took a train to Weybridge and he came and picked us up at the station."

"John Lennon picked you up at Weybridge station?"

"In a Mini. It was all a bit surreal. We spent the afternoon at his house at St. George's Hill, which is the most exclusive part of Weybridge. Lennon was very nice, entirely normal. He wasn't that much older than us, of course, and I think he was just a little lonely for normal conversation. The house was a mess. He and Cynthia had recently split, and none of the dishes had been washed or anything. At one point, we decided to have a cup of tea, but there weren't any clean ones, so we had to wash some up, and I can just remember thinking, 'Wow. I am standing at a kitchen sink washing tea cups with John Lennon.' My job for the interview was to look after the recording, while Maurice took the photographs. When we got back to Keele, Maurice decided to develop the film himself, to save money, and somehow ruined the lot. So there is nothing at all from one of the great days of my life. At the time, I thought I was going to have to kill Maurice."

We indicated that we all could understand that.

"Lennon never did anything like that again," Daniel went on. "It became known as the lost interview, though in fact it was never lost because I kept the tapes. Forty years later, we auctioned them at Sotheby's in London for £23,750. They were bought by the Hard Rock Cafe."

"Wow," we all said.

I decided it wasn't worth trying to impress everybody with my Leslie Charteris story.

"But your Ringo Starr story is very sweet," Daniel said generously to me.

John was reminded of a time when, as a fourteen-year-old boy in Manhattan, he saw Cheryl Tiegs come out of an apartment building and followed her for several blocks till she disappeared into another building. Cheryl Tiegs didn't mean anything to Daniel and Andrew, so they started talking between themselves about canings and ice-cold morning showers, but I was all ears about Cheryl Tiegs, of course, and made John several times retell the part about how he repeatedly walked briskly past her till he was about twenty or thirty yards ahead, then casually turned and walked back, so that he could see her face-on. John did this about eleven times in four blocks, but is pretty sure she didn't notice on account of his careful air of nonchalance. I loved that story.

And so passed a happy morning walking in the woods.

Our destination for the day was Minstead, a village in a glade in the northern part of the forest. Andrew had read that it was a good walk—which it indubitably was, through long stretches of undisturbed forest—and that Minstead had a lovely church. As a bonus, the churchyard contained the grave of Arthur Conan Doyle, creator of Sherlock Holmes.

It was spiritualism that brought Doyle to the New Forest just about a hundred years ago. Spiritualism became curiously popular at that time. Its adherents included not just Arthur Conan Doyle but also the future prime minister Arthur Balfour, the naturalist Alfred Russel Wallace, the philosopher William James, and the renowned chemist Sir William Crookes. By about 1910, Britain contained so many devoted spiritualists that they seriously considered forming a political party. But nobody outdid Doyle for devotion. He wrote some twenty books on spiritualism, became president of the International Spiritualist Congress, and opened a psychic bookshop and museum near Westminster Abbey in London. (The building was destroyed by a bomb in the Second World War. You would think he'd have seen that coming.)

The problem was that even by the elastic and forgiving standards of spiritualism and the paranormal, Doyle's beliefs grew increasingly loopy. He became convinced that fairies and other woodland sprites were real and wrote a book, *The Coming of the Fairies*, insisting on their existence. Through séances he developed a friendship with an ancient Mesopotamian named Pheneas, who gave him lifestyle guidance and warned him of a coming apocalypse. In the book *Pheneas Speaks*, Doyle revealed that in 1927 the world would be rocked by floods and earthquakes, and that one of the continents would sink beneath the seas. When these events failed to pass, Doyle conceded that Pheneas had got the year wrong (he'd been using a Mesopotamian calendar evidently), but that they would most assuredly happen sometime.

On the advice of Pheneas, Doyle bought a house near Minstead and there passed his days sitting quietly in the woods with a camera waiting hopefully for fairies to emerge (they never did) and his evenings holding séances at which he communicated with Britain's most eminent dead. Charles Dickens and Joseph Conrad both asked him to finish the novels they had left uncompleted at death, and the recently deceased Jerome K. Jerome, who had mocked Doyle in life, now sent a message through a third party saying: "Tell Arthur I was wrong." All this Doyle took as incontrovertible vindication of his beliefs. Remarkably, throughout all this Doyle continued to produce his celebrated Sherlock Holmes stories, all based on fastidiously rational thinking, and resisted the temptation, which must have been great, to have the great detective call on spiritualism to solve his cases.

In 1930, Doyle died (though in fact spiritualists don't die; they just get very still apparently) and was buried in the garden of his main home in Crowborough in Sussex. His wife was tipped in beside him when her time came, but in 1955 the house was sold and the new owners weren't keen on having skeletons cluttering up the garden, so Arthur and his wife were dug up and reinterred in the churchyard of All Saints, Minstead—a move that was not without controversy since spiritualists are not really Christian on account of their dogged refusal to die. Still, it must be said that the Doyles have been in Minstead churchyard for more than half a century and not caused any fuss.

All Saints is a handsome church, with a fine multilevel pulpit and an unusual side room, called a "parlor pew," which is essentially a small living room, with its own furniture and fireplace, where the owners of nearby Malwood Castle could watch sermons in homey comfort. We examined it thoroughly and appreciatively, then repaired to the nearby Trusty Servant pub for lunch. It is an old pub, but it has been modernized in an artificial style that I find vaguely irritating, like when a hotel puts some books in a bar and calls it The Library. The prices were astounding. A chicken, pesto, and mozzarella burger was £12.75. Confit of duck, with bok choy, pickled rhubarb, and red currants was £16.25. I would pay to have some of those things taken off my plate. But the place was full of people happily chowing this stuff down. Bitching bitterly, I parted with £8.50 for a cheese ploughman's.

After lunch we went and had a look at the Rufus Stone, which stands in a clearing about two and a half miles from Minstead and marks the spot where King Rufus—more properly King William II, son of William the Conqueror—had a bad day in the summer of 1100. Rufus was hunting with some cronies when an arrow fired by one Walter Tyrrell twanged into his chest and killed him more or less outright. Rufus was no great loss. He was short and fat, with lank blond hair and a ruddy complexion. ("Rufus" means ruddy). He was impious, licentious, and famously effeminate. He never married, and seemed wholly disinclined to produce an heir. Tyrrell maintained that the king's death was just an unfortunate accident—that his arrow ricocheted off a tree—but hardly anyone bought that story. Just to be on the safe side, Tyrrell fled to France, reportedly on a horse that had been shod with its shoes facing backward to confuse any followers.

The Rufus Stone is a simple black obelisk, about four feet high, with inscriptions on three sides. No one knows whether this was really the spot, or even close to the spot, where Rufus fell. Some authorities say he died at Beaulieu, a dozen or so miles away to the southeast. I know it was a long time ago, but I think it is interesting to find an English king commemorated so modestly.

—

The thing about walking is that, generally speaking, it is a great deal more fun to do than to read about, so I won't challenge your patience by telling you all about our third day other than to say it was jolly nice and that it took us past another literary connection in the form of the fallen estate of Cuffnells. This was once the home of Alice Liddell, who is better remembered by posterity as the Alice of *Alice in Wonderland*. I knew that Alice as a child in Oxford had provoked the unhealthy stirrings of Charles L. Dodgson, a stammering mathematician, and that he had written stories to amuse her, which became *Alice Through the Looking-Glass* and all that. But I had never paused to wonder what had become of her afterward. Well, the answer is that she turned into a beauty and lived a fairly unhappy life in the New Forest.

It might have been otherwise. Alice as a young woman was pursued by Leopold, Duke of Albany, youngest son of Queen Victoria. The young Ms. Liddell was both beautiful and intelligent; her genetic input would have done the royal family no harm at all. But the Queen rejected her because she was a commoner, so Leopold had to look elsewhere for breeding stock and Alice ended up with an amiable cipher named Reginald Hargreaves.

Hargreaves had grown up in and inherited Cuffnells, a magnificent house and estate half a mile outside Lyndhurst. Cuffnells was one of the finest homes in the district, with twelve bedrooms, massive drawing and dining rooms, and a hundred-foot-long orangery. There Reginald and Alice lived quietly and dully, and in increasingly straitened circumstances. Reginald was not much of a businessman, it seems, and kept selling pieces of the estate to make ends meet until there wasn't much of it left. The couple had three sons. Two died in the First World War and the third lived a life of dissipation in London. In 1926, Reginald also died, abruptly, leaving Alice alone and unhappy in a crumbling house. She became an ill-tempered recluse, and was mean to her servants. In 1934, she died aged eighty-two. Cuffnells, falling apart, was demolished a short while later. Today the space where Cuffnells once stood has vanished into woodland. You would never guess now that once a great house had stood there.

We parted the next morning, but there is a postscript to our adventure in the woods. The hotel we stayed at in Lyndhurst was called the Crown Manor House Hotel. It seemed a decent enough place to us all—not hugely friendly or charming or well run, but decent enough—but soon after our visit Andrew forwarded to each of us an interesting article from the *Southern Daily Echo* of Southampton, concerning the hotel's devotion to hygiene. The article stated:

> A Hampshire hotel has been ordered to pay more than £20,000 in fines and costs after preparing food in rat-infested areas. The Crown Manor House Hotel in Lyndhurst, which twice closed its kitchens after inspectors found evidence of the infestation, admitted five food hygiene offences in a case heard at Southampton Magistrates' Court. They included two offences involving the production, processing and distribution of food in areas where there was "an ongoing infestation of rats."

"I thought those peppercorns tasted funny," I quipped merrily, but I was genuinely astounded to read about this, and for two reasons. First, I was naturally a touch chagrined, as you might expect, to learn that I had been staying in a hotel that was so slyly squalid, but I was also, and almost equally, amazed to find that I could now read about this sort of thing in a daily newspaper. I worked for the *Southern Daily Echo*'s sister paper in Bournemouth for two years in the 1970s, and in that time I don't believe we ever ran a story about a filthy hotel or restaurant. That wasn't because there weren't filthy hotels and restaurants, I am sure, but because those things were secret.

Everything was secret in Britain then. Everything. There was even a law, the Official Secrets Act, designed to make sure that essentially no one could know anything. Honestly. It was quite extraordinary when I think back on it. Among matters that were classified in Britain in those days, ostensibly on grounds of national security, were: levels of chemical additives in foods, hypothermia rates among the elderly, the carbon monoxide levels of cigarettes, leukemia rates near nuclear power stations, certain road accident statistics, even some proposals to widen roads. In fact, according to the wording of Section 2 of the act, all government information was secret until the government declared it otherwise.

Sometimes all this became a little ridiculous. During the Cold War, Britain had a program of building rockets for the delivery of warheads, and naturally it needed to test them. It was notionally a top secret program. It even had a slick secret code name: Black Knight. The problem is that Britain is small and doesn't have vast deserts in which to conduct secret tests. In fact, there isn't any part of Britain that is really secret at all. For various reasons, it was determined that the best place to test the rockets was at a famous landmark and popular tourist site on the Isle of Wight called the Needles. The Needles are clearly visible from the British mainland, so the firing up of the rockets could be seen and heard for miles around. A friend of mine told me that whole communities used to turn out on the beaches of southern Hampshire to watch the smoke and flames. Even though the firings were visible to thousands, the tests were officially secret. No newspaper could report them. No official could speak of them.

Even better was the Post Office Tower in London. For over a decade and a half, it was the tallest building in Europe. It dominated the London skyline. Yet because it was used for satellite communications, its existence was officially a secret. It wasn't allowed to appear on Ordnance Survey maps until 1995.

So I was delighted to find that Britain's Food Standards Agency now makes public all its inspection reports. You can look up the ratings of any restaurant and food handler in the country. This, I discovered, provides hours of absorption. I checked out every restaurant I have ever gone to, and found that two of my favorites aren't nearly as keen on hygiene as I would like them to be, which is why you don't see me in them anymore. One striking feature is that many of the inspection reports are not very current. A good many are up to three years old. This is because local-authority food inspection budgets have been slashed. It is evidently more important, in this curious age in which we live, to save taxpayers' money than it is to be vigilant in ensuring that their local restaurants aren't poisoning them.

When I read about the court case against the Crown Manor House, I felt sufficiently moved to do something I had never done before: I opened an account with TripAdvisor, created a password, and submitted a review. It wasn't actually a review, but a message alerting customers that the hotel had been fined for having rats in its kitchens and directing readers to a link to the newspaper article. My feeling was that if I were considering booking into a hotel that had been fined recently for having rats in its kitchens, I would very much appreciate it if someone drew my attention to it. A few days later, TripAdvisor sent me an e-mail saying:

> We have opted not to publish your review as it does not meet our guidelines . . . We accept reviews that detail first-hand experiences with the facilities or services of an establishment. General discussion that does not detail a substantial experience will not be posted. No second-hand information

or hearsay (unverified information, rumors or quotations from other sources or the reported opinions/experience of others).

So there you have it. Criminal convictions, government hygiene ratings, and other secondhand information have no place on a hotel and restaurant ratings website. As I write, TripAdvisor gives the Crown Manor House Hotel high recommendations for both quality and cleanliness, and there is no indication that it has ever in the recent past been otherwise.

Let's pause for just a moment to incorporate a little context here. Think of the worst place you have ever eaten. In my case, it was a late-night kebab house in London, where meat of indeterminate origin permanently rotated on a heated spit. I am sure the meat was years old. I passed this kebab house regularly for years and the amount of meat on the spit never seemed to shrink or change. Yet one night when I was a little drunk (I know, hard to believe) and hungry, I went in and paid money for a grubby fellow in a slaughterhouse shirt to carve some slices off the slab and put them in a kind of pita-bread first baseman's glove, and I greedily devoured it. Grease ran down my chin. For weeks afterward my beard smelled like thousand-year-old mutton. Even now the thought of it makes me retch a little. I am sure you have eaten in places just as bad yourself. Well, here's the thing. Those terrible restaurants we have eaten in have probably never been fined £16,000, with £4,000 costs, for being disgustingly squalid. In your whole life, you may never have experienced a place so bad that it got a zero rating and had its kitchen shut down twice.

But then again you may just have been reading TripAdvisor recommendations. That's all I'm saying.

Chapter 8

Beside the Seaside

ENGLAND IS A COMPLICATED place. It has five different kinds of counties, all with different histories, purposes, and boundaries. First, there are historic counties—the ones that go way back in history—like Surrey, Dorset, and Hampshire. Most of these are still there, but some have been chopped into smaller pieces or even summarily dismissed and exist today only as partial relics or fond memories. Huntingdonshire was absorbed into Cambridgeshire forty years ago, but people still tell you that they live there. Middlesex hasn't been a county since 1965, but there is still a Middlesex County Cricket Club and a Middlesex University.

Then there are administrative counties, which exist principally to provide working boundaries for county councils. Administrative counties tend to pop in and out of existence like soap bubbles. Humberside was created in 1974, but disbanded in 1996. Rutland, conversely, was banished in 1974 and resuscitated in 1996.

The third kind of county are postal counties, whose boundaries may be different again. The outline of Cheshire, for instance, on the postal map is quite different from that of Cheshire on a historic map and different again from its administrative shape.

After postal counties come ceremonial counties, each of which has a Lord Lieutenant (or Official Twit), to preside over royal visits and other grand occasions requiring someone with a sword and a jacket with epaulettes, but otherwise ceremonial counties, like the Lord Lieutenants who serve them, have no known purpose.

Finally there is Cornwall, which isn't a county at all but a duchy—a distinction that the Cornish are very sensitive about. (You could say that it is a touchy duchy.)

And that is just English counties. Welsh and Scottish counties are separately confusing. The result of all of this, not surprisingly, is occasional confusion. When I worked on the Business News section of *The Times* in London we frequently had conversations at the copy editors' table that started with a question like:

"Where's Hull?"

"Up north," someone would answer confidently.

"No, I mean what county is it in?"

"Oh. Dunno."

"I think it's in East Yorkshire," someone else would say.

"I don't think there is an East Yorkshire," a fourth person would say.

"Really?"

"Don't think so. Well, maybe. Not sure actually."

"It doesn't matter," yet another person would interject, "because Hull isn't in East Yorkshire even if there is an East Yorkshire, which there isn't. Hull is in Lincolnshire."

"Actually, I think it's in Humberside. Or possibly Cleveland," a fifth or sixth person would add.

"Cleveland is a city in the United States," someone else would volunteer confidently.

"There's a Cleveland up north now, too."

"Really? When did that happen?"

"No idea. Not sure if it's a county or just an administrative unit."

These conversations could go on for hours and would generally end up with the person who started it all deciding that he would just put "Hull," and leave it at that.

The one corner of the country I knew about was Bournemouth and its smaller neighbor Christchurch because I worked in one and lived in the other for two years in the 1970s. Until 1974, Bournemouth and Christchurch were in Hampshire, but in that year English county boundaries were redrawn and Bournemouth and Christchurch were hefted into Dorset. The idea was to take some people out of overpopulated Hampshire and put them into underpopulated Dorset. But news of this change hadn't filtered through to everyone, so sometimes even into the 1980s a news article in *The Times* would place Bournemouth in Hampshire. Once when this happened I sauntered over to the Home News desk—which is to say the national news desk—and pointed out to the chief copy editor that they had Bournemouth in Hampshire.

"And your point is?" he said.

"Well, Bournemouth's not in Hampshire," I elaborated.

"I believe you'll find it is," he said, returning to his work.

"No, it's in Dorset. I worked for two years on the paper in Bournemouth. It was part of the condition of employment to know where we were."

The Home News editors didn't have a lot of respect for the Business News editors and I don't entirely blame them. We looked a little like Vince Vaughn's team in *Dodgeball*.

"We'll look into it," the chief copy editor told me.

"You don't need to look into it. It is a fact."

"And I said we'll look into it."

I don't remember my exact words from this distant remove, but I daresay "anus" was in there somewhere.

"Touchy fucker," the chief said as I walked off.

"He's an American," one of his colleagues pointed out gravely.

I looked in the final edition of the paper the next morning and Bournemouth was still in Hampshire. People on the Home News desk were by and large wankers, except for one or two who didn't rise quite that high.

Anyway, Christchurch is indubitably in Dorset, and, forty minutes after leaving Lyndhurst, so was I.

I have an abiding attachment to Christchurch. When my wife and I were newly married and I had my first grown-up job on the *Evening Echo* in Bournemouth, we lived for six months in a rented flat above a fish-and-chip shop in the outlying district of Purewell, then bought a bungalow in the even more outlying hamlet of Burton. It was a sweet white-painted cottage with a pretty garden and a distinctive copper beech on the front lawn, a perfect first home. We bought it from a kindly white-haired couple who had lived there for decades and were most concerned that we should look after the garden, which we solemnly promised to do and lovingly did for the two years we lived there.

I hadn't seen the house in years and wondered if it would look small now, the way fondly remembered places so often do. In fact, I didn't recognize it. I drove up and down our old road twice without spotting my own house, and finally parked and got out to have a closer look on foot. The only property I could find with a copper beech didn't look like ours at all.

I stood out front and checked a slip of paper to make sure I had the house number right. I did, but it was nothing like the house we had lived in and fussed over. The front garden was gone altogether, buried under asphalt. The most decorative objects on it were two garbage bins and a terra-cotta pot with a dead plant in it. A little enclosed glass porch that had served as a mini-greenhouse had been taken away for no visibly good reason. Even more pointlessly, a perky bow window, once the central feature of the house, was gone, too, replaced with a rectangle of aluminiumized double glazing.

Nearly all the other houses on the street had been similarly assaulted by owners looking for more parking and less maintenance. All the lovely gardens, all the well-tended prettiness of my day, were gone. It really doesn't pay to go back and look again at the things that once delighted you, because it's unlikely they will delight you now.

I continued on to Christchurch, fearing the worst, but in fact it was quite all right. Most of the good things were still standing and some of the ugly things—notably, a semi-industrial area formerly dominated by a large pale-blue gasometer—had been taken away. The gasometer zone was now occupied by stylish apartments and retirement homes with jaunty, if entirely imaginary, nautical names like The Moorings or Sea View Meadows, which I suppose are more romantic and commercial than Gasometer Way or Goodness Knows What's Buried Beneath Us Cottages.

The high street at first sight seemed pretty much unchanged. The buildings offered a pleasantly higgledy-piggledy mix of styles, sizes, and materials, yet formed a comfortable and coherent whole in that way that British towns seemed to do effortlessly for centuries and now often can hardly do at all. Though the buildings were the same, the businesses within them were completely changed. It is remarkable, when you think about it, how many types of shops have vanished from British high streets in only a few years: most butchers, greengrocers, fishmongers, ironmongers, repair shops, gas showrooms, electricity board showrooms, most building societies, travel agents, and independent bookshops.

Lots of post offices have gone, too. It's a sacrilege not to lament their loss, and I am genuinely sorry to see them go, but it has to be said there was scarcely a less pleasurable, more Soviet-style environment in which to pass half an hour than in a British post office queue. They were bureaucracy gone mad. At their peak you could (genuinely) conduct any of 231 types of transactions in a British post office—renew your TV license, collect pensions and family allowances, pay car tax, withdraw or deposit money in a savings account, buy savings bonds, mail parcels. All that was required of you was that you be white-haired, hard of hearing, and able to spend up to an hour hunting through a tiny coin purse for a 20p piece.

Despite all the changes in retail patterns, Christchurch's high street seemed to be thriving. The old Regent Cinema, which in my day was a dowdy bingo parlor, had been refurbished in an enlightened joint undertaking between the borough council and a nonprofit charity set up to run it. Now it offers a busy program of new and old movies, amateur and professional theatrical productions, talks and satellite broadcasts from places like the Royal Opera House and Royal Shakespeare Company, and a whole lot more. I was impressed. The restaurants in Christchurch are clearly better than they used to be, the pubs are cleaner, the supermarkets more exotically stocked. Christchurch was my new model community.

I had a look around Christchurch Priory—the biggest parish church in England, I believe, and very fine it is, too—then walked out past the flat where my wife and I once lived (the fish-and-chip shop was still there, I was pleased to see), then on a little-used path around the marshy harbor to the neighboring village of Mudeford, with long, dreamy views across the water to the stately gray hulk of the priory, and I thought that when England is lovely there isn't any place I would rather be.

I had lunch at a nice waterside café in Mudeford, then returned to the car and drove on the five miles or so to Bournemouth. When I did *Notes from a Small Island*, I stayed at the Pavilion Hotel in Bournemouth. It was a pleasant, old-fashioned place and I thought I would stay there again, but it turns out that the Pavilion was torn down in 2005. It took me some time to work this out, because when I googled "Pavilion Hotel, Bournemouth," I got responses from seventeen hotel-booking companies all faithfully promising to get me a room at the Pavilion Hotel at a very attractive rate. The first one turned out to be for the Pavilion Hotel in Avalon, California.

As usual I am left staggered by the Internet. How can anything be so useful and stupid at the same time? Does somebody somewhere in the Google universe really think that I am looking for any hotel in the world called the Pavilion and that one in California will do me as well as one in Bournemouth? I know these things are managed by an algorithm, but somebody still has to give it parameters. But then, I suppose, that is the thing about the Internet. It is just an accumulation of digital information, with no brains and no feelings—just like an IT person, in fact.

The bottom line is that seventeen companies promised that if I opened their pages they would book me into a hotel that in fact no longer exists. TripAdvisor's search entry indicated that the Pavilion Hotel in Bournemouth had a rating of 4.7 out of 5. "Book Pavilion Hotel and Save on Pavilion Hotel!" it shouted in strangulated English, so I clicked on its page out of curiosity and of course it turns out that when you reach the right page on TripAdvisor there is no Pavilion there because *there is no Pavilion there*. This is the thing that just drives me mad about the Internet, which is that the commercial parts of it operate on the assumption that there is no particular necessity for any part of it to be accurate, truthful, or reliable. When did that become all right?

Luckily, one thing Bournemouth has in abundance is alternative hotels and my wife had booked me into a boutique establishment— the Slightly Up Ourselves Hotel, I think it may have been called—on the East Cliff, where I dropped my bags, admired the arrangement of twigs in a bowl by the door, and hastened back out, eager to see the town. By chance, the hotel was by the bus stop where I used to get off for work each morning, so I decided to retrace the steps I took back then from bus stop to workplace to see how much I could recall.

I loved coming to work in those days. I was young, newly married, in my first real job. The English seaside was still something special then. Bournemouth was the queen of the south coast resorts and I felt lucky to spend every day in a place that other people saved up to visit occasionally. I rode each morning on a yellow double-decker bus from Christchurch, via Tuckton, Southborne, and Boscombe. I always sat upstairs, usually at the front, and experienced every journey like a seven-year-old on a school outing. Bounding off the bus on a hill above the sea, I walked a few hundred yards through the town, down one hill and up another, to the rather grand art deco offices of the *Echo* on Richmond Hill, one of several hundred people whose important job it was to get the town up and running each morning. I enjoyed the responsibility.

Early on I discovered a shortcut through a wooded cemetery tumbling down a hillside behind St. Peter's Church. One morning, when I stopped to tie a shoelace, I found that I was looking at the grave of Mary Shelley, creator of Frankenstein and widow of the poet Percy Bysshe Shelley. I had no idea that she was there, but then few people do. Mary Shelley only went to Bournemouth once, to visit her son who was living there, but she declared a wish to be buried there with her parents, the writer William Godwin and the noted feminist Mary Wollstonecraft Godwin—a somewhat odd request since they were long dead and had no connection with the town either. Nonetheless Mary's son dutifully had their remains brought from London and deposited beside his mother. Someone also tossed in the heart of Percy Bysshe (the only poet named for the sound of a match hitting water), who had drowned in Greece nearly thirty years before. It was his first visit to Bournemouth, too. So Bournemouth's most famous (and possibly most crowded) grave contains the last earthly remains of four people who had nothing to do with the place, three of whom never even saw it.

For years all this felt like my little secret—even people in Bournemouth, I found, didn't know about the grave—but when I passed it now I was interested to see that two bouquets had been laid on the lid, so someone must miss her. A couple of other mourners, lacking flowers, had left empty crisp packets, bless them, while someone else had placed an empty can of Carlsberg lager on the grave of a man named Duckett, who went to a greater reward, according to the inscription, in 1890.

Opposite the cemetery, where a small supermarket stood in my day, is now a large Wetherspoon's pub called, interestingly, the Mary Shelley. She really has been rediscovered. Around the corner there used to be a Forte's café where the coffee machine sounded like a jet taking off (and the coffee tasted like jet fuel with milk in it), and where I stopped each morning for a coffee and to study one or two of the broadsheets in a desperate daily effort to swot up on English life and current affairs. And from there, suddenly vaguely nervous, I proceeded to work.

Now it can't be argued that being a downtable copy editor on the *Bournemouth Evening Echo* was the most stressful and high-powered job in journalism in the 1970s, but it was stressful enough for me. The problem was that I knew nothing like as much as I ought to know to work safely as a journalist in Britain, and I lived in constant fear that my employers would discover the full extent of my ignorance and send me back to Iowa. Employing me was an act of kindness. I had only the barest working knowledge of British spelling, punctuation, grammar, and idiom, and almost no acquaintance at all with vast areas of the nation's history, politics, and culture.

I remember one day I was given a Press Association story to edit that I couldn't follow at all—or actually could only partly follow, which made it even more confusing. The story was clearly about declining stocks of seafood off the west coast of Cornwall, or something like that—it was all about bivalves and mollusks, I remember—but scattered through it were frequent unrelated references to a certain well-known northern railway station. I didn't know if this was a mistake or just the Press Association being eccentric in some way that I didn't yet understand. I had no idea what to do, so I just read the story over and over. For two or three paragraphs the story would make sense and then suddenly there would be a mysterious, seemingly nonsensical reference to this railway station.

As I sat there, paralyzed with uncertainty, a copy boy came past and dropped a slip of paper on my desk, and all suddenly became clear. The slip of paper was a correction, and it said: "In Cornish fisheries story, for 'Crewe Station,' please read 'crustacean.'"

And I thought then, "I will *never* master this country" and I was right. I never have. Luckily for me, the people I worked with were kind and patient and looked after me. By sad coincidence two of them, Jack Straight and Martin Blaney, died within a couple of weeks of each other in early 2015, which is why I mention them, in affectionate commemoration, here.

I looked now for the café where I used to have my morning coffee, but couldn't find it anywhere—couldn't even find the 1950s arcade of which it used to be a part—and then I strode up to Richmond Hill and examined the old and very slightly faded offices of the *Echo*.

They dropped "Evening" from the title a few years ago in recognition that no one wants an evening paper anymore, but they can't do anything about the consideration that hardly anyone wants a paper at all. The *Echo*'s circulation was about sixty-five thousand in my day, which wasn't very robust even then; it's under twenty thousand now. In one recent six-month period it fell by 21 percent. The *Echo* used to occupy the whole building, but now most of the downstairs belongs to a bar called the Ink Bar and a restaurant called the Print Room, both closed for refurbishment when I passed. But at least the *Echo* is still hanging in there. Since 2008, 150 local papers have closed in England, including some once major ones like the *Surrey Herald* and *Reading Post*. That's not good. Without local newspapers there's no one to tell you when somebody's been fined for having rats in their kitchens.

The *Echo* doesn't seem to be the only thing in Bournemouth that isn't quite what it once was. The whole of the town center was eerily quiet for a weekday afternoon. In my day, the streets of Bournemouth were nearly always busy—when I close my eyes and recall it, it's always sunny, with men in suits and women in summer dresses—but now it was nearly as empty as Sundays used to be. Bournemouth has always had an interesting downtown in that it consists of two shopping areas divided by the Pleasure Gardens, a long and lovely park with a bandstand, flower beds, and a little stream running through it. It used to be an agreeable intrusion, a leafy break from commerce when you were going from, say, Dingle's Department Store on one side of the gardens to Woolworth's on the other. But that was a pace for another age. Now people want to get everything accomplished in a hurry, and not have a lot of trees and lawns in the way, so they seem to have abandoned the heart of town altogether, on both sides of the park.

Some years ago they pedestrianized the Old Christchurch Road, a pleasantly curving shopping street, and gave it benches and tubs of flowers and smart brick paving, but over the years wherever the bricks have been lifted to renew pipes or do other groundwork, the intrusions have been roughly patched with asphalt, leaving behind long black gashes and unsightly rectangles. This is the problem with Austerity Britain. Repairs are either not made at all or are done in a slapdash fashion. There is a gradual deterioration until at some indefinable point the place stops being agreeable and instead becomes rundown and depressing. Welcome to Bournemouth. The tragedy for so many town councils is that they think they can quietly cut spending and no one will notice or care. The tragedy for the country may be that they are right.

But then again, perhaps not. Bournemouth's tourism numbers have plunged in recent years. Domestic visits fell from 5.6 million in 2000 to 3.3 million in 2011, and visitor nights in the same period more than halved from 23 million to 11.4 million. Bournemouth in my day prided itself on the range and elegance of its diversions. It had good theaters, stylish shops and restaurants, a renowned Sinfonietta Orchestra, and many other outposts of culture and refinement, but much of that is gone now. The Sinfonietta closed in 1999. The Winter Gardens went in 2002. The Pier Theatre followed more recently. A giant Imax theater opened on the seafront in 2002, but almost immediately ran into financial difficulties and closed three years later. In 2013, the council paid £7.5 million for the building just to tear it down. When I passed by now, the site was a giant hole in the ground.

But at least it still has the sea. Bournemouth boasts seven miles of golden beaches lined with cliffs and beach huts and indented here and there with steep wooded valleys called chines. There are still some very fine neighborhoods tucked up in those hills. I decided now to walk the four miles along the beachside promenade to Canford Cliffs, a neighborhood of old homes and considerable wealth at the top of Branksome Chine, and then back along the cliff tops.

It was a better day for walking than bathing—cool and overcast. Still, there were a fair number of people on the beach. Some were pretending to enjoy themselves. A few were doggedly sunbathing in defiance of the fact that the sky was a duvet of clouds. A small number were actually swimming, or at least bouncing in the waves. Years ago, when my wife and I were just dating, she took me on a day trip to the seaside at Brighton. It was my first exposure to the British at play in a marine environment. It was a fairly warm day—I remember the sun came out for whole moments at a time—and large numbers of people were in the sea. They were shrieking with what I took to be pleasure, but now realize was agony.

Naively, I pulled off my T-shirt and sprinted into the water. It was like running into liquid nitrogen. It was the only time in my life in which I have moved like someone does when a movie film is reversed. I dived into the water and then straight back out again, backward, and have never gone into an English sea again.

Since that day, I have never assumed that anything is fun just because it looks like the English are enjoying themselves doing it, and mostly I have been right.

Later that same day this lovely young English girl, this person in whom I was about to entrust my permanent happiness and well-being, took me to a seafood wagon and bought me a little tub of whelks. If you have never dined on this marine delicacy, you may get the same experience by finding an old golf ball, removing the cover, and eating what remains. The whelk is the most flavorless and indestructible thing ever to be regarded as a food. I think I still have one of them in a jacket pocket somewhere.

At some point along the way to Canford Cliffs you leave Bournemouth and enter the neighboring town of Poole. I used to think Canford Cliffs was a perfect place, apart from a curious shortage of pubs. But it had pleasant residential streets on the wooded cliffs above the sea, a lovely little library and a proper village center, and I was pleased to see now, as I hauled myself a touch breathlessly up the steep road from the beach to the village, that it was more or less unchanged from thirty-odd years ago. I was rather more dismayed, though not altogether surprised, to find that the village center had lost a lot of shops—there was no greengrocer, butcher, bookshop, hardware store, or proper tearoom, the things every good village must have if it longs for my goodwill and patronage. Long ago, when it had those things, I used to imagine how pleasant it would be to live in a big house in Canford Cliffs and stroll to the shops each day to run your errands, but now the greater bulk of those shops are occupied by realtors. The one thing you can do well in Canford Cliffs these days is buy property, but of course that is the last thing you want to do if you are living there already. Or indeed if you want a cup of tea.

The only place I could find for refreshment was a modest establishment called the Coffee Saloon, which, as the name suggests, is like a saloon that sells coffee. It was fine—the tea was perfectly all right, the service friendly—but it wasn't exactly the atmosphere I had in mind. As I sat drinking my tea, thinking that, with the best will in the world, this was not the most fun I had had in a long time, my cell phone rang.

It never rings. I had no idea where it was. I had to feel in every pocket and search through my backpack before I finally located it, down on the bottom under a couple of old whelks, on about the fifteenth ring. It was my wife. She sounded happy.

"You have a new granddaughter," she said. "Come home."

Chapter 9

Day Trips

I

STAND ON THE EASTERN slopes of Noar Hill in Hampshire and
you have a view that is pretty well unimprovable. Orchards,
fields, and dark woods sit handsomely upon the landscape. Here
and there village rooftops and church spires poke through the
trees. It is lovely and timeless and tranquilly spacious, as English
views so often are. It seems miles from anywhere, yet not far off
over the Surrey Hills is London. Get in a car and in an hour you can
be in Piccadilly Circus or Trafalgar Square. To me, that is a miracle,
that a city as vast and demanding as London can have prospects
like this on its very doorstep, on every side.

What accounts for the great bulk of this sumptuousness is the
Metropolitan Green Belt, a ring of preserved landscape, mostly
woods and farmland, encircling London and several other English
towns and cities with the single-minded intention of alleviating
sprawl. The notion of green belts was enshrined in the 1947 Town
and Country Planning Act and is to my mind the most intelligent,
farsighted, thrillingly and self-evidently successful land management policy any nation has ever devised.

And now many people want to discard it.

The Economist magazine, for one, has for years argued that the green belts should be cast aside as a hindrance to growth. As an *Economist* writer editorializes from a dementia facility somewhere in the Home Counties: "The green belts that stop development around big cities should go, or at least be greatly weakened. They increase journey times without adding to human happiness."

Well, they add a great deal to my happiness, you pompous, over-educated twit. Perhaps I see this differently from others because I come from the Land of Shocking Sprawl. From time to time these days I drive with my wife from Denver International Airport to Vail, high in the Colorado Rockies, to visit our son Sam. It is a two-hour drive and the first hour is taken up with just getting out of Denver. It is a permanent astonishment to me how much support an American lifestyle needs—shopping malls, distribution centers, storage depots, gas stations, zillion-screen multiplex cinemas, gyms, teeth-whitening clinics, business parks, motels, propane storage facilities, compounds holding fleets of U-Haul trailers or FedEx trucks, car dealerships, food outlets of a million types, and endless miles of suburban houses all straining to get a view of distant mountains.

Travel twenty-five or thirty miles out from London and you get Windsor Great Park or Epping Forest or Box Hill. Travel twenty-five or thirty miles out from Denver and you just get more Denver. I suppose Britain must have all this infrastructure, too, though I don't honestly know where most of it is. What I do know is that it isn't in the fields and farmland that ring every city. If that is not a glory, I don't know what is.

The arithmetic of the British countryside is simple and compelling. Britain has about 60 million acres of land and about 60 million people—one acre for each person. Every time you give up ten acres of greenfield site to build a superstore, in effect ten people lose their acres. By developing countryside you force more and more people to share less and less space. Trying to limit that growth isn't NIMBYism, it's common sense.

If it was only *The Economist* calling for the destruction of the green belt, my despair would be manageable, but lately the *Guardian* has decided to come down on the side of dismemberment, with a series of articles mostly suggesting that the green belt is a kind of elitist conspiracy that stops affordable housing from getting built. As Prof. Paul Cheshire of the London School of Economics puts it in one of the *Guardian*'s articles: "What green belt really seems to be is a very British form of discriminatory zoning, keeping the urban unwashed out of the Home Counties." Well, let me say at once that I have uttered huge amounts of tosh in my time, but I take my hat off to Prof. Cheshire.

The article in which the wise professor was quoted was "Six Reasons Why We Should Build on the Green Belt" by Colin Wiles, a planning consultant. This book is not a polemic, so I am not going to itemize his reasons for wanting to destroy the green belt or respond to each (though believe me I could), but on the other hand at least two of the ideas are so recklessly wrong, and so close to becoming received wisdom, that I can't let them pass without comment.

The first and most dangerous charge routinely laid against the green belt is that it isn't actually all that special, that much of the land is scrubby and degraded. Well, you decide. According to a study by the Campaign to Protect Rural England, green belts in England contain 30,000 kilometers of footpaths and other rights of way, 220,000 hectares of woodland, 250,000 hectares of top-quality farmland, and 89,000 hectares of Sites of Special Scientific Interest. That sounds to me like things worth keeping. If any green belt land is degraded, the answer surely is not to build on it but to make the owner improve it or sell it to someone who will improve it. Allowing owners to cash in on poorly managed land is the quickest way to get lots more poorly managed land.

The other common charge against the green belt is that it doesn't work, that it just forces people to move farther and farther away from cities to find affordable housing. Wiles offers nothing in the way of evidence to support this other than that he has noticed that a lot of people live outside London. If his view is going to have any credence, he needs to explain why Americans, who have no green belts and never have had them, have for over a hundred years been moving farther and farther out from their own cities. It isn't house prices that drive them out; the outer suburbs usually have the most expensive housing. What the people on the outer edge are always looking for, in fact, is the thing that England has already: countryside.

The one charge against the green belt that has some foundation is that it keeps a lot of land off the market. Yes, it does. That is actually the idea of it. But that land isn't sitting there doing nothing. It shelters wildlife, transpires oxygen, sequesters carbon and pollutants, grows food, provides quiet lanes for cycling and footpaths for walking, adds grace and tranquillity to the landscape. It is already under enormous pressure. Fifty thousand houses have been built on green-belt land in the last ten years. Sussex alone lost thirteen ancient woodlands to development in the same period, according to the Woodland Trust. We ought to be appalled to see this happening, not clamoring for more of it.

Southeast England is already as densely populated as the Netherlands, yet thanks to the softening influence of the green belt large expanses of it remain verdant and attractive and seemingly timeless—the England that most of us appreciate and love. There is absolutely no need to throw that away. The most conservative estimates show that there is enough brownfield land in England to build a million homes at average densities. Colin Wiles's article doesn't even mention the possibility of building on brownfield land. Why?

People are simply being misled. At about the same time the *Guardian* ran Wiles's article, it ran another article headlined "Why Surrey Has More Land for Golf Courses Than for Homes." This was based on a study by Paul Cheshire, the professor quoted above, which declared that houses in Surrey occupy about 2.5 percent of the county, less than golf courses. The point was to show just how dangerously skewed Britain's land use has become. But Radio 4's blessed and peerless fact-checking program *More or Less* looked into the figures, and found that Prof. Cheshire had been a little selective with his calculations. He counted only the space occupied literally by the houses themselves, not their gardens or any of the other land around them. So if all the houses in Surrey were squeezed together without any space in between, then they would indeed occupy less space than golf courses, but that was not what the report implied and it was certainly not the way the *Guardian* or any other publication interpreted it. When gardens are added back, Surrey's domestic properties turn out to occupy 14 percent of the county's land, roughly three times the average for England as a whole. There is, in short, nothing irregular about the volume of housing in Surrey and nothing to support the suggestion that its land has been profligately misused. But you can find wildly inaccurate interpretations of Prof. Cheshire's claim all over the Internet now. That's unfortunate, to put it mildly.

But enough of my disturbed ranting. Let's go for a walk and enjoy some of this lovely countryside while we still can. Thanks to the birth of my new granddaughter (Rosie, gorgeous, thank you), I was under instructions to stay near home for a couple of days, in case anyone could think of a way to make me useful, so I decided that I would have an outing or two in my own neck of the woods, beginning with a literary stroll to the homes of our two most celebrated local authors, Gilbert White and Jane Austen. Thus it was that I stood on Noar Hill enjoying the view and thanking God that unwashed people weren't allowed to see this.

A mile or so beyond Noar Hill is Selborne, a pretty village with two pubs and a good village store with a post office. In the middle of the high street is the house of Gilbert White, Selborne's most famous son. Gilbert White is a person that most people seem either to know a good deal about or know nothing at all about, though I suspect that many of those who place themselves in the first category would really be more at home in the second. He was a country parson, who was born in Selborne in 1720 and died there seventy-three years later and didn't do a great deal in between other than plant vegetables and watch the passing seasons. He lived quietly, never married, and was so unworldly that he thought the Sussex Downs "a mighty range of mountains." (They are not even big hills.) Through most of his life he kept notes and wrote letters, which became the basis for his extraordinarily enduring book, *The Natural History and Antiquities of Selborne,* which the writer Richard Mabey has called "one of the most perfectly realized celebrations of nature in the English language."

The book was nearly a lifetime in the making. It was published in 1788 when White was sixty-eight and just five years from the end of his earthly run. It takes the form of letters to other naturalists, often of a discursive nature, arranged in no particular order, but it has been amazingly influential. Samuel Taylor Coleridge, John Constable, and Virginia Woolf were among its great admirers. Charles Darwin said it inspired him to become a naturalist. In 220 years, the book has never been out of print. By one calculation, it is the fourth most published book in English.

White's house, called the Wakes, is now a museum, and a slightly odd one in that it is also devoted to the explorers Frank and Lawrence Oates, who had no connection to Gilbert White, Selborne, or even Hampshire. They are there simply because in 1955 a wealthy member of the Oates clan, Robert Washington Oates, gave money to buy the house on the understanding that some of it would be used to celebrate his cousin Lawrence and uncle Frank.

It makes an improbable but surprisingly splendid package.

Most of the house is given over to Gilbert White. In one of the front rooms downstairs is a life-sized, and very lifelike, model of Gilbert White himself. I was surprised to find that he was just a little guy—barely five feet tall and not more than a hundred pounds, I would guess—and of an open and amiable disposition if the model is anything to go by.

In a glass case nearby was the original manuscript copy of the *Natural History,* along with bound copies of almost every edition of the book ever printed (and there have been hundreds). White's own copy, according to the caption beside it, was bound in the skin of his pet spaniel. I am guessing that the spaniel died at a convenient moment and wasn't sacrificed specially, but the caption didn't say.

White lived much of his life in this house, and the rooms are mostly kept as he would have known them. The visitor can, for instance, step into Gilbert's snug study and see quills and parchment and some spectacles left on the desk, as if White has just stepped out. The far end of the house changes abruptly into Oates territory, which I thought would be a little ridiculous but was actually quite diverting. Of the two commemorated Oateses, Frank was unquestionably the lesser. He lived only from 1840 to 1875 and spent much of his short life battling ill health. He went exploring in Africa and the Americas in a curious, ultimately misguided attempt to build himself up through fresh air and adventure, but merely caught a fever and died somewhere along the upper reaches of the Zambesi River.

Far more memorable was his kinsman Captain Lawrence Oates, though he lived an even briefer life. He was one of the members of Robert Falcon Scott's ill-fated expedition to the Antarctic in 1910, which with great difficulty reached the South Pole only to find it planted with Norwegian flags, left a short while earlier by a party led by Roald Amundsen. Greatly disappointed and already physically diminished, Scott and his four men turned back, but ran into terrible weather, slowing their progress to a series of short, daily stumbles. They ran short of food and suffered wretched physical hardships. Descriptions of their frostbite are genuinely horrifying. Oates ended up in a particularly bad way and famously sacrificed himself so that the others might have a hope of living. Stepping to the flap of the tent, he said, "I am just going outside and may be some time." It was, Scott wrote in his diary, the "act of an English gentleman." I have no doubt he was wearing a dinner jacket. A point not often noted is that it was Oates's thirty-second birthday. His body was never found. Scott and the others perished soon afterward, dying in a whiteout just a short distance from a supply drop. Oates, it later emerged, couldn't stand Scott and blamed him for inadequate preparations.

The person I ended up most taken with, however, was not Gilbert White or an Oates, but a man named Herbert George Ponting, who was the official cameraman to the Scott expedition. Though an accomplished photographer, Ponting knew nothing about motion pictures—hardly anyone in 1910 did—but he learned through trial and error, and in the process produced some peerless footage of Scott and his team training for their epic expedition at their Antarctic base camp.

Ponting spent years refining the footage into a movie, called *Ninety Degrees South*. A ten-minute extract is shown continuously on a television in an upstairs room. I sat down out of mild curiosity and was instantly absorbed. Suddenly the people I had been reading about in the nearby displays were animate and real. They waved and smiled and moved about, albeit jerkily, cheerful in their preparations and obviously unaware that soon they would be dead. Ponting cut and recut the film for so long that by the time he was ready to share it with the world, the world had rather lost interest and the film was a commercial failure. Ponting was wiped out both physically and financially, and died more or less a pauper.

The Gilbert White museum seems to be the only place in the world where he is remembered.

I left Selborne by way of Gracious Street, which is not only prettily named but prettily arrayed with cottages, most of them wearing a comely cap of thatch. Then it was a long tramp up a steep slope and onto farmland, with yet another expansive outlook. Here, however, the view was dominated by a chain gang of electricity pylons marching dolefully across the foreground. I still have an old cutting from *The Economist*—I know I was just railing about *The Economist*, but this is different—from the time when Mrs. Thatcher was privatizing electrical distribution, observing that if the power companies were required to devote just 0.5 percent of their turnover to burying cables, that would provide sufficient funds to bury one thousand miles of cable a year. If the government had done that then, the cables would all be underground now.

But we have had enough bitching about assaults on the landscape for one chapter already, so let's just shield our eyes here and hurry down the slope to the pleasant village of Farringdon. There isn't a great deal to Farringdon, but I saw more of it than I expected to because I lost my way and ended up exploring a number of its lanes. This meant, happily, that I stumbled on an extraordinary building that I now know is called Massey's Folly. Large, ornate, and built of brick, it is a building of great charm and no evident purpose. From some angles, it looks grandly domestic, but from others it is more seemingly industrial, as if it might be an old mill or pumping station.

I passed two ladies walking dogs and asked them about it. They only knew a little, so I looked into it a bit more later, and what I now know is that it was built by a rich, eccentric local clergyman, Thomas Hackett Massey, who lived in Farringdon for sixty-two years, from 1857 to 1919. Massey apparently intended the building as a kind of village hall and nursery school, but just kept adding to it in a random and piecemeal manner. Massey's other notable feature—rather an unexpected one in a clergyman—was that he was a recluse. He erected a screen in the village church so that his congregation could hear his sermons but not look at him. In February 2014 Massey's Folly was put up for sale. At the time this book went to press, it still had not found a buyer.

Although the ladies didn't know too much about the village folly, they did know the way to Chawton and they escorted me to the edge of the village to show me a path through a housing estate and up into some woods, and with a cheery wave we parted ways and I continued on.

Soon afterward I crossed a narrow but excitingly busy highway, and made my way onto a disused railway line, now converted into a walking trail. This was the old Meon Valley Railway, which connected the market town of Alton in north Hampshire to Gosport in the south. Since not many people have ever wanted to travel between Alton and Gosport, the line was not a success and it closed to passenger traffic in 1955, only a little more than half a century after it was built. The track passed beneath some lovely brick bridges, now so overgrown as to be effectively part of the natural landscape. They were decorated with bands of bricks in contrasting hues—a touch of attractiveness that would never have been visible to anyone but engine drivers and track workers. It is amazing, the trouble Victorian engineers took to make things special.

Thanks to its obscurity, the Meon Valley line did have one special moment of glory. Four days before D-Day, the principal Allied leaders—Winston Churchill, Dwight D. Eisenhower, Jan Smuts of South Africa, and William Lyon Mackenzie King of Canada—met on the Royal Train, just south of where I now was, to discuss the final details of the invasion. The Meon line was chosen because it was so safely obscure, which I quite liked. Perhaps they should make that the motto for the region: "Welcome to East Hampshire. We're Safely Obscure."

Consulting my map, I discovered that I was getting a lot more history on this walk than I ever expected, for I was now on something called St. Swithun's Way. This is part of the Pilgrim's Way running from Winchester to Canterbury across the North Downs, and this in turn is part of the far more ancient track leading on to Stonehenge and Avebury. For at least a thousand years this route on which I was walking now was the Interstate 80 of the pedestrian world. St. Swithun himself may actually have walked where I was walking now.

It occurred to me that I had no idea who St. Swithun was, so when I got home I looked him up. He was Bishop of Winchester in about 850. One day he came across a woman who was distraught because the eggs in her basket had broken. With a pious wave, Swithun made them whole again. It was a good trick, I grant you, but I believe it would take more than nifty egg-fixing to get me to hike 130 miles from Canterbury to Winchester to venerate a bishop, yet that is what people did throughout the Middle Ages. Swithun became a cult. Cathedrals across England competed to get a piece of him. His head ended up in Canterbury, an arm went to Peterborough, and other parts of him were distributed hither and yon. It is a little ironic that the man who could put eggs back together couldn't keep himself in one piece.

In 971, Swithun's remaining bones were moved from one spot to another within Winchester Cathedral, and this coincided with a mighty storm. The date, July 15, became known as St. Swithun's Day, and spawned a legend commemorated in verse:

St. Swithun's Day, if thou dost rain,
For forty days it will remain:

St. Swithun's Day, if thou be fair,
For forty days 'twill rain nae mair.

Chawton is another sweet little village—this part of the world is full of them—tucked away down a side lane and not on the face of it a great deal changed from Jane Austen's day. Chawton Cottage, where Jane lived with her mother and sister, is a mellow brick building built close to the road. The interior is furnished simply, as it would have been in Austen's day, with a few good pieces of furniture but with a curious air of emptiness enhanced by the bare floors and empty grates. Knickknacks and personal effects are conspicuously absent from tabletops and mantelpieces, presumably because anything left out would be filched. The result, as with so many homes of famous people, is that you get a good notion of the walls and ceilings but not so much of the life of the person who lived there. That's not a bitter complaint, just an observation. It's the way it has to be.

Jane Austen lived in the house for eight years, from 1809 till 1817, and during that time did most of her most lasting work: wrote *Emma, Persuasion,* and *Mansfield Park,* and revised and prepared for publication *Sense and Sensibility, Pride and Prejudice,* and *Northanger Abbey.* The prize item of the house is Jane's small round writing table, where all her books were scratched out. A group of Japanese visitors were gathered around it now, discussing it in low, reverential whispers, which is something I find the Japanese do exceptionally well. Nobody gets more out of a few low grunts and a couple of rounded vowel sounds stretched out and spoken as if in surprise or consternation. They can carry on the most complex conversations, covering the full range of human emotions—surprise, enthusiasm, hearty endorsement, bitter disagreement—in a tone that sounds awfully like someone trying to have an orgasm quietly. I followed them from room to room, enthralled by their conversation, until I realized that I was becoming part of it, and that they were casting glances at me with something like unease, so I bowed apologetically and left them to admire an old fireplace with low moans of expressive rapture.

When Jane Austen left the house, in the summer of 1817, it was to go to Winchester, sixteen miles to the west, to die. She was only forty-one, and the cause of her death is unknown. It may have been Addison's disease or Hodgkin's lymphoma or a form of typhus or possibly arsenic poisoning, which was surprisingly common in those days as arsenic was routinely used in making wallpapers and for coloring fabrics. It has been suggested that the general air of ennui and frailty that seemed so characteristic of the age may simply have been generations of women spending too much time indoors taking in gently toxic vapors. In any case, three days after St. Swithun's Day 1817 she breathed her last.

I was very pleased I went, though not quite so pleased to discover on emerging that the skies had darkened significantly and that I was about to walk home eight miles in the rain.

II

The National Trust, Britain's foremost conservation charity, is a wonderful organization. There can be no doubt about that. It safeguards 160 historic houses, 40,000 archaeological sites, 775 miles of coastline, and 250,000 hectares of countryside. It even owns and manages fifty-nine villages. The world is unquestionably a better place for having the National Trust in it. So here is my question: Why does it have to be so very annoying?

I mention this because my next port of call was the ancient Trust-owned village and megalithic site of Avebury, which manages to be both fabulous and exasperating in about equal measure. Avebury village is an attractive place with a post office, shop, some pleasant cottages, a manor house, a thatch-roofed pub. It's an entirely conventional village except that scattered through and around it are great, angular standing stones. Some are quite massive and clearly took huge effort to maneuver into place. The largest of them weigh up to a hundred metric tons.

The stones at Avebury are not smooth and picturesquely grouped as at Stonehenge but rough-edged and of varying sizes, which gives them a more primitive and sinister air. The scale of Avebury, rather than the beauty of it, is what takes your breath away. The outer circle of stones covers twenty-eight acres, and that is only part of a much greater pageant of antiquity. The immediate environs also include two other fragmentary stone circles, a giant bank and ditch, processional avenues, and barrows by the, well, barrowload. Yet Avebury is only a shadow of what it once was. Today it has seventy-six standing stones. Once there were over six hundred. Even so, it remains the largest stone circle in Europe, fourteen times bigger than Stonehenge.

The size and complexity of Avebury and the fact that a village stands in its midst make it awfully hard to get your bearings, and the National Trust does precious little to help. There are no information boards or usefully sited maps to help you get oriented, absolutely no boards providing interpretation. If you want to know what you are looking at, you have to buy a guidebook. The directional signs point only to places where you could spend money—the shop, the museum, the café. It would be a kindness if they gave you a map of the site when you paid for parking and admission, but that is not the National Trust way. They like to charge for every individual thing. The day cannot be too far off when you have to pay for toilet paper by the sheet in a little booth manned by a volunteer.

Within minutes of arriving, I had paid out £7 for parking, £10 for a ticket to the manor house and garden, and £4.90 for the small museum, and I still couldn't find my way around the stones, so I went into the gift shop and bought a big handsome map for £9.99, which meant that I had spent £31.89 at Avebury without even having had a cup of tea. So I went and had a cup of tea (£2.50) and studied my map. Then, feeling ever so slightly grumpy, I went and wandered among the stones and everything was suddenly fine, for Avebury is both awesome and entrancing.

Modern Avebury is almost entirely to the credit of an extraordinary man named Alexander Keiller. Keiller was born in 1889 into marmalade, as it were. His family made the famous Keiller marmalade in Dundee, Scotland, but his parents died young and Keiller grew up as a very rich orphan. When he came of age, he left the running of the business to an uncle and devoted his own energies to fast cars, skiing, a breathtakingly active sex life, and several harebrained business pursuits. His investments included a "wind-wagon," a car powered by an airplane propeller mounted on its back. The only problem was that the propeller was liable to slice unsuspecting passersby into salami-sized pieces and so the business failed. Keiller then invested in a car with seats that folded down to become a bed, but unfortunately the business folded before very many seats did.

When he was not hurling his money into foolish business ventures, Keiller devoted himself to "exploring the range of sexual practices," as the *Dictionary of National Biography* delicately puts it. According to his biographer Lynda J. Murray, Keiller bemused a young woman named Antonia White by asking her to climb into a laundry basket "wearing nothing but a mackintosh so that he could poke her through the wicker work with an umbrella." Quite how Keiller found pleasure in this and whether Ms. White complied are questions not addressed in Murray's otherwise thorough biography. With some like-minded men, he founded a club whose members took turns having sex with a willing (and presumably resilient) prostitute, then sat with whiskies and compared notes on the experience. Despite (or, for all I know, because of) these quirks, Keiller enjoyed a steady string of mistresses and four marriages.

In 1924, aged thirty-five, Keiller visited Avebury for the first time and instantly found a new calling. Avebury at that time was not the glorious, manicured treasure we find today. The stones, Murray relates, stood amid "a jumble of pigsties, derelict corrugated buildings, crumbling cottages, and an old garage which was in need of renovation. The whole area was overgrown with shrubs and trees and the remaining stones of the circle were overshadowed by indiscriminate building." Many stones were toppled. Others had been broken up in earlier times and used as building materials. When Keiller arrived just fifteen stones were still standing.

Keiller bought Avebury Manor and invested his wealth and considerable energies in a farsighted program of excavation and restoration. He wasn't universally popular in the village because of his inclination to tear down cottages and barns that interfered with his excavations, and because he booted some elderly tenants out of an estate cottage so that he could park a mistress there. But there is no question that the archaeological work he funded was world class and made Avebury what it is today. Keiller spent nearly twenty years excavating until in 1943, his health failing, he sold out to the National Trust. He died the following decade, pretty well forgotten.

I was particularly keen to see the manor house as I assumed it would be filled with Keiller's personal curios and archaeological treasures. But no. In what must be the cheesiest thing the National Trust has ever done, it had allowed the house to be made into a set for a now-forgotten BBC television series. The idea of the series was to decorate each room in the style of a different period, reflecting the ages through which the house has stood. It probably sounded like an excellent notion on paper. The problem is that it was clearly executed by designers and crews who build sets for a living. If you ever go to a television studio the thing that most immediately strikes you is how slapdash it all is. Props and furnishings that look perfectly all right on screen are, up close, patently fake. I was once on the set of *University Challenge,* a popular British quiz show. From the front it looks fine, but step behind and you see that it is really just a lot of plywood and duct tape.

Each room of the manor house looked like it was done in about twenty minutes. Just one small room was devoted to the period of Keiller's residency, and it told you almost nothing about why he came to Avebury and what he achieved there. The other rooms had nothing whatever to do with the monuments outside.

The accompanying museum, in a nearby stable block, was only fractionally less disappointing. Avebury is a World Heritage Site for a reason. It is an astonishing, fascinating place, yet the museum seemed perfunctory and uninspired, as if it were fulfilling an obligation rather than reflecting an enthusiasm. We know almost nothing about the people who built Avebury—their language, culture, beliefs, pastimes, where they came from, even what kind of clothing they wore. They are a complete mystery. Yet they had the ambition and organizational skill to build the greatest stone circle in Europe. But any sense of wonder this instills must be supplied by the visitors themselves.

Of these there were plenty, I must say. I was surprised at how popular Avebury has become. By eleven in the morning, the crowds were pretty thick. I had to wait in line to get through a kissing gate, and was very glad I had had my cup of tea already because there was quite a line at the café now as well.

Just over a mile from Avebury is something about as amazing and possibly even more memorable than Avebury itself: Silbury Hill. This is not a National Trust property, so the Trust doesn't draw visitors' attention to it. That is unfortunate, for Silbury Hill is a wonder. It is 130 feet high—about the height of a ten-story building—and is entirely made by hand. It is the tallest artificial prehistoric mound in the world. There is nothing like it anywhere else. It is covered in grass and is uniform all the way around. It is sensationally lovely to look at. It is genuinely perfect. It deserves to be world famous.

Silbury Hill is easily reached from Avebury across some fields. The walk was very pleasant, but the path was largely overgrown and clearly not much used. I had to push my way through a lot of nettles and brambles. I didn't see another soul. You can't walk up Silbury Hill—it is too fragile—but you can stand and stare at it for as long as you like. I could have stayed for most of the day, I think—it is that arresting. Its construction involved an almost unimaginable amount of labor, yet it has no known purpose. It is not a burial mound. It holds no treasures. It is nothing but soil and rock painstakingly shaped into a large pudding-shaped hill. All that can be said for certain is that at some point in the massively distant past, for reasons unknown, some people decided to make a hill where none had stood before. Even where the material in the hill came from is a mystery. It is not as if there is a 130-foot hole nearby. The landscape is perfectly undisturbed, yet somehow and for some reason people were able to bring in enough soil and rock to build a small mountain. Extraordinary.

But that's not all. Across a busy highway—one must waddle smartly, rucksack jiggling—and a quarter of a mile or so up a sloping track is the West Kennett Long Barrow, a large burial chamber. This, too, I had all to myself. The view from the top of it was extremely fine. In the foreground was Silbury Hill, shapely and majestic. In the middle distance, glinting in the sunshine, were a couple of hundred cars parked in the National Trust parking lot, with still more coming in all the time. All around in every direction were lovely low hills and rich-looking farmland.

The barrow itself, however, didn't at first glance seem terribly thrilling. It is just a long, grassy mound that has settled so well into the landscape that it seems almost a natural feature. But looking around more closely, I discovered an entrance, semi-hidden behind a massive rock, and I crept in. The whole became immediately sensational. Here, I could see that the barrow was made from massive stones, many as big as anything at Avebury, hefted into position—goodness knows how—to form walls and ceilings. The barrow is three hundred feet long. This was a massive undertaking. It was built fifty-five hundred years ago, but as far as could be told fewer than fifty people were interred there in a period of only twenty-five years or so. The bodies were arranged by sex and age. More than that, no one will ever be able to say.

I was so glad that I had traipsed up here. I went and stood on the roof of the barrow again and surveyed the view, feeling like a conqueror, pleased to have it all to myself.

"And this part of the day didn't cost me a penny," I said proudly, hands on hips.

Chapter 10

To the West

I

ONE DAY IN THE London Library I came across two books that changed my life, or at least the small part of it that is concerned with British highways.

The first was a slender work called *Report of the Departmental Committee on Roads (1944),* published by His Majesty's Stationery Office, which addressed the issue of road numbering and how it might be improved after the war. I was captivated to think that while all the rest of the Allied world was training for D-Day, a parliamentary committee in Westminster was focused on the perhaps-not-quite-so-pressing issue of postwar road numbering. I imagined twenty men sitting around a table in some underground bunker, white plaster dust settling onto their heads and shoulders from the reverberations of German bombs falling nearby, and the chairman saying: "And now to the matter of whether the B3601 should be upgraded to arterial status between Slumpton Dumpton and Great Twitching. Who would like to open the discussion?"

Beside the departmental committee report on the shelf was a plumper, more recent work called *A,B,C and M: Road Numbering Revealed,* by Andrew Emmerson and Peter Bancroft. This explained in exhaustive detail—and when I say "exhaustive" I am using the word with a rare degree of precision—the history and methodology of British road numbering.

I was surprised to learn that there *is* a system to British road numbering, but then I remembered that it is a British system, which means it is not like systems elsewhere. The first principle of a British system is that it should only *appear* systematic. That is the nub of it really. It is what sets British systems apart from those created by less idiosyncratic peoples. All British systems are like this, I find. Just look at the English language, and the rules of spelling, grammar, and punctuation. Who but the British would come up with spellings like "eight" and "island" that are obvious strangers to phonetics, or a word like "colonel," which clearly has no "r" in it, but proceeds as if it did? Or look at the British constitution, which isn't written down on a single piece of parchment headed "Constitution," as you might expect, but is scattered all over the place in drawers and filing cabinets and no doubt in old trunks from which the key was lost in the time of Anne of Cleves. No one knows what is in the British constitution because it doesn't actually exist except as a notion. Or look at the old money, with its florins and half crowns and thrupenny bits, and imagine what it was like in the days when people had to add tuppence ha'penny to one shilling four nibblings or whatever.

With respect to roads, it works like this: Britain has three main kinds of roads: A roads (the major highways), B roads (smaller, back highways), and motorways (superhighways). England is divided into six sectors defined by the A roads emanating from London. So you start at the top with the A1 (London to Edinburgh), then move in a clockwise fashion to the A2 (London to Dover), A3 (London to Portsmouth), and so on all the way around to the A6 (London to Carlisle). In principle, all the roads in each sector are assigned the same initial digit, so that the A11 and B106 are both in sector 1 (i.e., between the A1 and A2), while the A30, A327, and B3006 are all in sector 3. In theory, therefore, if you wake from a coma and don't know where you are, you have only to determine the number of the road you are on, and if it starts with a 1 you know that you are somewhere between London and Edinburgh and to the east of the A1 but west of the A2, and can start to plan your life accordingly.

So far, so good.

What makes the system enchanting to people like Emmerson and Bancroft is that it doesn't actually work. It never could. That is, as I say, the brilliance of it. For one thing, roads must leave their assigned sectors in order to proceed across the country. The A38, for instance, starts in Zone 3, as it ought to, but trespasses into Zones 4, 5, and 6 as it travels from Devon to Nottinghamshire. The A41 actually starts and finishes in Zone 5. It's called the A41 because—well, I don't know why. The rule—I am not making this up; no one could—is that roads may venture into other zones and retain their number as long as their direction of travel is clockwise and not anticlockwise, though this rule has exceptions, too.

It is often suggested that the British do these things for the pleasure of confusing foreigners, but that is quite wrong. The British don't give a shit about foreigners. They do it to confuse themselves. I can't say why that is because the British won't tell me. It is not something you can talk to them about because frankly they are in a bit of a state of denial over it. If you suggest to any British person that there is anything odd or irregular about any part of a British system—let's say, just for the sake of argument, about weights and measures—they get very slightly huffy and say, "I don't know what you are talking about."

"But it's full of meaningless units like bushels and firkins and kilderkins," you point out. "They make no sense."

"Of course they make sense," the British person will sniff. "Half a firkin is a jug, half a jug is a tot, half a tot is a titter, half a titter is a cock-droplet. What's not logical about that?"

There really is no talking to them about it, so I don't know why they do it, any more than I know why they think that cricket is worth five days of close attention or jam makes a cake delicious. It's just the way they are.

But having said that, I have come to appreciate with the passing years that being unsystematic gives life a richness and unpredictability that endows even the simplest undertakings with an air of challenge and uncertainty.

Compare finding your way around London with finding your way around Paris. As everyone knows, Paris is divided into arrondissements. These are numbered sequentially in a clockwise fashion. Once you have spent ten minutes with a map of Paris, you will understand arrondissements forever. London uses postal districts for organizing itself. These begin logically enough in the central area, with W1 beside W2 and WC1 beside WC2, but then it all unravels as you move outward because outside central London the districts are numbered alphabetically after the names of postal sorting offices. That means that SW6 and SW18 stand side by side. N15 abuts N4 and N22. SE1 is twelve miles from SE2. (Moving east from SE1 you cross, in this order, SE16, SE8, SE10, SE7, SE18, and a corner of SE28.)

What all this means in practice is that the only way to understand the layout of London is to spend years studying it. If you haven't done your homework and you try to travel from SE1 to E4, you could end up anywhere. There are people in London living in doorways or under railway bridges because they couldn't find E4. They all made the mistake of assuming it was in East London, when in fact, as anyone who has studied a map knows, E4 is actually a *northern* zone. In fact, it is the northernmost of all London postal zones. That is, of course, why it is called E4.

The downside in all this is that you can easily cross a line and become too interested in road numbering or London postal districts or almost anything, and the next thing you know you have joined a society and receive a quarterly newsletter, possibly even pay money to go on organized excursions. This is the point at which you should seek medical help.

Anyway, I can't pretend to really understand British systems, but I can tell you that on the fine spring morning when our story resumes I made my way west through Hampshire and Dorset principally along the B3006, A31, and A354 but with an interesting discontinuity on the A3090 between Hockley Viaduct and Oliver's Battery, and, after taking advice at a filling station as to the best route between Romsey and Blandford Forum, reached Lyme Regis in late morning.

I have a great fondness for Lyme Regis, based almost exclusively on a hotel my wife and I stayed there many years ago over a wintry weekend as an extravagant treat when we were young and poor. It was a small hotel on the cliff top with long views across a cold sea. I think it had once been a private home, and it had seen better days, but to us it was the height of elegance because it had its own bar and there was a sweets trolley—which is to say, a wheeled cart laden with puddings and trifles and other rich treasures—at dinner. When the sweets trolley came rattling out each evening, every head in the dining room craned eagerly, believe me. The hotel was run by one harried, irritable man who seemed to be engaged in a long-term battle with the hotel infrastructure. I remember ordering a pint of lager in the tiny bar, and for the next ten minutes watched as he held a glass to a spigot that coughed and sputtered while he waggled the handle impatiently. At length he presented me with a glass about three-quarters filled with what seemed to be warm shaving foam. "I'll have to change the barrel," he muttered unhappily, as if I were being unreasonable with respect to beverages, and disappeared through a door. We never saw him in the bar again.

Lyme Regis remains a fine town, with a very steep high street, called Broad Street, leading up from Lyme Bay to a feast of wooded hills, which formerly were made up exclusively of large Victorian houses, but now seem also to incorporate a great many municipal parking lots. Lyme clearly struggles to accommodate the number of people who wish to drive through its narrow streets and leave their cars to sun while they amble around looking for refreshments and knickknacks. For a long time, the principal gift shop item in Britain seemed to be mugs, tea towels, and other kitchen items that said "Keep Calm and Carry On" on them, but now the thing seems to be to have planks of wood bearing inspirational messages like:

"Live Well, Love Much, Laugh Often"

or

"This Kitchen Is Seasoned with Love"

or

"Life Isn't About Waiting for the Storm to Pass. It's About Learning to Dance in the Rain."

Every gift shopwindow in Lyme Regis, and there are many, had at least a couple of signs like this. I wanted to put stickers on them that said: "Caution: These Signs May Induce Bulimia," but I guess there is a market for them. I walked around Lyme Regis pleased with the thought that nearly all my shopping in life is behind me. One of the great pleasures of dotage is the realization that you have pretty much everything you will ever need. Apart from a few perishable essentials like lightbulbs, batteries, and food, I require almost nothing. I don't need any more furniture, books, decorative bowls, lap rugs, cushions with messages expressing my feelings about animals or housework, hot-water-bottle covers, paper clips, rubber bands, spare cans of paint, dried out paintbrushes, miscellaneous lengths of electrical wire, or any kind of metal objects that might one day theoretically come in handy for some as yet unimagined purpose. Thanks to years of travel at other people's expense, I have a lifetime supply of soaps, small bottles of shampoo, aromatic lotions, sewing kits, and shoe mitts. I have over eleven hundred shower caps and require now only a reason to use them. I am so well prepared financially that I have money in a range of currencies that no longer exist.

I am especially set for clothes. I have reached the time of life where all I want is to wear out the clothes I have and never get another thing. I think many men of a certain age will nod in agreement when I say there is a real satisfaction when you wear something out and can finally discard it—a feeling of a job well done. It's not always easy. I have an L.L.Bean shirt that I have been trying to wear out for nearly twenty years. I wear that shirt up to two dozen times a month. I have washed the car with it. I have used it to clean the grate on the barbecue. I hate that shirt. I didn't actually particularly like it the day I bought it. But I will wear it out if it kills me.

And so I walked about Lyme Regis with a slightly superior air, looking in windows and thinking, "No, I don't need a dog basket or a plank of wood with a sentimental message on it or a new paperback thriller written with the blessing and possible light assistance of James Patterson or anything else for sale in Lyme Regis, but thank you very much for offering."

I had a cup of coffee in a stylish deli, and went down to the seafront and walked along the Cobb, the magnificent curving seawall made famous by John Fowles in *The French Lieutenant's Woman*, and there admired the views along the coastline.

I have walked this stretch of coast a few times and it is rolling perfection. When I first came to Dorset, nobody called it anything but the Dorset coast, but now it is the Jurassic Coast World Heritage Site, which is obviously a lot more impressive. There is a certain irony in the fact that Britain gave the world nearly all its most important geological names—Devonian, Cambrian, Silurian, Ordovician—but that the one epoch that everybody knows about is named for the Jura Mountains in France, even though the Dorset coast is actually the best place in the world to see Jurassic outcrops.

There is, or at least always was, a sensational walk west from Lyme Regis to Seaton along a hanging path that has sheer cliffs above and below. Large signboards at each end warned you that for the next seven miles the path was inaccessible from sea, land, or air and that if you got in trouble rescue teams couldn't airlift you out. This made the walk seem pleasingly dangerous and daring. Little did I know that it actually was. A big section of cliff face collapsed in early 2014, carrying away the path with it, though fortunately no walkers. The path has since been rerouted inland; it seems unlikely that the original can ever be reopened.

Dorset's unstable cliffs have claimed many lives and a good deal of property over the years. One notable casualty was Richard Anning, who tumbled over a cliff in Lyme in 1810 and never got up again. Anning himself isn't remembered now, but his daughter Mary is. She was just ten when her dad died, leaving the family in poverty, but Mary almost immediately embarked on a long career of excavating and selling fossils that she found along the sea strand. She is commonly credited with being the person referred to in the tongue twister "She sells seashells by the seashore."

To say that Mary Anning had an affinity for excavation is to put it mildly. In a career of more than thirty years she found the first British pterodactyl, the first complete plesiosaurus, and the finest ichthyosaurus. These were not the kind of fossils you could stick in your handbag: the ichthyosaurus was seventeen feet long. Excavating them took years of delicate, patient, expert toil. The plesiosaur alone occupied ten years of Anning's life. She not only extracted with the utmost skill, but also provided lucid descriptions and first-rate drawings, and in consequence enjoyed the respect and friendship of many leading geologists and natural historians. But because important finds were rare and the work slow, she spent most of her life in straitened circumstances at the best of times. The house where she lived is now the local museum, and it is, let me say at once, a perfect little institution. If you go to Lyme Regis, don't miss it.

The other memorable thing about Mary Anning, incidentally—though there wasn't anything incidental about it to those around her—was that she seemed a curiously unlucky person to be close to. In addition to her father tumbling over a cliff, one of her sisters died in a house fire and three other siblings were killed by a lightning strike. Mary, sitting right beside them, was miraculously spared.

I'd have happily stayed longer but I had tracks to make. I was still sixty miles from Totnes, in Devon, where I had booked a room for the night, and as anyone who has traveled in the region in summer will know, sixty miles in the West Country is a very long way. Besides, I had one other place I wanted to stop en route: Torquay.

II

The British are an ingenious race. There can be no question about that. Their contribution to the world's comfort and knowledge is way beyond what, measured proportionately, ought to come off a little island in the North Sea. Some years ago, Japan's Ministry of International Trade and Industry made a study of national inventiveness and concluded that in the modern era Britain had produced 55 percent of all the world's "significant inventions," against 22 percent for the United States and 6 percent for Japan. That is an extraordinary proportion. But cashing in on them has been another matter altogether, and Torquay offers a salutary example of that in the shape of the now forgotten figure of Oliver Heaviside.

Heaviside was born in London in 1850, but passed much of his life in Torquay, a stately resort built around a lovely bay on a stretch of south Devon coastline known, just a touch hyperbolically, as the English Riviera. It remains a fine, old-fashioned town, with a promenade, some noble buildings, and a harbor picturesquely filled with pleasure boats, the whole backed by hills containing pink and cream-colored villas. It was to one of these hillside villas, where Heaviside lived and worked and died, that I directed my attention first.

Heaviside was short, ill-tempered, and hard of hearing, which no doubt contributed to his testiness. He had flaming red hair and a beard and, if surviving photographs are a reliable guide, a permanently crazed look. Children apparently followed him down the road and threw things at him. But he was possibly the greatest modern British inventor of whom no one has ever heard.

He was entirely self-taught. As a young man, he worked for a few years in telegraph offices, but quit that job at the age of twenty-four and never held another. Instead he moved to Devon and devoted himself to the private study of electromagnetism. Working from a flat above his brother's music shop in Torquay, Heaviside made a number of important breakthroughs. For years people had been puzzled by how radio signals followed the curve of the earth instead of shooting off in a straight line into space. Even Marconi couldn't explain how his radio messages reached ships that were over the horizon. Heaviside deduced the existence of a layer of ionized particles in the upper atmosphere which was bouncing radio signals back. It became known as the Heaviside layer.

Heaviside's most singular contribution to modern life, however, was devising a way to boost telephone signals while simultaneously eliminating distortion—two things that had long been thought impossible. It would be difficult to overstate the importance of Heaviside's breakthrough. It made instantaneous long-distance communications possible and in so doing changed the world.

Heaviside's house was on Lower Warberry Road, a very pleasant residential street, up in the hills above the bay, lined with some big houses, many of which have been converted into flats or nursing homes. I can think of worse places to end up than in an old house overlooking the sea at Torquay. Heaviside's residence was a cream-colored building, hidden behind a high wall. Heaviside had just a room or two upstairs. After Heaviside's time, the house spent some years as a small hotel, then gradually slid into dereliction. In 2009 it was damaged in a fire, probably accidentally started by a squatter. Today it remains abandoned, hidden behind high walls and plywood hoardings. There is supposedly a blue plaque on the building commemorating Heaviside, but I couldn't see it anywhere from the road. I don't imagine too many people come to look.

Extraordinarily, Heaviside didn't bother to patent his invention. The patent was filed instead by AT&T, which had nothing to do with the discovery but nonetheless went on to become one of the largest corporations in the world thanks in large part to its unrivaled lead in long-distance telephony. Heaviside should have ended up a multimillionaire but instead passed his last years living in angry poverty in a bedsit in Torquay with children following him down the road taunting him.

It is remarkable how often Britons invent or discover something of great value, then fail to cash in on it. The list of things invented, discovered, or developed in Britain that benefited Britain barely or not at all includes computers, radar, the endoscope, the zoom lens, holography, in vitro fertilization, animal cloning, magnetically levitated trains, and Viagra. Only the jet engine and antibiotics are British inventions from which the British still benefit. I had just read an interesting book called *The Compatibility Gene* by Daniel M. Davis, a professor at the University of Manchester, who noted in passing how two medical researchers, Derrick Brewerton in Britain and Paul Terasaki in the United States, had coincidentally made the same important breakthrough in the understanding of genes at the same time in the 1970s. Terasaki formed a company to exploit the commercial potential of his discovery and grew so wealthy that eventually he was making donations of $50 million a time. Brewerton wrote a book on arthritis and chaired a committee devoted to saving a beach near his home on the south coast. Somebody needs to explain to me why that seems so inevitable.

Heaviside wasn't the only famous resident of this steep and pleasant neighborhood. Peter Cook, the comedian, was born a short distance away on Middle Warberry Road in a house then called Shearbridge, now called Kinbrae, and I decided to walk up there now and have a look. It took me some time to work out that although the streets are parallel and clearly from the same family, they don't seem to be on talking terms because there was almost nowhere where they connected. So I walked quite a distance before finding my way to Kinbrae, which proved to be a biggish house divided, not terribly attractively, into apartments. I stood looking at it for a good while, without anything like a real thought in my head, then turned and, still thoughtless, walked through pleasant streets back downhill to the town.

It was only a little after three o'clock, so I had time for both a cup of tea and a look at the town. It seemed to be an awfully long day. When I got back to the town, Torquay was surprisingly quiet. I spotted a café that looked agreeable, but when I reached the door a man was emerging to lock up.

"Sorry, we're closing," he said.

"Oh," I said, surprised. "What time do you close?"

"Five o'clock."

"Oh," I said again. "What time is it now?"

He looked at me as if I was a little bit slow.

"Five o'clock."

"Of course," I said. I showed him my watch. "Battery's been playing up."

He pointed to a shop down the street. "I think they're open till five thirty. You might get a battery there."

I thanked him and went to the designated shop where a man of about fifty sat impassively at a counter. He looked like he hadn't moved a muscle for at least twelve hours. I passed him the watch and explained that the battery seemed to be going.

He examined the watch for half a second and passed it back. "We don't handle these," he said flatly.

"You don't handle what? Timepieces?"

"Mondaine. We don't handle Mondaine."

"Oh. Do you know anyone who does?"

He shrugged. "You can try Jones."

He didn't actually say Jones. He used another name, but because I am kind I am giving it a pseudonym. I managed to coax a street name out of him and a nod of the head to indicate the approximate direction of this alternative possibility.

"Thank you," I said and then abruptly leaned across the counter and with two forked fingers poked him sharply in the eyes. Actually, I didn't do that. I just imagined it. But imagining it made me feel better.

I hurried along to Jones's—for some reason this was beginning to feel urgent—to find another fellow of equally sweet disposition.

I explained my problem and passed him my watch. He looked at it and passed it back. "Can't help you," he said.

"Why?"

"Haven't got the batteries in stock. Sorry."

At least he said sorry, but I could tell he didn't mean it. I said thank you and left. It was clearly too late to do anything else in Torquay, so I retrieved my car and drove off in the general direction of Totnes. I quite like Torquay and might one day come back, but I can tell you this now: where watch batteries are concerned, they can go fuck themselves.

Chapter 11

Devon

SOMETIMES IT DOESN'T PAY to be first. Britain not only invented the train, but embraced rail travel with more alacrity and enthusiasm than most other nations and ended up with far more capacity than it ever needed. Tracks were laid all over the place as early enthusiasts rushed into the business. The Isle of Wight, an area of 147 square miles, had fifty-five miles of track operated by eight separate companies at one point.

By the time the network was nationalized in 1948, it was antiquated, incoherently structured, and losing money hand over fist. Its holdings included not only trains, stations, repair depots, and the like, but also fifty-four hotels, seven thousand horses, a fleet of buses, some canals and docks, the Thomas Cook travel agency, and a film company. The enterprise was so diverse and slackly managed that no one knew how many people the new company employed; estimates ranged loosely from 632,000 to 649,000.

By 1961, things had grown so bad that the prime minister, Harold Macmillan, instructed his transport secretary, Ernest Marples, to sort things out. Marples was already a contentious figure. As cofounder of a leading construction company, he had made a fortune building roads for the government before becoming part of the government himself. When Opposition members objected that it seemed a little corrupt for a minister of transport to oversee state projects that could easily benefit his own company, Marples came under pressure to dispose of his shares. His first plan was to sell them to his business partner on the understanding that he could buy them back later at the original price. When told that that still wasn't quite ethical, Marples came up with a more straightforward arrangement: he sold them to a company secretly controlled by his wife.

Marples appointed Richard Beeching to the job of consolidating the railways, at the enormous annual salary of £24,000—more than double what the prime minister was paid. Beeching was a portly, prissy-looking man with a caterpillar mustache, a bad comb-over, and a striking absence of relevant experience. A physicist by training, he was technical director of the chemical company ICI. Though he knew no more about railways than the average rail passenger, Beeching was an able enough administrator, and anyway it didn't take a lot of vision to see that the railways needed attention. Beeching commissioned a study which showed that the situation was even worse than thought. Some lines were barely doing any business at all. The Invergarry and Fort Augustus line in Scotland was found to be carrying an average of just six passengers a day. The little Llangynog-to-Mochnant line in Wales had average daily earnings of less than £1. Altogether, one half of Britain's rail network accounted for 96 percent of business, while the other half generated just 4 percent. The obvious solution was to close the unproductive parts. In March 1963, Beeching produced a hefty document called *The Shaping of British Railways,* universally known then and ever since as the Beeching Report, in which he proposed to shut down 2,636 stations, about one-third of the total, along with two hundred branch lines and some five thousand miles of track.

The sacrificing of so many stations for the sake of economic efficiency gave Beeching a notoriety that clings to his memory yet. Had Beeching confined himself to the obscure parts of the network, he would probably never have attracted so much opprobrium, but in a burst of reforming zeal he also recommended closing several prominent stations—Inverness, King's Lynn, Canterbury, Stratford-upon-Avon, Hereford, Salisbury, Chichester, Blackburn, and Burnley, among many others—and that stirred a furious response.

In point of fact, none of the aforementioned stations closed. Indeed, many of the cuts that followed had little to do with Beeching at all. The Labour Party came to power in 1964 with its own program of rationalizations. Harold Wilson, the new prime minister, spared the well-known stations but closed an additional fourteen hundred that Beeching had not mentioned at all. The cuts were particularly devastating for seaside towns in the West Country. Lyme Regis, Padstow, Seaton, Ilfracombe, Brixham, and many others lost their services. Several resorts are said never to have recovered. Once there was a service called the Atlantic Coast Express. Wouldn't it be wonderful to have something like that now? Today the fastest train to the west, from Paddington station in London to Penzance at the western tip of Cornwall, takes five and a half hours to travel 280 miles, for an average speed of about fifty miles an hour. I have ridden it several times. It is like rigor mortis with scenery.

His work done, Beeching returned to ICI and was given a peerage for services to evisceration. Although Beeching wasn't responsible for all the cuts commonly attributed to him, he was no hero. About a third of the cuts he proposed were, by any measure, shortsighted or regrettable. It has also been suggested that many of Beeching's figures were collected intentionally during quiet times—at seaside resorts out of season, for instance—to make certain lines look particularly underutilized. One of the services that Beeching wanted to ax was the Exeter to Exmouth line. It survived and now carries a million passengers a year, suggesting that Beeching's assessments were not always reliable or even necessarily honest.

Ernest Marples likewise was elevated to the peerage at about the same time, but soon afterward fled the country to escape arrest for tax fraud. He died in France in 1978, never having returned to Britain or having shown the slightest inclination to be other than an odious, oily-haired Tory wanker.

So thanks to a scattering of long-dead politicians, my travel across Devon and Cornwall could not be done by train. Nor, I was wearied to discover, could I go by bus either, so poor were local services. To get from Totnes to Salcombe, a distance of nineteen miles, would involve separate journeys from Totnes to Brixham, Brixham to Dartmouth, Dartmouth to Torcross, and Torcross to Salcombe, and then the same again in reverse, but the buses were so infrequent that it would take days to make the full return journey anyway.

So I had no choice but to drive, and it took forever. All the roads were narrow and full of blind corners and tight spots. At every village and hamlet lines of parked cars meant that the roads were not wide enough for two cars to pass, so everyone had to take turns letting other cars through. It was all surprisingly good-natured and agreeable because everyone was considerate and no one cheated. This was the English at their best—like the England that used to exist everywhere, in which you considered the needs of others along with your own on the assumption that they would do likewise with you.

I stopped at one point and counted as a string of twenty-eight cars gratefully accepted my gesture of deferral. They all waved to me a sincere but distracted thanks as they simultaneously squeezed through a tight space between me and a cottage built hard by the road. Whether they wished it or not, all those cars were now part of a convoy slowly making its way across south Devon. Eventually a driver in the distance flashed his lights for me to come through, and I discovered that I was now the head of a convoy of my own.

At least two dozen cars were reliant on me to create openings and squeeze through blockages. I found I quite enjoyed the responsibility of it, and I am happy to say I led them successfully to Salcombe with hardly any losses along the way.

Salcombe is a famous yachting community, picturesquely sited on a sweep of green hills overlooking a preposterously pretty cove. The last time I was there, some twenty years ago, you could drive into the village and park by the harbor, but those days are long gone. Today there is a park-and-ride lot on a hilltop just outside the village. Even from a distance I could see there was a queue to get into the lot, but I spotted a space in a lay-by across the road and darted into it with an abrupt and daring maneuver that prompted six or eight other motorists to honk their horns and flash their lights in a spontaneous gesture of admiration.

I walked into the village along the crest of the hill and then down a steep curving road, past cottages that all had jaunty nautical names and the trim but impersonal look of second homes. The population of Salcombe, I read somewhere, increases tenfold during the summer season, from two thousand to twenty thousand. This was definitely the summer season. But even when crowded to bursting, it is a lovely place. In the harbor, little boats with triangular sails floated on the glassy water like party favors. A tangy smell of marine life hung in the air. Gulls cawed and wheeled overhead, dropping splatty white cluster bombs on rooftops and pavements. Goodness knows what those gulls eat, but it certainly keeps them regular.

Salcombe is smart and prosperous and lively. Everyone was dressed like a Kennedy at Hyannisport. I had to get a sweater out of my bag and tie it around my neck to keep people from staring. They all had a robust, healthy, sea-sprayed look about them. These people didn't walk from place to place, they *bounded*.

The main street in Salcombe is Fore Street. The *Daily Telegraph* has deemed it the sixth coolest street in Britain. I have no idea how they make such an assessment, though I suspect, this being the *Telegraph*, that it has little to do with science or much real thought. The shops were unquestionably upmarket. At the Casse-Croûte Deli, the special of the day was Brie and asparagus tart made with organic cider, which I was pleased and relieved to see. How often have I had to decline a Brie and asparagus tart because the cider wasn't organic. It occurred to me that in my lifetime British food has gone from strange and unappetizing to strange and unappetizing again with about fifteen years of glorious, unself-conscious tastiness in between. Call me an unreconstructed heathen, but the sooner we get back to a national diet of chips with gravy and that sort of thing, the happier I will be. In my day every restaurant meal started with prawn cocktail and finished with Black Forest gateau and we were all a lot happier, believe me.

Everywhere in Salcombe was packed. I stood not the slightest chance of sitting down with a cup of coffee or organic tart, so I decided to go for a walk and retraced my route back up to the hilltop and along the road toward Kingsbridge. About a mile along, a narrow, beckoning lane ran off to the right through glorious countryside. From my hilltop vantage point, I could see the Kingsbridge estuary poking its skinny arms into various clefts in the middle distance. I had left my Ordnance Survey map in the car, so I couldn't see where the local footpaths were, but I thought I could amble down the lane to the next village and maybe find a nice, forgotten pub for lunch. I walked for perhaps a third of a mile, unable to see anything beyond the thick hedges pressing in on both sides, then came around a bend and to my dismay found a giant piece of farm machinery coming up the lane toward me. It entirely filled the available space and was roughly brushing the hedges on both sides. There wasn't any possibility of my standing aside for it, and no gaps for farm gates anywhere along the way to retreat into, so I had no choice but to turn around and walk briskly all the way back up the hill to where I had started, acutely aware that just behind me, moving at a speed just fast enough to be menacing, was a giant piece of machinery that could flatten me like a piece of dropped chewing gum if it elected to. I turned from time to time to the driver to mime a kind of apology for being in his way, indeed for existing at all, and to indicate that I was moving as fast as I could, but found not the tiniest hint of warmth or compassion in his grim, set expression. The faster I tried to move, the more he seemed to speed up. At the top of the hill, I bent double gasping for breath and he sped past without a look of acknowledgment.

"You're welcome, you hayseed fuck!" I called, but I don't think my words had the wounding effect I wished for. I can only hope that later he reflected on this and felt bad about it, or perhaps that he got a terrible disease and died.

I returned to the car and drove a dozen miles along yet more slow but glorious roads to Torcross, a hamlet on a dramatic sweep of coastline overlooking Start Bay. To the north from here stretches a duney expanse called Slapton Sands, so similar to the beaches of Normandy that they used it for a dress rehearsal for D-Day in the spring of 1944. Amid great secrecy, thirty thousand American troops were loaded onto landing craft and taken out onto the bay to practice coming ashore, but by chance nine German torpedo boats spotted the activity and cruised at will among them, blowing the landing craft out of the water with ease and causing all kinds of mayhem. No one from the Allied side, it appears, had thought to line up suitable protection for the exercise, so the U-boats were able to move about unimpeded.

One of those watching the carnage was Eisenhower himself. Nobody seems to know how many people died. Numbers range from 650 to 950 or so. An information board at Torcross says 749 American soldiers and sailors died. Whatever the exact figure, far more Americans were killed that night than died in the actual landing at Utah beach just over a month later. (Casualties were much higher at Omaha beach.) It was the most lopsided rout America suffered during the war, yet nobody has ever heard of it because news of the disaster was withheld, partly for purposes of morale, partly because of the general secrecy surrounding the invasion preparations. What is most extraordinary is that the Germans, having chanced upon a massive collection of boats and men engaged in training exercises just across the sea from the Cherbourg peninsula, failed to recognize that an invasion of northern France was imminent.

Here at last I got a walk in. I strolled up onto a big hill above Torcross village, a taxing climb but worth it, to a field high above the bay. The field was extensively land-mined with cow pats, but no cows were about, I was pleased to see. The view took in the mighty sweep of Start Bay, which is surely one of the very loveliest in England. To the south an attractive white lighthouse stood on a distant eminence called Start Point. To the north at Stoke Fleming, there was some other tower—a church steeple, I decided—and in between sprawled the most exquisite, effortlessly perfect combination of fields, clustered villages, farmhouses, and wandering roads.

Just at this point a herd of cows appeared over a rise and decided to come and have a look at me. They weren't aggressive, just stupid. All they wanted was to be with me. But of course as soon as they got near they became skittish, which meant they were capable of panicking and trampling me into a shape and consistency not unlike the glistening pats they left everywhere. I didn't want to panic them, so with an air of stoic resignation I let them escort me to the gate. Returning to sea level, I went for a walk along the sand dunes, which was hard on the ankles but at least free of cows.

Wishing for a cup of tea, I drove on to the historic town of Dartmouth, famed for its gorgeous setting on the River Dart and home of the Royal Naval College. On the outskirts, an illuminated sign beside the road told me on no account to drive into town but to use the park-and-ride system, but I went anyway to see if they were lying. They weren't. Dartmouth was heaving and it was impossible to park, so I went all around the one-way system and back up the steep hill to an extraordinarily distant park-and-ride lot, where I should have gone in the first place. Parking cost £5, which seemed outrageous to me, bearing in mind that all I wanted was a cup of tea and that I was severely inconveniencing myself already for the sake of their economy, but I felt slightly mollified when I discovered that the charge was reduced to £3 after 2 p.m. So I rode a bus back into town and had a shuffle around, which is what tens of thousands of other people, most of them of about my age and socioeconomic background, were doing. This, I realized, is my future: a dotage spent mooching around in places like Dartmouth, visiting shops and tearooms, bitching about crowds and costly, inconvenient park-and-ride schemes.

Dartmouth used to be filled with charming shops, though I guess I should allow that that was more than twenty years ago when most places were filled with charming shops. Today it seemed to be mostly small, busy cafés and gift shops selling planks of wood with foolish sentiments on them. Dartmouth long had a celebrated independent bookshop, Harbor Books, run by Christopher Milne, son of A. A. Milne, but that closed in 2011, so I was pleased to see a new bookshop in town, the Dartmouth Community Bookshop, a not-for-profit cooperative. It is very small and on a back street, but at least it is a living bookshop and I hope the people of Dartmouth support it. I went in and talked to the manager, Andrea Saunders, and she told me that it was doing well, which I was pleased to hear. But, her books aside, if you gave me a £100 gift certificate I would struggle to spend it in Dartmouth unless it was to make kindling.

I had a cup of tea, then transferred myself to the waterfront, where the town overlooks the broad estuary of the River Dart. This was very much more agreeable, indeed quite beautiful, and I suddenly remembered why someone might choose to pass time here. Out of the corner of my eye I noticed a little oik of a kid about thirteen years old in a Chelsea Football Club shirt sitting at a bus stop eating a bag of potato chips. When I came back a few minutes later, the boy was gone and the bag was on the ground. There was a bin three feet away. It occurred to me, not for the first time, that if Britain is ever going to sort itself out, it is going to require a lot of euthanasia.

I stayed two nights in Totnes while in south Devon and liked it very much. It is a trim and well-kept place with an interesting range of shops—like Dartmouth used to be, in fact. There was a little more in the way of New Age crystals and that kind of thing than I personally require, but also some interesting galleries and antique shops. I went in four shops one morning as a kind of experiment. At one I was given a friendly good morning by a lady of about my own age, at another I received a wordless nod and small smile— not unfriendly, but not exactly lavish—and at the other two I was completely ignored by the people in charge.

I can never decide which is worse, the titanic indifference of the average British shopkeeper or the suffocating attention of American ones. It's a tough call. Recently I was in New York and on an impulse I went into an Aveda shop. My wife likes Aveda shampoo (she likes anything that costs more than it ought to) and I thought I might surprise her with a little gift.

"Hello," said the nice young woman who was in charge, "can I help you find something?"

"Oh, no thanks, I'm just looking," I replied.

"What's your pH?" she asked.

"I don't know," I answered. "I didn't bring my soil test kit." I gave her my friendliest smile. I don't believe she knew I was joking.

"Have you tried our new performance shampoo?" she asked and thrust a cylindrical green bottle a little more into my face than I would say was altogether a good idea. "It is made with 100 percent plant-surfactants and cleanses gently while engaging the senses."

"I am really just looking, thanks," I said again. What I was actually looking for was a price sticker. I'm a generous soul—anyone will tell you that except for those who know me fairly well—but there is a limit to how much I will pay for shampoo, even for someone who has given me children.

As I bent to examine some bottles on a lower shelf, I became aware that the sales assistant was studying the top of my head.

"Have you tried our exfoliating shampoo?" she asked.

I straightened up. "Miss, please," I said, "I just want to browse quietly and alone. May I do that, please?"

"Of course," she said and took a step back. She was silent for a nanosecond, then stepped forward again. "I'd recommend the exfoliating for you," she said.

She had, I realized, Retail Tourette's Syndrome, a compulsion to blurt advice. There was nothing she could do about it. Whatever I touched or looked at, she would have to comment on. In the end, I had to leave the store. On the plus side, I think she saved me $28.50.

So the manifest impassivity of British shopkeepers doesn't bother me nearly as much as it does my wife. Still, you do sometimes wonder if it would kill them to say hello. Sometimes I just have this sneaking suspicion that it might help them win some repeat business if they didn't make it quite so clear how much they loathe you coming into their shop and touching things. Then again, as my wife always points out, no matter how warmly or not they receive me, I am still not going to buy anything because I think everything costs too much and I have everything I need already.

—

From Totnes, I headed to Dartmoor, land of hills and heath, of wild ponies and stone footbridges (called clapper bridges) across tumbling rills. I had just read *In Search of England* by H. V. Morton, which is always described as a classic, presumably by people who have never read it because it is actually quite dreadful. It was written in 1927 and consists largely of Morton motoring around England and slowing down every twenty miles to ask directions of a besmocked bumpkin standing at the roadside. In every village he went to Morton found a man with a funny accent and fuck-all to do, and had a conversation with him.

On Dartmoor he stopped at Widecombe-in-the-Moor and asked an old man leaning on an ash stick whether they really sang the old folk song "Widecombe Fair," for which Widecombe is, not surprisingly, famed.

"Oi zur," the man replies. "We zings it after a zing-zong zometimes afore 'God Save the King'! Oh, aye, zur!"

The impression you get from *In Search of England* is that England is a cheerful, friendly place, peopled with lovable halfwits with comic accents, so it is a little ironic that the book is so often cited as capturing the essence of the nation. An even greater irony is that Morton eventually soured on England because it wasn't fascist enough for him. He moved to South Africa in 1947 and lived the last thirty-two years of his life there, forgotten by the world but happy to have servants he could shout at. The only thing I remembered from the book was that he made Widecombe-in-the-Moor sound awfully pretty and I was curious to see to what extent it remained so. I am happy to say it is still a gorgeous place. It has a lovely church with a magnificent tower, a green, a pub, and a shop, and stands amid a symphony of rocky hills. I said good morning to an old fellow by the churchyard, but he didn't say "Oi zur," or anything amusingly rustic at all.

I drove up into the hills and parked in a parking area—just a rough clearing really—presumably put there for walkers, and got out with my trusty walking stick and map. It was a splendid morning. The hills were sprinkled with sheep and wild ponies and granite outcrops called tors. Dartmoor gets almost eighty inches of rain a year, making it one of the dampest of English regions, which is of course saying a great deal. Because the drainage is poor, the water gathers into what are locally known as "feather beds"—pools of water just covered over with moss. These are practically indiscernible, with the consequence that outsiders frequently step into them and then vanish with a startled glug, or so it is said. I didn't actually believe this, but I stayed on the paths nonetheless.

I couldn't for the life of me work out where I was on the map. I couldn't even find Widecombe. A stiff breeze kept trying to refold the map for me. (Only later, when I was back in the car, did I realize that the map was printed on both sides and that I had been looking at the wrong side.) Wherever exactly I was, it was a lovely walk with top-of-the-world views. Eventually I came to a trig point—always an excitement on a country stroll for they usually indicate that you have reached a summit. "Trig," if you don't know, is short for triangulation, and a trig point is a small concrete pillar with a brass inset on the top to which a surveying instrument was once attached in order to make an accurate map of the landscape. Every trig point is within sight (albeit distantly) of two others, so that each is at an apex of a triangle. I am not at all sure how a series of triangles gives you a map of Britain—and please don't write to tell me; I'm not saying I want to know—but somehow it does and that's what matters. Sarah Palin named her son Trig. I wonder if he knows that he is named after a concrete block.

The whole of Britain was retriangulated between 1932 and 1962, which is what accounts for all the trig points you find on any walk in the hills. Nowadays of course it is all done with satellites, and trig points aren't needed, so many of them are vanishing, either through neglect or because they are intentionally removed, which I think is sad.

I expect there is somewhere in Britain a Trig Society. I also imagine that now that I have written this they will ask me to come and speak at their annual meeting. So let me say here that I miss trig points a lot, but not that much.

Chapter 12

Cornwall

I

FOR SOME TIME, I have believed that everyone should be allowed to have, say, ten things that they dislike without having to justify or explain to anyone why they don't like them. Reflex loathings, I call them.

Mine are:

Power walkers.
Those vibrating things restaurants give you to let you know when a table is ready.
Television programs in which people bid on the contents of locked garages.
All pigeons everywhere, at all times.
Lawyers, too.
Douglas Brinkley, a minor academic and sometime book reviewer whose powers of observation and generosity of spirit would fit comfortably into a proton and still leave room for an echo.
Color names like taupe and teal that don't mean anything.
Saying that you are going to "reach out" to someone when

what you mean is that you are going to call or get in touch
with them.

People who give their telephone number so rapidly at the
end of long phone messages that you have to listen over
and over and eventually go and get someone else to come
and listen with you, and even then you still can't get it.

Nebraska.

Mispronouncing "buoy." The thing that floats in a navigation channel is not a "boo-ee." It's a "boy." Think about it.
Would you call something that floats "boo-ee-ant"? Also,
in a similar vein, pronouncing Brett Favre's last name as if
the "r" comes before the "v." It doesn't, so stop it.

Hotel showers that don't give any indication of which way is
hot and which cold.

All the sneaky taxes, like "visitor tax" and "hospitality tax"
and "fuck you because you're from out of town tax," that
are added to hotel bills.

Baseball commentators who get bored with the game by
about the third inning and start talking about their golf
game or where they ate last night.

Brett Favre.

I know that is more than ten, but this is my concept, so I get
some bonus ones. Now you might think that driving in the West
Country of England in the summertime would be on my list, but
it doesn't qualify because it's an obvious and rational loathing. It's
the same reason you can't put men who wear cravats or people
who take signs to sporting events so that they can be on TV. It
has to be something that some people don't necessarily agree with,
and no one can dispute that driving in the West Country in the
summertime is a nightmare.

It took me over an hour to cross the Tamar Bridge, which was
only one lane wide going west. What on earth were they thinking

when they built it? That was in 1961, at the very time they were try-ing to put motorways everywhere, but in the one spot where a bit of expansiveness would have made obvious sense, they decided to economize. Go figure.

Beyond Plymouth, traffic would zip along for a couple of miles, then back up for hundreds of yards at a roundabout, creep for-ward in increments of two feet for about ten minutes, then speed up again, only to be repeated at the next roundabout, and there were lots of roundabouts.

And so I made my fitful way across Cornwall, past turnings for Looe, Polperro, Fowey, and a succession of other coastal villages. I was tempted to nip down and have a look at one or two of them, but all the roads to the sea were dead ends and at each I could see long lines of RVs and cars loaded with bicycles and kayaks head-ing toward the water, and knew that it would take an hour or more to reach the village and then there would almost certainly be no place to park. Nonetheless, just beyond St. Austell, bored and res-tive, I impulsively took a turning for Mevagissey.

Rarely have I more immediately regretted something that I knew I would immediately regret. The road to Mevagissey was twisting and slow. It took forever to reach the outskirts, where there was a single large parking lot. Cars were queuing to get in. I asked the attendant if I could just turn around. He said of course, and then recognized me, which pleased me. (It doesn't happen very often. Ask any author.) His name was Matthew Facey, and he wasn't the parking lot attendant but the owner. The lot has been in his family for years and it keeps him busy in the summer, but his real passion is photography. I looked at his website later and he is very good. Anyway, we had a nice chat and he urged me to come back out of season, which I promised to do.

On the way back to the A390, the main road to Penzance, my destination for the night, I passed a sign for "the Lost Gardens of Heligan" and made an abrupt, impetuous turn down a side lane, bringing a moment's unscheduled excitement to two cyclists and a motor home. I had never heard of this place, but I was curious to know how you lose gardens. The Lost Gardens of Heligan turn out to be the work of Tim Smit, a Dutchman who has lived in England for years and who is also responsible for the popular Eden Project, a giant nature center and botanical expo a dozen miles to the north on the other side of St. Austell.

Heligan was once a great estate, set high on a rolling hill above the sea, with a staff that included twenty-two gardeners. But Heligan fell on hard times and the gardens lapsed into weedy ruin. When Smit and his business partner, John Nelson, came along in 1990, the gardens had been untended for seventy years. Smit and Nelson decided to restore them. It was a monumental task. After seventy years, not much was left even in outline. Two and a half miles of woodland paths had vanished. Greenhouses had fallen in on themselves. Walled gardens were chest-deep in brambles. More than 750 fallen trees had to be cleared away before real renovations could begin. It seemed an impossible task, but Smit, who had trained as an archaeologist at Durham University, brought an archaeologist's rigor to the task. The upshot is that after years of hard labor, the gardens were restored and today are splendid and thronged, as they deserve to be.

They cover a huge expanse, much of it woodland, and I must say I was grateful to stretch my legs after so many hours in the car. The woodland walks seem to go on for miles. At first I thought that is all Heligan was, just woods and ferns, but then I came across a walled cutting garden, full of bright, nodding blooms and dancing butterflies. In the distance the sea was just visible, a bright pale blue beneath a matching sky. It was all very fine. In the café I had a refreshing cup of tea and a lovely dry piece of cake—cautiously flavorful in the British style, satisfying but not so delicious that you would want a second piece for a month or so—and returned to the road feeling gloriously restored, like Heligan itself.

—

Once every springtime for several years I took a train from London to Penzance, at the very bottom of Cornwall, and spent the night there before continuing on the next day to the Scilly Isles to attend the Tresco Marathon. The marathon was held on behalf of the Cystic Fibrosis Trust. I didn't run the marathon myself, needless to say, but attended as a kind of cheerleader and just walked around and shouted helpful, distracting remarks to the runners as they struggled past. The Tresco Marathon was one of the most wonderful things ever. It was held at the same time as the London Marathon, and it existed because the chef at the island hotel, a guy named Pete Hingston, realized he could never run in London on behalf of his little girl, Jade, a cystic fibrosis sufferer, because it was too busy a time to leave Tresco. So with his wife, Fiona, he started a marathon on Tresco and it rapidly blossomed.

Because Tresco is small and can only hold so many visitors, entries were limited to a hundred runners, which made it both exclusive and intimate. There are people in the world who collect marathons, and Tresco was one of the hardest to bag. The course was also very tough. Because of the island's size, runners had to do eight laps around it, which included eight ascents of a long hill. Marathons don't usually require you to run up a hill eight times. Many of the runners were there because of a personal connection to cystic fibrosis, and ran on behalf of siblings or partners or children. On at least one occasion, the runner had cystic fibrosis herself; however long you live, you will never see anything more heroic or moving than a person with cystic fibrosis completing a marathon. It was just the best thing ever. It really was. And at the end of the day, having run a marathon, Pete went off to the hotel and spent an evening cooking.

The only downside in getting to Tresco is getting to Tresco. Formerly there were two ways. One was to take the ferry. This is the way I came on my first visit, and I have to say it was a curious experience. All the passengers—and there weren't very many— went below and lay down on whatever horizontal surfaces they could find. Many covered their faces with their coats, as if hiding. Just after we left port, the snack bar closed. All this seemed a little strange, and then we hit the open sea and began to roll and pitch in a weirdly restrained but emphatic way. I am not the most experienced of sailors, but I have been on a few boats in my time— including once through the Beagle Channel in South America, which isn't so much a water passage as a trampoline for boats— and I can say that I had never encountered anything quite like this. It wasn't rough, but just slowly, cumulatively, peculiarly unsettling. The problem, as it was explained to me later, is that the ferry must have a flat bottom to get in among the shallows around St. Mary's, the main port of the Scillies, but this means that it sits on the water like a cork, which guarantees a lot of motion even on the smoothest days. In rough weather, I was told, it bounces so much you can have the novel experience of being sick on the ceiling.

One person on Tresco (whose identity I am sworn not to disclose) told me that once he made the sea crossing from Penzance in winter, and when the ferry reached Land's End, where the currents of the English Channel, Irish Sea, and North Atlantic come together in a foamy vortex, the ship could make no headway. For something like two hours it just rode the bouncy waves, unable to go anywhere, until finally the winds relented or tides changed or something, and the ship was suddenly able to chug forward and complete the twenty-five-mile crossing. But when it reached St. Mary's, the waves in the harbor were too big for it to dock.

"The captain announced that he was going to give it one more try and if that failed we'd have to turn around and go back to Penzance, into even rougher seas," my informant told me. "I swear to you, no exaggeration, I was holding on to a lifesaver and I was seriously thinking of jumping overboard and taking my chances of swimming to the dock. That's how bad it can be. Luckily, however, the waters calmed for a minute and we were able to tie up at the quayside. You have never seen twenty people get off a ship faster."

The only other way to get there was on a giant helicopter. I wasn't too crazy about the helicopter either because its record was not entirely flawless. In 1983, when it was operated by British Airways, the Scilly helicopter crashed in poor weather. Twenty people died. I took the helicopter several times and it was always fine, but it did rather feel like something that should have been in the Imperial War Museum in the Korean War section. The helicopter service was ended in 2012, on economic grounds, and what used to be the Scilly airfield in Penzance is now a giant Sainsbury's supermarket. Today if you want to get to Scilly, you brave the ferry or fly in a small airplane from one of three mainland airports.

In 2010, after ten years of heroic existence, the Tresco Marathon was likewise canceled on economic grounds after a sponsor pulled out. So the Tresco Marathon is just history. There is no question about it. We live in dispiriting times.

I was pleased to be back in Penzance. My usual hotel was closed for refurbishment, so my wife had booked me into a boutique hotel at the other end of town. I dropped my bags and hit the streets, keen to get in a walk before dinner and to see how Penzance had changed since I was last there.

Penzance ought to be fabulous. It has a superlative setting overlooking St. Michael's Mount, a romantic castle on a rock nearly identical to but much less well known than its namesake across the English Channel in Brittany. It has a long and agreeable promenade and a harbor that could be lovely with a little paint and imagination, and perhaps one or two sticks of dynamite. Its streets are narrow and beguiling. The terraced houses have a neighborly feel and often enjoy bewitching views. It must be splendid to look out your bedroom window first thing in the morning and know what kind of day it's going to be from the color of the sea.

There isn't anything about Penzance that isn't promising. Yet it is a sad and fading place. I walked through the town and was struck by the number of businesses that had gone since my last visit. The Star Inn was boarded up. A restaurant called the Buttery was gone. Several shops were dark and empty. The London Inn was still going but didn't look to be thriving. A sign by the door said: "This is a public house, not a public toilet." I was glad to see that the management had taken a stand on the issue, but I can't say it struck me exactly as an inducement to enter. The Ganges Indian restaurant, where I had often dined, was also gone, though I wasn't altogether surprised. It was so bad that it wasn't even within hailing distance of being dreadful. I was generally the only customer. The service was always excellent.

Across the street from the Ganges was a good pub called the Turk's Head. I looked through the window now and it was heaving with a Saturday night crowd, so I walked down the street to another good pub, the Admiral Benbow, and it was even fuller. I went back to the Turk's Head and waded into the throngs at the bar. It took an age to get a pint, but to my joy when I turned from the bar I spied a tiny table being vacated and I grabbed it. When I asked a passing waitress about food, she was happy to take an order, but was candid in telling me that service was going to be very slow. The upshot was that for the rest of the evening about every forty minutes the waitress would bring something to my table, and assure me that I hadn't been forgotten. Generally what she brought was something that would help me with my food when eventually it came—salt and pepper shakers, silverware wrapped in a paper napkin—but once she brought a slice of bread and butter, which I devoured more or less in a single gulp, like a frog with a fly. At about 8:40, I got a bowl of soup, steaming and delicious, and after a further long interval I received my main course of fish and chips. In between, I had a little bowl of tartar sauce, a pat of butter, and many pints of beer. I also learned that if you drink a sufficient amount, dinner ceases to matter very much.

At about 10 p.m., the waitress asked me if I wanted dessert, and we immediately agreed that I was unlikely to live long enough to enjoy it, so we just settled on another pint of beer and the bill. It was quite a wonderful evening in the end—but then when did anyone ever drink seven or eight pints of beer and not have a good time?

Afterward I discovered that it is possible to get so drunk that you walk a mile and a half in the wrong direction to the hotel you used to stay at and then spend thirty minutes circling the building wondering why it is covered in scaffolding and your key doesn't work in any of the doors. I don't remember anything in detail after that, but I woke up the next morning on top of my bed in the correct hotel, wearing one shoe but otherwise fully dressed, and in the posture of (and feeling remarkably like) someone who has just fallen out of a tree.

II

Isn't it amazing how many people in the world hate you? Most of them you will never even meet, and yet they really don't like you at all. All the people who write software at Microsoft hate you, and so do most of the people who answer phones at Expedia. The people at TripAdvisor would hate you, if they weren't so fucking stupid. Almost all frontline hotel employees detest you, as do airline employees without exception. But nobody, absolutely nobody, hates you as much as the people who make English bus shelters. I've no idea why, but their most earnest wish, the single-minded thought that carries them through every working day, is to make sure that no user of a bus shelter in the United Kingdom ever experiences a single moment's comfort. So all they give you to rest on is a red plastic slat, canted at an angle so severe that if you fail to maintain a vigilant braced position you will slide off, like a fried egg off Teflon.

I mention this here because after breakfast the next morning I went for a walk along the seafront and passed a new bus shelter that didn't even have a canted rail in it, but just a simple pole—like a scaffolding pole, but shinier—resting on three legs. I went into the shelter and tried it just out of interest. It actually hurt to sit on. Goodness knows what a pensioner would make of it. And the shelter was ugly, too. Bus shelters in Britain used to be like little cottages, with pitched roofs and built-in wooden benches. Now they are just wind tunnels with advertisements.

So my question is a serious one. Why do these things have to be so horrible? Britain used to have a kind of instinct for producing jaunty, agreeable everyday objects. I don't suppose any other nation has devised more incidental infrastructure about which one can feel a kind of connectedness and fondness—black taxicabs, double-decker buses, pub signs, Victorian lampposts, red mailboxes and phone booths, the absurdly impractical but endearing policeman's helmet, and much more. These things were not always especially efficient or sensible—it could take an almost superhuman amount of exertion to heave open a cast-iron phone booth door if there was a wind blowing—but they gave life a quality and distinctiveness that set Britain apart. And now they are nearly all gone. Even black cabs in London arc giving way to Mercedes vans with automatic doors that you get shouted at by the driver if you try to open yourself, and the police are dressed in yellow vests that make them look like the people who repair railway lines. In countless small ways the world around us grows gradually shittier. Well, I don't like it at all.

—

I was headed to Mousehole, a famously pretty fishing village. The curious name (pronounced *mowz-ull*) is of uncertain provenance, but probably comes from some old Cornish word. The village is about three miles along the coast road from Penzance. It was a fine morning, and quiet because it was Sunday. The views across Mount's Bay were glittery and serene. Somewhere between the village of Newlyn and Mousehole itself I came upon the old Penlee Lifeboat Station, and that brought me up short because I knew it was famous for something but I couldn't immediately think why. An information board beside the station filled in the details that my memory couldn't supply. This was the site of an act of great but tragic heroism some thirty years earlier.

On the evening of December 19, 1981, a small cargo ship, the *Union Star,* on its maiden voyage from Holland to Ireland, got in trouble in heavy seas near here. It had been a wild day and by early evening the storm had turned into a Force 12 gale. As well as its normal complement of five crew, the *Union Star* was carrying the captain's wife and two teenage daughters so that the family could celebrate Christmas together in Ireland. In the worst possible conditions, the ship's engines failed and it began to drift helplessly. When word of a Mayday call was brought into the village pub in Mousehole, the lifeboat captain, Trevelyan Richards, selected seven volunteers and they set off at once for the station. With great difficulty the Penlee lifeboat put to sea and found its way to the stricken ship, where it managed somehow to get alongside and to get four people off. That in itself was an extraordinary achievement. Waves were up to fifty feet high.

Captain Richards radioed that they were bringing the four rescued people to shore and then would go back for the others. That was the last message ever sent. The presumption is that in the next moment a wave dashed the boats together and both sank. Whatever happened, sixteen people lost their lives. The Penlee station was never used again, but has been left just as it was that night as a permanent memorial.

I had never really stopped to consider what an extraordinary thing the Royal National Lifeboat Institution is. Think about it. A troubled ship calls for help, and eight people—teachers, plumbers, the guy who runs the pub—drop everything and put to sea, whatever the weather, asking no questions, to try to help strangers. Is there anything more brave and noble than that? The RNLI—I looked this up later—is an organization run by volunteers, supported entirely by public donations. It maintains 233 stations around the coast of Britain and averages twenty-two callouts per day. It saves 350 lives a year on average. There are times when Britain is the most wonderful country in the world—genuinely the most wonderful. This was one of them.

All this only deepened my admiration for Mousehole, which is in any case an absolutely lovely place. Its streets are narrow and crazily twisting. Many are too narrow for cars. Several lanes are more like passageways than streets. At the foot of the village stands a little harbor surrounded by a protective wall. The tide was out so the boats lay aslant on seaweed and mud. The sea beyond sparkled in the morning sun. St. Michael's Mount shimmered, like a galleon in stone, across the bay. Standing on the quayside was the Ship Inn, a most perfect-looking pub. This was where the lifeboat men had set off from. On the front wall was a plaque in memory of its former landlord, Charles Greenhaugh, who was one of the eight Mousehole men to die that night. Because it was early on a Sunday morning, the village was quiet and everything shut, so I just shuffled around a little, admired the view, then took a long, rather pensive walk back to Penzance.

In Penzance, I stood beside my car with a book of maps opened to Cornwall, trying to think what to do next when my eye fell on a place that I hadn't been to, or even thought of, for forty years: Tintagel.

And so I had my next destination. I am not actually quite sure why because I don't have deep and happy memories of it. I didn't even like it the first time, but I felt a kind of compulsion to see it again. I think the very fact that I hadn't seen it for forty years made it automatically of interest. I was curious not so much to reexperience Tintagel, but just to see how much, if any, of it came back to me.

Tintagel, if you don't know it, is a promontory with a ruined castle, traditionally associated with King Arthur, standing high above a crashing sea on a bleak stretch of Cornish coast between Newquay and Bude. It is only about seven or eight miles off the A39, the main road through north Cornwall, but the lanes leading to it are so mazelike and slow that it feels like much more. On my first visit, I walked there from the nearby town of Camelford, little realizing that I would have to step into hedges every time a vehicle passed—which mercifully wasn't all that often—and was dumbfounded to find that the route was both farther and more confusing than was indicated by the inch or so of space it took up on my map. As I stood at an unsignposted crossroads, map open, confused, a battered, ancient car pulled up alongside me and a window crashed down.

"Going to Tintagel?" said a woman with a refined voice.

I bent down to look in the window. A second woman was in the front passenger seat. "Why, yes," I said.

"Hop in. We'll give you a lift."

I squeezed gratefully into a backseat that was tiny already and more or less filled to the ceiling with suitcases and travel gear. I sat with my legs hooked over my ears. We took off with a throaty *vrooom*—one of the few times in my life that I have experienced actual g-forces. I don't know what kind of car it was, but the woman drove it as if she were Stirling Moss and this was the Nürburgring.

She appeared to be short and almost perfectly round. Her companion, a woman of similar years, was tall and lean. I remember thinking that they could go to a costume party as the number 10.

The round one—the driver—began probing me with questions. What was I doing in Britain? Where had I been so far? She was particularly eager to know what I liked and disliked about their little island. I answered diplomatically that I liked it all.

"There must be something you don't like," she insisted.

I could see at once that this was a scenario without a winning outcome, so I said no, really, I liked everything.

"Surely there must be *some*thing you don't like," she persisted.

"Think hard," urged her companion.

"Well, I am not crazy about the bacon," I said.

"You don't like our bacon," said the round woman and in the rearview mirror I could see her eyebrow arch nearly to the ceiling. "And what is wrong with English bacon, pray?"

"It's just different. We have it crisp in America."

"And you think that's better, do you?"

"It's just the way I am used to it, I suppose."

"When I was in Sunt Lewey," said the thin one abruptly, "I had something they called hotcakes. Can you imagine it—cakes for breakfast."

"They're not really cakes," I pointed out.

"Yes, they're called hotcakes. I specifically remember," the thin one insisted.

"What are they like, dear?" asked the small, round one.

"Well, they're rather like our pancakes."

"They *are* pancakes," I said. "It's just a different name." But the women weren't listening to me at all now.

"And they have them for breakfast?"

"Every day."

"Never!"

"They were most peculiar. And they eat pizza pie."

180

"For breakfast?"

"No, for lunch and dinner. But it's not a pie at all, it's a kind of bread with tomato sauce and cheese on it."

"Sounds dreadful."

"Oh, it is," agreed her companion. "Quite dreadful."

"Do you eat pizza pie?" the round one asked me accusingly now.

I allowed that sometimes I did.

"And you prefer it to English bacon?"

This question was too confusing to answer, so I just made some speaking shapes with my mouth, but no words came out.

"It's very odd that you would like pizza pie but not English bacon. Don't you find that odd, dear?" the short round one said to the thin one.

"Most peculiar," agreed her friend. "But then Americans *are* quite peculiar if one is completely honest about it."

The round one was looking at me narrowly in the mirror. "And what else don't you like?" she said.

I was going to maintain my stance of diplomacy, but I found myself, against my own wishes and better judgment, saying, "Well, I am not actually crazy about the sausages either."

"Our sausages? You don't like our sausages?"

"I prefer the American ones."

I was dismissed from the conversation again.

"Did you have sausages in Sunt Lewey, dear?" asked the round one of her friend.

"Yes, and they were most peculiar. They were small and rather spicy."

"Ooh, I don't like the sound of that."

"No," agreed the thin one.

The round one was looking at me critically again.

"Well, I hope you are not starving in this country. You seem to dislike everything."

This was actually more or less correct, but I said, "No, I like everything else." Then after about five minutes, I added: "It's Saint Lewis, by the way. It's pronounced *Saint Lewis,* not *Sunt Lewey.*" This was received with silence and I realized that our experiment in transatlantic friendship had come to an end. We parted ways in the central parking lot in Tintagel, and the last words I heard were the tall one saying, "*Most* peculiar. And rather ill-mannered, don't you think?"

I parked now in the same spacious parking lot and ventured onto the high street. I had no recollection whatever of the community of Tintagel and could immediately see why. It was a spectacularly unmemorable place, consisting primarily of a single street lined with shops selling mostly New Age tat. It was very busy with tourists, and all the cafés and tearooms were packed.

I didn't remember the castle either, but that is not entirely surprising since there is no castle to remember. It is just a few scraps of ruined wall standing on a windy platform of grass and rock 190 feet above the sea. The history of Tintagel Castle is a little obscure. It enters the literary record in a twelfth-century work by Geoffrey of Monmouth called *History of the Kings of Britain.* The story as told by Geoffrey was that the King of Britain, Uther Pendragon, fell for the beautiful wife of the Duke of Cornwall. Alarmed, the duke had his dear wife locked up in the stony fastness of Tintagel Castle while he went off to fight battles in some distant place. Uther, not to be denied, had his crafty wizard, Merlin, transform him into the very likeness of the duke and in this guise the king gained entrance to Tintagel. There he had his way with the duke's unsuspecting (or at least uncomplaining) wife, and thus turned the duke into the first Cornish patsy, so to speak. The beautiful duchess soon afterward discovered that she was pregnant. The child of this union was King Arthur.

One of a great many difficulties with this story was that Geoffrey was writing six hundred years after the events described and, as far as can be told, was making everything up anyway. If Arthur existed at all, he could have been any of several historical figures, only some of whom had a connection to Cornwall. Arthur's seat, Camelot, may actually have been on the other side of the country in East Anglia. It has been suggested with some plausibility that the name Camelot may have come from *Camulodunum,* the Roman name for Colchester, in Essex. What is certain is that Arthur, Uther, Merlin, and all the others never saw Tintagel Castle for it wasn't yet built.

I had a respectful look around and read the information panels, then descended to sea level to have a look at a natural feature called (again without historical basis) Merlin's Cave, then trudged all the way back up to the cliff tops. I walked back into the village to find that it was still packed with people, almost none of whom seemed to be heading for the castle but were evidently content to nose around in the shops looking at candles and tarot cards and the like.

On my first visit, all those years ago, after viewing the castle I returned to the parking lot, hoping that my lady friends would take pity on me and convey me back to the known world—it was, however faint, my only hope—but the space where their car had been was bare. So I walked out of town on the road on which we had come in, presumably without a great deal of thought as to how foolish it was to leave the only inhabited place for miles just as darkness was falling. I can't imagine what outcome I hoped for, but before long I was hungry and cold and pretty well lost. It was at this point that I came across a lonely farmhouse—and this is, let me say, an absolutely true story—with a B&B sign out front. I could hear quite a lively argument going on inside even before I reached the door. It stopped at once when I pushed the buzzer. After a minute, the door was opened very slightly by a haggard-looking woman. She didn't speak but just looked at me with an impassive expression that said: "What?"

"Do you have a room for the night?" I asked.

"A room?" She seemed astounded. I expect she had more or less forgotten that she had a sign out front. Then, remembering, she said quickly: "It's a pound."

Confused as always, I thought she was describing the nature of the lodging. "A pound like where dogs sleep?" I asked in tentative dismay.

"No, it costs a pound."

"Oh," I said. "That'll be fine."

She showed me to a room at the back of the house on the ground floor. It was a bit cold and spartan, with a narrow bed, bedside locker, a chest of drawers, and a sink with just a cold tap, but clean.

"Is there anywhere around here I can get something to eat?" I asked.

"No."

"Oh."

"I could do you something. Won't be much."

"Oh, that would be great," I said, sincerely grateful. I was starving.

"Cost you another pound."

"Fine."

"Wait here. I'll bring it when it's ready."

She left me in the room. Almost at once the most ferocious shouting ensued from a room nearby. It was clear that I had now become part of the argument. Over the next half hour, doors and drawers slammed and voices were continually raised in anger. Something heavy—possibly a toaster—crashed against a wall. Then abruptly all the noise stopped. The next moment my door opened and the woman brought a tray in. It was a wonderful, enormous meal. It included a large slab of cake and a can of beer.

"Leave the tray outside the door when you've finished," she

said, then left and the arguing resumed at an even more intense and angry pitch than before. I ate quietly, half expecting my door to fly open at any moment and a man about seven feet tall in bib overalls to be standing there with an ax, but that never happened. Once the woman shrieked and said, "Put that down!" and then things like "You just dare" and "Go ahead, you sick bastard." There was the sound of a struggle and a chair being knocked over. Then it went quiet for a while and then there were more ructions and the sounds of things being flung. I didn't know whether to intervene or escape out the window. Instead I sat on the edge of the bed and ate my cake. It was delicious.

I went to bed about 8 p.m.—there was nothing else to do—and listened to the fighting in the dark. After about an hour it moved upstairs, where it continued intermittently until about eleven when at last the house grew quiet and we all slept.

In the morning my haggard hostess brought me an enormous, lovely breakfast on a tray. "You need to go when you finish that," she said. "I'm going out and I don't want to leave you alone here with him." She put the tray on the chest of drawers, accepted two pounds from me and departed. A few minutes later I heard a car go down the driveway.

I ate the breakfast in about seventeen seconds, gathered up my things, and stepped out of my room for the first time since arriving. Down the corridor a man was standing at a mirror adjusting a tie. He looked at me without expression, then returned to the tie.

I let myself out the front door and walked briskly and without a backward glance the four miles to Boscastle, where I got on the first bus that was going anywhere. This was in 1972. Except for my few visits to Penzance, I hadn't been back to Cornwall since.

Chapter 13

Ancient Britain

I DIDN'T DO STONEHENGE justice when I went there in *Notes from a Small Island,* but in those days it really didn't do itself justice. Back then, the parking lot and visitor center stood conveniently but unattractively near the stone circle, just off the busy A344 highway. The visitor center had the warmth and charm of an army barracks. The exhibitions were grudging, the snack bar grubby. The whole thing was commonly termed a national disgrace.

Well, what a transformation. Today, discreetly tucked away behind a neighboring hill, there rises a sleek new reception area, glassy and inviting, with a generous exhibition space incorporating informative displays and space-age technology. The old parking lot and visitor center and a good stretch of the old A344 have been taken away and grassed over, a blissful improvement. Once there were plans also to put the very busy A303, which skirts the southern edge of the site, into a tunnel, which would have made Stonehenge the silent and solitary wonder it once was, but that plan was eventually rejected as too expensive. Still, with the recent improvements, Stonehenge is a thousand times better than it was until just a couple of years ago.

Not everyone is entirely happy with the new arrangements. For many overseas visitors Stonehenge is just one stop on a whirlwind day tour from London that also takes in Windsor Castle, Bath, and sometimes Stratford-upon-Avon, too. It used to be that such visitors could get the complete Stonehenge experience—see the stones, look around the gift shop, discover to their dismay that there were no nachos or pizzas for sale, buy a box of fudge to eat until something cheesier became available, visit the restroom, put on a plastic poncho because it was evidently time to look a little ridiculous, then climb back on their tour bus and depart—all in about ten minutes. Now, with the new visitor center more than a mile from the stones, it takes that long just to drive to the site, which is more time than people doing the south of England in a day can comfortably spare.

I, however, was enchanted from the moment of arrival. The admission price of £14.90 brought only a small cry of pain to my lips. The new exhibition space was excellent—or as excellent as these things can ever be. It is an impossible task. The exhibition must satisfy people with brains, interests, and language skills of all different capacities, and it must keep the crowds moving along, to accommodate the steady flow of new arrivals from behind, so it can't invite lingering. But once we have allowed for that, it is awfully good.

Much of our knowledge about Stonehenge is surprisingly recent. For most of my lifetime, Stonehenge was thought to date from about 1,400 BC, but now it is known to be a thousand years older than that, and a large part of the surrounding earthworks are older still. The cursus, a giant oval ditch nearly two miles long, predates Stonehenge by hundreds of years, as do many of the burial mounds and processional avenues. Something about this site drew people long before anyone decided to erect stones there. Many came long distances—from as far as the Alps and the Highlands of Scotland—but for what purposes precisely will probably never be known.

Nothing of course is more mysterious than the great stone circle itself. The Stonehenge we see today was built from two types of stone: sarsen, an immensely hard sandstone that forms the giant uprights, and bluestone, which was used for the smaller encircling stones. The sarsens were brought from the Marlborough Downs, which are generally described as nearby, but you try dragging an eighty-thousand-pound rock twenty miles over open ground and see how often you use the word "nearby." Today seventeen of the big stones are still standing, but once there may have been thirty. The smaller but more numerous bluestones—eighty or so of them altogether—came 180 miles from the Preseli Hills of western Wales. That is truly extraordinary. How did people in lowland England know about the existence of special stones on a mountaintop in distant Wales? If they thought the stones were sacred, as they clearly must have, why didn't they build their shrine in Wales? Why go to the immense effort of bringing them all the way to Salisbury Plain? It wasn't to help complete the great stone circle that we see today. We now know that the bluestones were brought to Stonehenge five hundred years before the great stone circle was built. This is another new fact, known only since 2009. As with everything at Stonehenge, the more we learn the more wondrous and inexplicable it becomes.

When I first came to Stonehenge in the early 1970s, you were still allowed to wander among the stones, to touch them and lounge against them and perch upon them. Soon afterward, however, that practice was stopped in the interests of preservation and everyone was made to stay on an outer encircling path, which is clearly a shame. At the new visitor center they have addressed this problem by placing two full-sized replica stones—one a bluestone, one a sarsen—just outside. Visitors can thus feel and inspect both types of stone before they see the real thing, which is a great help. Sarsen is a sandstone, but harder than granite. The display block at the visitor center lies on its side on wooden rollers, to show how it is believed the stones were moved. It is an excellent presentational stroke because it conveys the immensity and weight of the thing instantly.

Most people travel to the Stonehenge circle from the visitor center on a conveyance called a land train, but a discerning few elect to walk—a much better option because it gives you a chance to settle into the landscape and get a sense of the spaciousness of Salisbury Plain. You see the stones for the first time from about a half mile away and below you as you emerge from a stand of trees at the top of a long, low hill.

At first sight, they seem surprisingly modest, dinky even—we are used, after all, to seeing big buildings in our world—but with a little effort you can imagine the awe it must have evoked in people who had never encountered anything larger than a hut. And it actually takes no effort at all to be struck silent by the beauty and perfect majesty of it. You realize at once that this is one of the most beautiful and extraordinary things ever created by humans, and it is all the more remarkable for being totally without precedent. The wonder of Stonehenge isn't just the energy and organizational skills necessary to get it built, but the vision of it.

How, in every sense of the word, did they do it? How did anybody get the idea, how did they persuade hundreds of people to join in the endeavor, how did they find and select the right stones, haul them across the country, shape them to perfection, heave them into position? How anyone could conceive such a harmonious assemblage in a world with nothing to compare it with is a mystery way beyond answering. And it was all done by people who had no metals to work with, no tools sharper than flint or antler.

Why Stonehenge was built where it was is a question not easy to answer, even speculatively. The site is not especially prominent. It isn't served by a mighty river or bounded by natural grandeur. The materials necessary to construct Stonehenge were all far away. There must have been other places easier for pilgrims to reach. Yet, for some reason, unknown numbers of people invested vast amounts of energy and thought into making one of the most literally perfect structures ever made. The fastidiousness of it is staggering. The Stonehenge site slopes slightly, but the builders allowed for that and made the uprights different heights so that the lintels would remain perfectly horizontal all the way around. The stones are not standing on top of the ground, like dominoes on a tabletop, but are embedded in the earth, in some cases up to a depth of eight feet, to keep them from toppling. Somebody wanted them still to be standing forty-five hundred years later. The sides of the lintels are gently curved, so that they can neatly fit a circular structure. This was a meticulously engineered monument.

And yet despite their having taken all that care, it now appears that Stonehenge was used for no more than a couple of generations and then abandoned. What made people walk away from it is likely to remain forever the biggest mystery of all.

As you might expect, all this left me in a reflective frame of mind. Trudging back up the long, low hill, I wondered idly what the builders of Stonehenge would have created if they'd had bulldozers and big trucks for moving materials and computers to help them design. What would they have created if they had had all the tools we have? Then I crested the brow of the hill with a view down to the visitor center, with its café and gift shop, its land trains and giant parking lot, and realized I was almost certainly looking at it.

I was headed for the county of Norfolk, in the region known as East Anglia, but the Natural History Museum in London had a special exhibition that was highly relevant to East Anglia, so I stopped there on the way. The Natural History Museum is a glorious, over-wrought building with a massive central hall dominated by the skeleton of a *Tyrannosaurus rex*, which seems to be poised to attack and devour anyone coming through the front entrance, which in fact wouldn't be a bad idea at all these days.

I remember the Natural History Museum from years ago as being packed with excellent stuff and seeming almost infinite. The long downstairs corridors, softly lit and tranquil, were filled with tall glass cases of stuffed animals of every imaginable type. It was like being in a frozen zoo. You could study the animals closely, observe their steady gaze and fur and musculature, get a sense of their strength or fleetness, marvel at life's diverse ingenuity. It was fascinating, even thrilling. Above all, I remember the Natural History Museum as being almost empty of other visitors and very quiet, like a library.

Now it is never calm or empty. Like so many popular tourist destinations in Europe, it is permanently bright and noisy and horrible. Where a long gallery full of stuffed animals and glass cases used to beckon there is now a gift shop. It is not even a gift shop really. It's a toy store. Gone are the days when you could fob your children off with a pencil case and an eraser. This was like Hamley's, the famous children's emporium on Regent Street.

The crowds were loud, intense, and mostly foreign. The atmosphere was that of a Middle Eastern souk or the streets around a football ground before a big game. Nothing about it was agreeable. I threaded my way through the throngs to the special exhibition I had come for, "One Million Years of the Human Story," which was all about the first people in Britain. I had been wanting to see it for some weeks but particularly I wanted to see it now when I was en route to East Anglia, for that is where the human story in Britain begins.

People, it turns out, have come and gone a lot in Britain. The country has been occupied and abandoned at least seven times. These comings and goings don't always make a lot of sense. Half a million years ago Britain had a fairly substantial population, but then for about one hundred thousand years no one was in Britain at all, as far as can be told, even though that was a period when the climate was mild and food abundant. At other times when the country was covered in ice hundreds of feet thick, people clambered over every obstacle to get there. Throughout the whole of the long haul of the Paleolithic era, people came and went in ways that seemed perversely at variance with what nature was telling them to do. I suppose it could be said they still do.

In 2000, an amateur archaeologist named Mike Chambers, while walking along the beach at Happisburgh, Norfolk, noticed a flaked flint sticking out of a crumbly sea cliff in a stratum where worked flints shouldn't be. A team of academic archaeologists moved in and over the next five years extracted thirty-two more pieces of worked flint—that is, human artifacts—which proved to come from an extremely remote past, left by a people so distant from us in time that we know nothing about them. The Happisburgh people were not modern humans. They are usually assigned to a species called *Homo antecessor,* which means "first people," but that's just a guess. They left no direct traces of themselves, only the flinty remnants of their industry. Whoever they were, they were the earliest beings yet found in Britain, from nearly a million years ago (hence the name of the exhibition).

At least two other early species of human came and went in Britain before *Homo sapiens* arrived: *Homo heidelbergensis* and *Homo neanderthalensis* (which is to say the Neanderthals). Out of all the incursions, the only permanent one so far is the present one, and that dates from just twelve thousand years ago, which means that Britain is actually one of the more recent places in the world to become inhabited by modern people. In this sense it is much younger than the Americas or Australia.

The exhibition was everything an exhibition should be— thoughtful, informative, blissfully quiet. I was one of just three visitors, no doubt because it was also rather expensive at £9. (The museum itself is free.) The curators had assembled much that had never been brought together before—the earliest Neanderthal skull in Britain, the world's most ancient spear, hand axes and scrapers of all shapes and sizes, including those found at Happisburgh—so you could follow the whole story of human occupation over nearly a million years. But the most mesmerizing features were two life-sized, and wholly lifelike, models—one of a Neanderthal, the other of an early modern human. They were made by two Dutch brothers, Adris and Alfons Kennis, who have a genius—that's really not too strong a word—for human reconstructions. The models were fashioned to look like individuals, not archetypes, so that entering the room was like being with an actual, living Neanderthal and an equally actual early human, a quite uncanny experience.

The Neanderthal was short, about five feet four inches tall, but solidly built and rugged-looking. Neanderthals are a wonderful mystery. Their brains were bigger than ours, for one thing. They lived through ice ages, so needed clothing, but left no evidence that they ever learned to sew. For a long time it was thought that we didn't breed with them, but now we know that we are 2 percent Neanderthal ourselves. I don't know why scientists have been so resistant to the idea of interbreeding. You look at the modern humans that a lot of us have slept with and it is hardly a surprise if a Neanderthal maiden or two might have twinkled by the campfire light. Among the genetic gifts the Neanderthals passed on to us, it seems, is red hair, bless them. Alongside the Neanderthal, the early modern human looked delicate, almost wispy. He was several inches taller but considerably less robust. There is no question that a Neanderthal could easily beat us up. So, too, presumably could their women, which may be why we are only 2 percent Neanderthal instead of 50 percent. Those bitches were too scary for us.

Nearby was a plaster model of the head of a *Homo antecessor*, looking uncommonly happy for some reason. *Homo antecessor* was an entirely new species discovered in northern Spain in 1994. They have never been found anywhere else. No one actually knows that the Norfolk people were *Homo antecessor*. They are assumed to be because they come from the right age, but they could be something else altogether, including even a new species. The model in the Natural History Museum suggested a human-like creature that was good-natured but none too bright, but this, too, is just a guess.

The exhibition ended, inevitably, with a pop-up gift shop. I don't blame the museum exactly. This is what happens when institutions are told to offer free general admission but also somehow pay their own way. I wouldn't be at all surprised on my next visit to find the space occupied by a Tesco Express mini-supermarket.

I went and had a look at the rest of the museum. The displays everywhere were dated and threadbare. The room on "Creepy Crawlies," which I don't think has changed since I took my own kids there in the 1980s, is relentlessly jokey in a way that makes you want to shoot yourself through the head. Many of the signs were half worn away; this was slowly becoming the Na ural Hist ry Mus um. The labels everywhere were hopelessly lacking in enthusiasm and thought. In the ecology section, a picture of a dolphin, head out of the water looking cheerful and friendly, was accompanied by this message (given here in full): "In 2004 MPs [members of Parliament] called for an end to sea bass fishing in Southwest England following pressure from campaigners to reduce the number of dolphins drowned in trawler nets each year." I'm sorry, but we just have to look at this ridiculous statement for a moment. First of all, 2004 was a long time ago. Has anything happened since then? Certainly nothing has happened to this label since then. How many MPs called for action? Three? Five hundred? What? Did they introduce legislation? Was it acted on? Was there a reason for particular concern about sea bass fishing in Southwest England? Why not all fishing around Britain—or even all fishing in the world? Even when this information was fresh, it was lame and inadequate.

Now it is just out of date and an embarrassment to museumology, or whatever is the word for what these people do. All the museum was like this. The stuffed animals in glass cases that once enraptured my children have been put in storage, presumably deemed too old-fashioned for twenty-first-century display.

The mezzanine overlooking the grand hall used to have a good section on anthropology on one side and yet more stuffed animals on the other. Now the anthropology section is just an empty corridor and the other side is fully occupied by a café—one of at least five in the building. Slowly it dawned on me what's going on here. The Natural History Museum can't afford to be a museum anymore, so the directors are stealthily turning it into a food court. Now when I bring my grandchildren, we can sit with refreshments and I can tell them how it used to be. "Over there where that ice cream machine is used to be a glass case with a polar bear in it. Drink up and I'll take you down and show you where the blue whale used to be. We can get some curly fries there." It won't be as informative or educational, but I expect it will be financially viable.

Just beyond this new upstairs café was a lone glass case, and for a moment I thought I had come across an overlooked relic of the way the museum used to be when it was exciting and interesting, but it was a false alarm. It was essentially just an advertisement for Down House, Charles Darwin's home in Kent, now preserved as a museum. There wasn't any information about Darwin's life and achievements, nothing about the *Beagle* voyage or evolution or anything that could be called mildly instructive, just a recommendation to go and see his house.

It didn't say anything at all about what the snack facilities were like, however, so I decided not to chance it.

Chapter 14

East Anglia

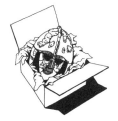

I

ON A LOVELY BRIGHT summer's morning, I was walking the Norfolk coast path between Holkham and Blakeney when I came around a bend and found the way temporarily blocked by a woman and her dog. I stood with the woman and we watched together as the dog dolefully extruded three soft lozenges onto the path.

"Don't you think that's a little disgusting, right on the path and all?" I asked in a tone of genuine inquiry.

"I'm local," she said as if that explained everything. She was well spoken.

"And that gives you the right to let your dog shit on the paths?"

"I'm going to cover it," she said irritably, as if I were needlessly belaboring the point. "Look," she said, and scuffed some leaf litter over it, converting the dog's deposit from a conspicuous hazard into a kind of fecal landmine. "There," she said, and looked at me with satisfaction, as if this had solved everything.

I stared at her for a long moment, with something like awe, then raised my walking stick high into the air and calmly beat her to death. When she was quite still, I rolled her ample, Barbour-clad body off the path and into the marshy reeds where it sank with a satisfying glug. Then I checked my map and resumed my walk, wondering if there was any place in Blakeney where I could get a cup of tea at this hour.

I like Norfolk. I lived there for ten years until 2013 and have grown convinced that there is nothing wrong with it that a few hills and a little genetic variability wouldn't fix. For the benefit of the foreign reader, I should perhaps explain that Norfolk has a long-standing reputation for inbreeding. As my son Sam used to say: "Norfolk: too many people, not enough surnames." I am not for a moment suggesting that the rumors are entirely true, but I will say that when the police do DNA checks after crimes they sometimes have to arrest as many as twelve thousand people.

The other thing for which Norfolk is famed, incontestably, is flatness. Much of it makes tabletops look varied and interesting. But if none of Norfolk is exactly spectacular, parts of it are at least very fine and nowhere is that more true than along the north Norfolk coast. For the ten miles or so between Wells-next-the-Sea (and how pretty a name is that?) and Cley it is buffered on the seaward side by great expanses of salt marsh. These are intercut with channels, some quite deep, that fill with water remarkably swiftly when the tide comes in. It is very easy to lose your way in the chill and wispy fogs that sweep in off the North Sea and to find yourself stranded on a steadily shrinking island of marsh.

North Norfolk is popular with well-to-do second homeowners from London; it is often called Chelsea-on-Sea. But it was blessedly quiet after the West Country. The coast here has the best and most intelligent rural bus service I know. Some years ago, Coasthopper, the company that runs the service, got rid of all its slow, full-sized buses and invested in a fleet of small buses called Hoppers, with the promise that there would be a bus in each direction at least once every half hour. Because the service is so dependable, it has proved remarkably popular with locals and visitors alike. One of the drivers once told me proudly that it is the best-used rural bus service in the country. If you are walking the coast path, it gives you the flexibility to break the walk at any point if you get tired or the weather turns stormy. It also means that you can park your car at somewhere like Holkham or Wells, walk along the coast to Sheringham, then get a bus back to your car. That is what I was doing now.

Several attractive villages of brick and flint stand along the way, notably Blakeney and Cley, but I like to stop for lunch at a place called Cookie's at Salthouse. Cookie's is what in America would be called a crab shack, and it has been there forever. It used to be filled with angry handwritten notices telling customers all the things they were not permitted to do. This included not seating themselves, not asking for a table until they had ordered, not requesting any deviations from the written menu, and above all not consuming anything not bought on the premises, including oxygen and sea views, if I remember correctly. I kept looking around for a sign that said, "Actually, Why Don't You All Just Fuck Off and Leave Us in Peace?"

They seem to have calmed down a good deal at Cookie's now and the signs are fewer and more restrained, which I can't help feel is kind of a shame. I like a place that has a bit of spirit. Anyway, the food is great and very reasonably priced. You can berate me all you want if the price is right. I had a big plate of seafood and it was divine.

Beyond Salthouse the walk is close to the sea and over sand and gravel and along the tops of giant dunes for a couple of miles before climbing upward onto big grassy fields seventy or eighty feet above the sea. It is all lovely. I was doing a long walk—eighteen miles from Holkham to Sheringham—but the terrain at least was undemanding. Just before I reached Sheringham, the air was pierced by a shrill whistle, loud enough to make me start, and off to my right a steam train passed, chuffing away and filling the air with a long chain of white smoke. This was the North Norfolk Railway, a preserved line run by volunteers as a tourist attraction. Even from a fair distance, I could see that the train was packed. Hundreds of happy people were on an eighteen-minute journey from Holt to Sheringham at a speed much slower than they had used to get to Norfolk, on a conveyance almost certainly less comfortable, and they were in heaven.

Very few things are more reliably astounding than the British when they are enjoying themselves, and I say this with a kind of cautious admiration. They have the ability to get deep and lasting pleasure out of practically nothing at all. Give them a form of transportation that was becoming obsolete in the time of Clement Attlee and they will flock to it. Did you know, Britain has 108 steam railways—that is surely 106 or so more than any nation needs—run by 18,500 volunteers? It is an extraordinary fact but a true one that there are thousands of men in Britain who will never need Viagra as long as steam trains are in operation.

And steam trains are only a small part of the Diversions No One But the British Would Want. Britain also has a Water Tower Appreciation Society, a Society for Clay Pipe Research, a Pillbox Study Group, a Ghost Sign Society (which finds and then becomes excited about faded advertisements painted on the sides of buildings) and a Roundabout Appreciation Society. Are you following what I am saying? There are people who spend their free time, not at gunpoint, traveling around seeking out the most interesting and satisfying roundabouts. (How do they even tell when they have found one?)

I recently happened upon a website for the Branch Line Society, which exists to visit and celebrate little-used rail lines. Here is an extract from their newsletter describing a day out attended by 160 people—160!—in 2013:

We took the Up Relief at Parson Street from the first available crossover and stayed "relief" through to Bristol Temple Meads where we took the Up Through, before reversing at Bristol East Jn and terminating in platform 9 only one minute down. With 302 miles and 61 chains under our belts, we waved our good byes to the train crew, stewards and passengers—and promptly started counting the huge pile of booking forms we had collated during the day for the Power Haul Tracker on 3rd November!

It is that exclamation mark that brings joy to my heart. And this was just a tiny part of what they get up to at the Branch Line Society. Here are some of the other exciting days they have had: "Toton Center to Trowell Junction," "Thrumpton West Junction to Retford West Junction (High Level Platform 2)," "Dinting West Junction to Dinting East Junction, avoiding Glossop" (and who could blame them?), and my favorite of all, "Irk Valley Junction to Oldham Mumps."

I can't tell you what comfort this brings me. Any time I am feeling low, when I am tempted to think that life is pointless and empty, I go to one of these societies' websites and read about their latest outings, and I realize just how rich my life is.

In Sheringham, I climbed onto a cheery Hopper bus and rode back to Holkham to collect my car. It wasn't actually *my* car, but a rental car from Norwich, and I really didn't want to have it at all, but there is no way to see East Anglia without a car. Then I drove back to Sheringham, parked with difficulty, and had a very modest look around the town on my tired old legs.

Sheringham, a fading resort overlooking the North Sea, is the nicest not-very-attractive town I know. It doesn't have a super-abundance of charm, I don't think it has a single decent pub, and not much in the way of memorable restaurants, but it has a well-supported little theater and a most commendable range of utilitarian shops of the type that have mostly vanished from the rest of Britain: greengrocer, fishmonger, a couple of butchers, a bookshop and stationer's, and a splendid hardware store called Blyth and Wright that sells everything. A big part of the reason that Sheringham still has these things is that for fourteen years the town successfully fought to stop Tesco, a supermarket chain, from opening a big store in the town center. But Tesco is nothing if not relentless and after much patient maneuvering it eventually won permission to build there. I had a look at the new Tesco and it was busy, but then so too was the high street. I stopped in a shop—a real, independent shop—to buy a bottle of water and asked the proprietor if the new Tesco had made much difference. He nodded grimly. "It was already hard. Now it is getting bloody impossible. Come back in a few months and I guarantee that a lot of the shops on this street won't be here."

"That's sad," I said.

"Bloody tragedy."

"But then again," I pointed out, "your shop is kind of a dump, you didn't say hello when I came in, and you give every appearance of being a miserable old git."

"You're absolutely right. I really should try a lot harder, shouldn't I?"

"Much harder," I agreed. "But the sad thing is you won't. You'll just bitch away as if your failing business is everybody's fault but your own."

"You are so right. Well, thank you for helping me to be a better shopkeeper and possibly even a better person. I hope you'll come again."

Actually we didn't have that conversation. He just handed me my change without saying thank you or giving me the least reason for ever wanting to step into his shop again, cheerless prick.

I stayed the night in the Burlington Hotel, a large and dark establishment on the seafront for which I have an unaccountable affection. I have never been in the Burlington when I didn't wonder if I was the only guest in the place, but somehow it hangs in there. Perhaps my semiannual visits are all the business they need. While grooming for the evening, I turned on the television just in time for the local news, which in this part of the world always means a report of a factory closure in Lowestoft. I am amazed that there are any factories left to close in Lowestoft, but they always seem to find another one. It is generally an obscure business that is the last of its type in Britain.

"Britain's last remaining kelp sniffer is to close its doors after 160 years," the newsreader will gravely intone. "Two hundred and fifty employees, some of whom have been with the firm since the nineteenth century, are to lose their jobs." The next night it will be Britain's last remaining cockle flayer, flange trimmer, oyster chafer or other improbable-sounding enterprise. I didn't catch the nature of the business on this evening because I was drying my hair with a noisy blower and turned it off only to hear: "Staff have been offered alternative employment at the company's production facility in Ho Chi Minh City."

Scrubbed to a pink freshness and attired in clean clothes, I had a drink in the hotel's empty bar, followed by dinner at a nearly empty restaurant nearby, returned to my room, and fell into bed and slept like a baby.

II

In the morning I woke to watery sunshine, and after breakfast in the Burlington's large but empty dining room drove twenty miles down the coast to Happisburgh, a remote and lonely but good-looking village roughly halfway between Sheringham and

Great Yarmouth. Happisburgh is dominated by a tall, lovely light-house with three red stripes. A sign in the neighboring parking lot informed me that this was "the only independently run lighthouse in the Uk." Now I am very sorry, but how can you possibly pass a lifetime in a country and not know how to abbreviate it? Why did you bother going to school at all? Why did your teachers turn up in the morning? Apart from this minor outburst of illiteracy, Happisburgh seemed to be an entirely agreeable place. It is pro-nounced, incidentally, *hays-burra,* or even just *hays-brrrrr.* Norfolk specializes in odd pronunciations. Hautbois is *hobbiss,* Wymond-ham is *windum,* Costessey is *cozzy,* Postwick is *pozzik.* People often ask why that is. I'm not sure, but I think it is just something that happens when you sleep with close relatives.

Happisburgh rarely attracted the attention of outsiders until 2000 when the flint scrapers found there by archaeologists were dated to nine hundred thousand years ago. These were the oldest human artifacts ever found this side of the Alps. The unexpected-ness of this can hardly be exaggerated.

Nobody else in the world was this far north at that time. These were the most out-of-Africa people on the planet. That is a truly extraordinary fact. They had the whole world to themselves and they chose Happisburgh—and this was before it had a film evening on the second Tuesday of every month organized by the Corona-tion Hall Film Club. And people think Happisburgh is slow now.

Happisburgh was of course a very different place then. Britain was connected to the rest of Europe by a land bridge and Hap-pisburgh stood where the Thames met the sea. Today the Thames enters the North Sea ninety-five miles to the south, but a million years ago this was a broad and nutritious estuary.

This stretch of English coastline has been fighting a losing battle with the sea for centuries. The cliffs along the seafront stand some thirty or forty feet high and are made of loose sand and little else. Signs of slippage are evident everywhere. Lots of properties have fallen into the sea over the years and more now are clearly not far off following. In some places, homes stand on the very brink of fresh cliff edges. Just by the parking lot, a steepish path led down to the sea, but the tide was in and the beach was underwater. I went down as far as I could, but there was nothing to see, so I returned to the cliff top and followed it north toward a trailer park.

Just below the site was the spot where ancient footprints had been exposed the year before. A storm washed away a covering layer of sand, and the footprints of half a dozen individuals, permanently impressed in rock, were exposed to daylight probably for the first time since they were made in soft mud almost a million years ago. They are the oldest footprints in the world outside Africa. Archaeologists studied and recorded them, then allowed nature to cover them again. The cliff edges are dangerously unstable, but I crept close and looked over as much as I dared. Directly below me, where waves washed against the cliff, was the spot where the footprints had been found. There was something eerily splendid in standing almost on the very place where people from a time before modern humans tramped about in an unimaginably distant past.

Happisburgh was also the scene of one of Britain's worst nautical tragedies, in the winter of 1801, when one of its greatest warships, HMS *Invincible,* was driven onto a sandbank during a storm and broke up. Four hundred men drowned in the freezing waters. Nearly 120 bodies washed onto the beach and were buried in St. Mary's churchyard. I strolled up there now. St. Mary's is a striking church with a 110-foot-high square tower, which is pretty high but seems even higher against the big, empty skies of Norfolk. The church looks to be a safe distance from the shore, but at the present rate of coastal erosion, it has been calculated, the sea will claim it in about seventy years. Faced with this tragic prospect, the British government is doing what governments always do when confronted with a problem that doesn't need an immediate solution: nothing.

I drove a dozen miles back toward Sheringham along wandering lanes, through lush and sunny farmland to the coastal village of Overstrand. It is hard to believe, but this was once one of the most fashionable resorts in Europe. On a summer's afternoon in the early years of the twentieth century, a visitor to Overstrand might run into Winston Churchill, Ellen Terry, Henry Irving, or Sidney and Beatrice Webb. It was called the "Village of Millionaires." Lord Hillingdon, owner of Overstrand Hall, used the house for just two weeks a year but famously kept three butlers and an army of understaff on permanent alert in case he showed up unexpectedly, which he never did.

My interest was with a property called the Sea Marge and with the forgotten magnate who built it, Sir Edgar Speyer. Speyer was a German who spent most of his life outside Germany. He was born in 1862 in New York City to wealthy German parents, then went to England in his twenties to look after the family interests there. He made a fortune as a financier, built much of the London Underground, and became a generous patron of the arts. When the Proms got into financial difficulties, he stepped in and saved it. He became pals with King George V, our friend from Bognor, took out British citizenship, was knighted for his services to the arts, and was appointed to the Privy Council. He gave generously to hospitals and funded the Antarctic expedition of Robert Falcon Scott. When Scott died, he had a letter to Speyer in his pocket.

Speyer was, in short, a nearly ideal human being, except that it seems he wanted Germany to win all its wars and take over the world. This is, of course, occasionally a problem with Germans. Speyer's house is a hefty edifice in the style of an Elizabethan manor standing on cliffs above the sea. Rumors have often had it that Speyer signaled German ships from the terrace during the First World War. It is an appealing image, but a slightly preposterous one. For a start, what would he tell them? ("Bit rainy here. How you?") He had no access to information that would be of special value to the German war effort and it was unlikely that he would expose himself to the obvious risk of being observed.

Speyer's real problem was that he was Jewish at a time when even the most enlightened members of society tended to be at least lightly anti-Semitic. Lord Northcliffe, owner of the *Daily Mail*, spoke for his generation when, in noting the proliferation of Jewish businessmen in England, he remarked drily, "We shall soon have to set the Society column in Yiddish." Northcliffe loathed Speyer and persecuted him mercilessly. Eventually Speyer fled to America under a cloud of suspicion. A parliamentary committee stripped him of his honors and branded him a traitor, which he was insofar as he longed for a German victory.

The Sea Marge is now a hotel. I trespassed onto its grounds and looked over the garden wall at the sea, then wandered inside, wondering if anyone would challenge me, but no one did. There didn't seem to be anything at all to recall Herr Speyer, so I wandered out again and went to have a look at the village, which was tidy and quite arrestingly normal.

It is a small miracle that it has survived as well as it has. Norfolk is the most out on a limb of English counties. It has terrible roads and a generally appalling rail service. When we first moved there, the train services were operated by a company called WAGN, which I assumed was short for "We Are Going Nowhere." That company lost the franchise eventually and it was given to a Dutch company, but if there have been any improvements I haven't seen them. The upshot is that getting to the east coast of Norfolk requires immense reserves of fortitude and time mixed with an eccentric desire to be on the east coast of Norfolk.

—

Just beyond Overstrand is Cromer, another old seaside resort, with a grand old hotel, the endearingly named Hotel de Paris. I can't imagine where it gets its business from. I was here to see Cromer's pier, which I think may be the best and handsomest in the nation. Once there were about a hundred piers in Britain, but today there are barely half that number and a great many of them—Bognor springs to mind, or it would if there was anything left in it capable of springing—are falling down or are scarcely worthy of the name. Cromer's was badly damaged by a winter storm in 2013, and I'd heard that there was talk of tearing it down, which would have been beyond a tragedy, but happily it was repaired and seems as good as new now.

A few years ago, when Daniel and Andrew and I were walking this section of coast, Daniel discovered to his great and improbable excitement that the pier's little theater was staging a show of songs from the Second World War, and that one of the performers was someone he had once worked with. Daniel insisted that we go to that day's matinee. I was frankly dubious, but in the event enjoyed myself immensely. The performance was well attended, mostly by elderly people who arrived on buses from nearby nursing homes. I believe Daniel, Andrew, and I were the only members of the audience not sitting on incontinence pads. The cast consisted of just three performers, but they were excellent. It helped a lot that the female singer was pretty and talented and that the whole thing lasted only a little over an hour.

Cromer is a pleasant, old-fashioned place and I had a good look around it, then returned to Sheringham and had another look around it for want of anything more sensational to do. Then I returned to the Burlington Hotel, and sat very quietly until it was a respectable enough hour to go and have a drink.

III

You can't go to East Anglia and not visit Sutton Hoo. Well, you can obviously, but you shouldn't. The Sutton Hoo story begins with a man named Col. Frank Pretty, who didn't do much of anything for the first fifty years or so of his life, then did rather a lot in quite a short period. He married a middle-aged spinster named Edith May, moved with her onto a big estate called Sutton Hoo near Woodbridge in Suffolk, fathered a son, and then abruptly died, on his fifty-sixth birthday.

Left on her own with a small son and large, lonely house, Mrs. Pretty took up spiritualism and developed an interest in the twenty or so grassy mounds that stood on heathland about five hundred yards from her house. Deciding to excavate them, she contacted the Ipswich Museum, which put her in touch with a curious figure named Basil Brown.

Brown was a farm laborer and odd-job man with no archaeological training. He had dropped out of school at twelve, but he continued to educate himself through private study, and acquired certificates of attainment in geography, geology, astronomy, and drawing. My own interest in him began when I lived in Norfolk and discovered that he had married a girl from our village and lived with her for some years on a neighboring property called Church Farm. Brown had a rustic Norfolk accent his whole life and was often likened in appearance and manner to a ferret, but he had a genius for archaeology. He spent nearly all his free time cycling around Norfolk looking for likely archaeological sites and, to an almost uncanny degree, often finding them.

Brown agreed to have a look at Mrs. Pretty's estate, but had no great expectations. The mounds, it was well known, had been extensively picked over in the past. That was probably why the job was offered to Brown rather than someone of greater stature. Mrs. Pretty gave Brown a small salary and lodgings in the chauffeur's cottage, and lent him two estate workers as assistants. Brown and his team had no special tools. They used jugs, bowls, and sieves brought down from the pantry. The most delicate work was done with pastry brushes from the kitchen and a bellows from the library. In the summer of 1938, Brown dug trenches through three of the mounds, but found nothing. Undaunted, he returned the following summer and excavated what is now called mound one. Almost at once he found a piece of metal, which he correctly deduced was a ship's rivet and that this was a ship burial. This was quite an insight for there was no history of ship burials in Britain—this is still one of only two ever found—and anyway the mound was a mile or so from water. Nobody had ever found a ship burial this far inland. The only reference work Brown could find to guide him was a heavy volume in Norwegian from 1904 describing the excavation of the Viking ship *Oseberg* from western Norway.

It is important to remember that Brown didn't find a ship. He found the *impression* of a ship—the indentations of a long-vanished structure. It was intensely delicate work—like trying to excavate a shadow. But what a payoff. Brown had found the greatest haul of treasure ever recovered in Britain—jewels, coins, gold and silver plate, armor, weapons, and decorative objects of every sort. The goods came from as far away as Egypt and Byzantium. No one knows who was buried in the ship, or indeed that anyone actually was, for it contained no remains. It may be that every bit of the body percolated away in the acidic soil, or it may be that the occupant was cremated and his ashes sprinkled among the relics. The person most often cited as the most likely occupant is Raedwald, king of the East Angles, but that is just a guess.

When it was realized how priceless a find this was, government archaeologists rushed in and Basil Brown was roughly cast aside. For years, his role in the discovery was either unmentioned or discussed with condescension. A typical assessment was that of the archaeologist Richard Dumbreck who described Brown as "having the appearance of a ferret" and said that he excavated "like a terrier after a rat. He would trowel furiously, scraping the spoil between his legs, and at intervals he would stand back to view progress and tread in what he had just loosened . . . The sad thing is that with training he might have been a brilliant archaeologist." In much the same way, I suspect, with enough training Dumbreck might have become a decent human.

The discovery of the Sutton Hoo treasure came at exactly the wrong time, just as war was breaking out, and all excavations were halted for the duration. The military took over Mrs. Pretty's estate and used it, amazingly, for tank training. When archaeologists returned after the war, they found tracks running right through the excavations. Mrs. Pretty gave the recovered treasure to the British Museum. It remains the single most valuable donation ever made to the museum by a living person. Curators spent years cleaning the finds. The biggest challenge was a golden helmet, which had broken up into more than five hundred fragments. A team of experts spent years trying to put it all back together, but ended up with several pieces left over and a helmet that other experts said was patently unwearable. For the next twenty years, that is what visitors to the British Museum saw. Finally, in 1971, the whole was taken apart again and reassembled into the form it has today, which uses all the pieces and is presumed to be correct. It is one of the most arresting and beautiful objects in the British Museum.

Basil Brown spent another twenty years riding his bicycle around East Anglia and sometimes farther afield, finding Saxon and Roman artifacts and even occasionally an entire farmstead or settlement. He retired in 1961, but lived until 1977, when he died aged eighty-nine. He occasionally went to the British Museum to look at the Sutton Hoo horde. He was never officially honored for its discovery.

I enjoyed a long walk around the site. The mounds are a fair hike from the visitor center. There are about twenty altogether, though all of them are much lower than they once were because of plowing and plundering, and several are barely visible at all. You can also now visit the Prettys' house, which is decorated as it would have been in Mrs. Pretty's day. Each room had a laminated information card giving details of Mrs. Pretty's life there. These contained many errors of spelling and punctuation, which is a little unfortunate, but at least they attempted to convey useful information. I don't remember the house being open in 2009, when I last visited, but then I don't remember things I saw two weeks ago.

The visitor center was stylish and bright, and the displays are interesting and informative and give a good impression of what the burial would have looked like when it was new and again when it was found centuries later. The actual treasures are all at the British Museum, but the exhibition includes some very good replicas. I had a sandwich and a cup of tea in the café and was feeling so benignly pleased with the whole experience that I didn't bitch even privately to myself that the sandwich was a little dry and cost roughly double what, in a reasonable world, it should have. Well, maybe I did bitch inwardly just a little, but I didn't say anything grumbly to anyone and that is surely a mark of progress.

I drove on to Aldeburgh on the Suffolk coast. Aldeburgh is a smart and good-looking town, well supplied with fashionable retailers, locally owned boutiques and cafés, and a good bookshop. Somebody needs to explain to me how it is that Aldeburgh and Southwold, another resort just up the road, remain thriving and chic while so many other resorts are dying. It can't have anything to do with accessibility or underlying beauty—Aldeburgh and Southwold are harder to get to and no more attractively situated than Bognor Regis and much less blessed by nature than Penzance—so what does explain it? I am genuinely at a loss to say.

Once, in my more ambitious days when I made a television

program for the BBC about the problem of litter in Britain, in the touchingly naive belief that people might want to do something about it, I visited a beach cleanup at Aldeburgh being undertaken by the Marine Conservation Trust, to interview the saintly souls who were doing the work. From them I learned that every kilometer of shoreline in Britain contains on average forty-six thousand pieces of litter, mostly tiny bits of plastic, much of which ends up in the stomachs of birds in fairly staggering amounts. In one study, 95 percent of fulmars washed ashore along the North Sea were found to have plastic in their stomachs—and not just a little but a lot: forty-four pieces on average. Transparent bags, meanwhile, choke a great many turtles because they mistake them for jellyfish.

From the Suffolk team I also learned that about ten thousand containers fall off ships each year. Sometimes after a period of years the container doors pop open and the contents float to the surface. One of the volunteers I met, an artist named Fran Crowe, showed me a potato chip packet she had picked up—one of several thousand that had washed onto the beach at Aldeburgh. The chips inside had long since dissolved, but the packets themselves were in pristine condition. The one Fran Crowe showed me bore a price label of 3p and came with an offer expiring on December 31, 1974. It had been under the water for forty years before becoming part of a fiesta of flotsam in Suffolk.

I mentioned that once when I was in the Scilly Isles I saw lots of clear plastic glistening on a beach at Tresco and it turned out to be thousands of saline drip bags, all empty, produced by a British company in Lancashire, but with writing in Spanish.

"Happens all the time," Fran said. She once came upon a beach containing hundreds and hundreds of bicycle seats. She has also found computers, refrigerators, and vacuum cleaners. Lots more floats than you would ever expect, it seems.

—

I spent the night in Dunwich at a jolly nice pub called the Ship. Dunwich is an odd place in that it mostly isn't there anymore. In the twelfth century, it was one of the most important ports in England, nearly three times the size of Bristol and not that much smaller than London. It was home to four thousand people and boasted eighteen churches and monasteries. But in 1286 a mighty storm swept away four hundred houses, and further storms in 1347 and 1560 took away much of the rest. Today most of the original Dunwich is underwater. St. Peter's Church is nearly a quarter of a mile offshore, and some people with no attachment to acoustic reality claim that you can still hear its bell ringing late at night if you listen carefully. All that is left of Dunwich these days is a beach café, a few houses, a ruined priory, and its chirpy pub.

In the evening, in a desperate effort to keep from starting to drink too early, I went for a longish walk and ended up at the seafront. Ships, prettily lit, slid across the horizon, presumably headed for or coming from Felixstowe, just around the corner to the south.

I had just read in *The Economist* that Felixstowe is now the world's leading exporter of empty cardboard boxes. The world sends Britain its products and Britain sends back the boxes. It isn't that Britain is more vigilant than other nations about gathering up old cardboard, but more that other nations don't export it. They recycle it. Britain prefers to send its discarded packaging abroad for expert handling by poorly paid people in distant places. In 2013, the United Kingdom exported more than one million metric tons of cardboard, considerably more than any other nation proportionate to its population.

And with that proud thought to sustain me, I walked back up to the Ship to toast, in my own private way, my adopted nation.

Chapter 15

Cambridge

O N THE PLATFORM AT Cambridge station was a poster for a book by Jeremy Clarkson, a popular television presenter and columnist who has fashioned a very lucrative career out of being cheerfully boorish. The poster had a photo of Clarkson looking adorably doleful and a caption that read: "Dads. Everything they say. Everything they do. Everything they wear. Its all completely wrong." Oh, the wit. But note the absence of the apostrophe in "its." I know it is way too much to ask that a television presenter should take an interest in the literacy of his posters, but surely someone at Penguin ought to care.

We have now reached a level in which many people are not merely unacquainted with the fundamentals of punctuation, but don't evidently realize that there are fundamentals. Many people— people who make posters for leading publishers, write captions for the BBC, compose letters and advertisements for important institutions—seem to think that capitalization and marks of punctuation are condiments that you sprinkle through any collection of words as if from a salt shaker. Here is a headline, exactly as presented, from a magazine ad for a private school in York: "Ranked by the daily Telegraph the top Northern Co-Educational day and Boarding School for Academic results." All those capital letters are just random. Does anyone really think that the correct rendering of

214

the newspaper is "the daily Telegraph"? Is it really possible to be that unobservant?

Well, yes, as a matter of fact. Not long ago, I received an e-mail from someone at the Department for Children, Schools and Families asking me to take part in a campaign to help raise appreciation for the quality of teaching in Great Britain. Here is the opening line of the message exactly as it was sent to me: "Hi Bill. Hope alls well. Here at the Department of Children Schools and Families . . ."

In the space of one line, fourteen words, the author has made three elemental punctuation errors (two missing commas, one missing apostrophe; I am not telling you more than that) and gotten the name of her own department wrong—this from a person whose job is to promote education. In a similar spirit, I received a letter not long ago from a pediatric surgeon inviting me to speak at a conference. The writer used the word "children's" twice in her invitation, spelling it two different ways and getting it wrong both times. This was a children's specialist working in a children's hospital. How long do you have to be exposed to a word, how central must it be to your working life, to notice how it is spelled?

People everywhere have abandoned whole elements of grammatical English, and I don't understand it. I was watching a Brian Cox television documentary in which he was standing in a field in Mexico talking about bombardier beetles when he said: "The bombardier beetle and me, and in fact every living thing you can see, are exposed to the same threat . . . Me and my friend the beetle have both reached the same solution." Now don't get me wrong. I have great respect for Brian Cox. He has a brain so big that it crosses whole time zones, and he is normally impeccable with the language, so why on earth would he say "the bombardier beetle and me" when it is surely more natural, and clearly more respectable, to say "the bombardier beetle and I"? Soon after this, I watched a documentary by another eminent young scientist, Adam Rutherford, and he said: "Now I've got just 33 vertebrae in my spinal column, but Belle here [a boa constrictor] has got 304, and the amazing thing is it's the same handful of genes that determine how many vertebrae both me and her have."

Then I heard Samantha Cameron, wife of the prime minister, say to a television interviewer, "Me and the kids help to keep him grounded."

So here is all I am saying about this. Stop it.

I thought it would be quiet in Cambridge on a Sunday, but it was the very opposite. The streets were teeming with tourists and shoppers, as if there were a festival on, but it was just the usual Sunday shuffle, people passing their day of rest by aimlessly wandering between shops, with lunch and an occasional hot beverage and day-old pastry thrown in. It used to be that on Sunday mornings the only people you would see in a commercial district were vagrants searching through litter bins. In those days the only shops open on Sundays were gas stations and newsagents, so all you could buy were cigarettes, sweets, and newspapers. If you had forgotten to shop for food on Saturday, you had a candy bar and a glass of water for dinner.

How the world has changed. Now there were more people on the streets of Cambridge than lived in Cambridge. Some streets were packed primarily with locals, some primarily with tourists. Every few steps some cheerful young person would thrust a leaflet at me for some kind of a tour—walking tour, ghost tour, hop on / hop off bus tour. Every shop doorway and postcard rack, indeed every available space within sight of a historic building, was crowded with gaggles of foreign youngsters, usually with matching backpacks. I wanted a coffee, but the cafés were filled to overflowing, so I went to a John Lewis department store on the presumption that I would find a quiet café there, up on the top floor, with views over rooftops. John Lewis stores always have a café with a view over rooftops, and it did here, too, but it was packed, with a queue stretching back to the Keep Calm and Carry On giftware section. At least two dozen people hadn't even reached the plastic trays yet. The idea of creeping along behind people who couldn't decide between a pain aux raisins and a fruit cup, or who wondered if they could just have a daub of Dijon on the side and were happy to stop the line while some hapless skivvy went down to the cellars to fetch a new jar, or who got to the cash register and didn't have the right money and had to send a search party to fetch Clive—well, I couldn't face that. So I gave up on coffee and went and looked at televisions because that's what men do in John Lewis stores. There were over three hundred of us, moving solemnly up and down the rows of televisions, considering each in turn, even though the televisions were all essentially identical and none of us needed a television anyway. Then I examined laptops—tapped the keys, opened and closed the lids, nodding ruminatively, like a judge at a vegetable-growing competition—and finally waited my turn to listen to the demonstrator Bose headphones. I dropped the headphones onto my ears and immediately I was in a tropical jungle— and I mean right in it, aurally immersed—listening to cawing birds and skitterings in the undergrowth. Then I was in Manhattan at rush hour with murmured voices and honking horns. Then in a cleansing spring shower with just an occasional crack of thunder. The fidelity was uncanny. Then I opened my eyes and I was back in John Lewis in Cambridge on a Sunday. It was perhaps little wonder that six men were waiting behind me for a turn on the headphones.

I strolled over to Trumpington Street and to the Fitzwilliam Museum, which to my mind is Cambridge's most luscious treasure. I only recently discovered the Fitzwilliam. I had always supposed it to be small and charmingly overstuffed with treasures, like Sir John Soane's Museum in London, but in fact it is vast and grand and airy, like the British Museum transported to a secondary street in Cambridge. Uniquely among Cambridge institutions, it was only moderately busy. Better still, the café had empty tables. Suppressing a whoop of joy, I ordered an Americano coffee and a piece of walnut cake, which was small, dry, and expensive, just the way the English seem to like it, and thus was able, twenty minutes later, to embark on an exploration of the Fitzwilliam's echoing galleries in a refreshed state.

It occurred to me that I had no idea who the Fitzwilliam behind the museum was, so afterward I looked it up. It was Richard Fitzwilliam, seventh Viscount Fitzwilliam, who in life never did much of anything other than spend a good deal of it in France, where he sired three children illegitimately by a ballet dancer. Beyond that his private life is "deeply obscure," according to the *Oxford Dictionary of National Biography,* which knows a thing or two about being deeply obscure. Fitzwilliam died in 1816, never having married, and left his art and a large sum of money to Cambridge University to build a museum in his name, which it faithfully did.

The Fitzwilliam Museum doesn't normally attract a great deal of attention, but in 2006 it leapt into the news when a visitor named Nick Flynn tripped on a loose shoelace and swept three precious Qing vases off a windowsill, smashing them to bits and causing damage of between £100,000 and £500,000, depending on which part of the Google universe you consult. Photographs of the aftermath of the occasion, available on the Internet, show that Flynn's trip was possibly the greatest shoelace fall in history, for he managed to sweep clear a windowsill that was perhaps fifteen feet long and leave the vases in thousands of small pieces on the floor. Police arrested Flynn on the suspicion that the damage was intentional, but the charges were subsequently dropped. "I actually think I did the museum a favor," Flynn told the *Guardian* sometime afterward. "So many people have gone there to see the windowsill where it all happened that I must have increased the visitor numbers. They should make me a trustee." Not surprisingly, the museum did not do that. Instead, it wrote to Flynn and politely asked him not to come back anytime soon. It was all it could do.

I had read that the vases had been repaired and were back on display, though now safely behind tempered glass. I asked an attendant where they were and she directed me to a glass case that I had in fact just been peering into. The repairs are so good as to be essentially invisible. I had to look hard a second time to see even the tiniest line of repair. Speaking as someone who has never glued anything without also at the same time unintentionally gluing at least three other things, I was impressed.

I spent an hour and a half in the Fitzwilliam, not counting snack time, and then strolled around the corner to the Scott Polar Research Institute Museum, which, let me say right now, is one of the best small museums in the country, but it was closed, alas. So I went to the Whipple Museum of the History of Science, but it was closed, and then to the Sedgwick Museum of Earth Sciences, and the Museum of Classical Archaeology, and they were closed, too. The Museum of Zoology was closed altogether for refurbishment. To my joy, I found that the Museum of Archaeology and Anthropology was open on Sunday, but it was closing for the day just as I arrived.

"Perhaps I'll come back tomorrow," I said.

"We're closed on Mondays," said the man.

So I just wandered around. By happy accident, I cut down a back street called Free School Lane and chanced upon the building that was home of the famous Cavendish Laboratory from 1874 to 1974. Somebody once observed to me that probably no small patch of earth has produced more revolutionary, earth-changing thinking than an area a few hundred yards across in the center of Cambridge. Here at various times you have had Isaac Newton, Charles

Darwin, William Harvey, Charles Babbage, Alan Turing, John Maynard Keynes, Louis Leakey, Bertrand Russell, and more other original thinkers than I could list here. Altogether, ninety people from Cambridge have won Nobel Prizes, more than any other institution in the world, and the greater portion of these—nearly a third—came out of this anonymous building on Free School Lane. A plaque on the wall noted that this was the building where J. J. Thomson discovered the electron in 1897, but there was nothing at all to indicate that this was also where the structure of DNA was revealed by Francis Crick and James Watson or where James Chadwick discovered the neutron or Max Perutz unraveled the mystery of proteins. Twenty-nine members of the Cavendish have won Nobel Prizes, which is more than most countries. Four members won in 1962 alone: James Watson and Francis Crick in Physiology or Medicine and Max Perutz and Sir John Kendrew in Chemistry.

It was in the Cavendish in 1953 that Crick and Watson were photographed together posed before a model of the DNA molecule that looked as if it had been built from parts taken from an Erector set. I once asked someone from the Cavendish lab why the model isn't on display anywhere. It is, after all, surely one of the most famous scientific models of the twentieth century. He told me that the model in the photographs wasn't the actual model they had used. That had been dismantled. Crick and Watson had to assemble a new one for the photographers. Meanwhile, people had begun taking pieces from the kit as keepsakes, many of which subsequently ended up being sold as collector's items. As a consequence, the model has essentially duplicated itself, just like real DNA, as there are more pieces floating about now than existed in 1953. That, I was told, is why it is not on display in a museum.

My favorite Cavendish person is possibly Max Perutz, who spent forty years of his life working out the structure of a single protein, hemoglobin. It was such a challenging proposition that it took him fifteen years just to figure out how to go about it.

Perutz was a spectacular hypochondriac. He carried a card with dietary instructions in five languages, which he sent to the kitchen wherever he dined. He refused to be in rooms where candles had recently been burned or that had been cleaned with any of several common cleaning solutions and disinfectants (even though he wanted everything around him disinfected). Because of chronic back pain, at symposia he would often introduce a speaker, then lie down in front of the lectern for the duration of the talk. Sometimes he delivered lectures himself while supine.

I am also an admirer of Sir Lawrence Bragg, who won the Nobel Prize for his work on X-ray crystallography in 1915. Bragg later became president of the Royal Institution in London. He loved the work, but missed gardening, so he took a job as a gardener one day a week at a house in South Kensington. The woman who engaged him had no idea that her gardener was one of the most distinguished scientists in Britain until a friend came for tea one day and, looking out the window, casually asked: "My dear, why is the Nobel laureate Sir Lawrence Bragg pruning your hedges?"

Late in the afternoon I walked back to the railway station. I'd wanted to take a train onward to Oxford, but it turned out I was nearly fifty years too late for that. The line from Cambridge to Oxford—known affectionately as the Varsity Line or sometimes the Brain Line—was closed in 1967. Today the fastest journey between the two cities (which are just eighty miles apart, you understand) takes more than two and a half hours and involves two changes of train.

I decided to break the journey in London and travel on to Oxford in the morning. At the station I bought a one-way ticket to London and proceeded to platform one, the London platform. When I lived in Norfolk and traveled regularly between there and London, I had to change trains at Cambridge each time. This usually meant getting off one train just in time to see the other departing. So I am well acquainted with Cambridge station and know from experience that the people who run it don't like to give away too much information. Every visit there is a little like being a guest on the game show *Would I Lie to You?* On this occasion, a train looking very like a London train pulled in at platform one and stopped there. But the TV screens said: "This Train Terminates Here" and clearly intimated that it would be foolhardy to board it because it might at any moment leave to go to a depot at Royston or someplace equally desperate and unwelcome.

So about five hundred of us stood around looking at the empty train for ten minutes or so. Eventually a few brave souls got on, and then there was a kind of rush, like when they opened up the Oklahoma Territory to settlers, as nearly everyone hurried to get a seat. But we all had to remain poised to leap off again if it turned out that this train really was headed for servicing (or, a better idea still, retirement) at Royston. In the event, it turned out we had all guessed correctly. This was and indeed always had been the London train. So we won the game. Our prize was that we got to ride to London seated. The thirty or forty people who had remained on the platform because they trusted the television screens got to play a new game called Standing in the Vestibule All the Way to London.

I noticed that I was seated at a window with a good view of the Jeremy Clarkson poster that I had noted earlier and this got me to thinking about ignorance again, in the universal sense. I had recently read about something called the Dunning-Kruger Effect, which is named after two academics at Cornell University in New York State, who first described it. The Dunning-Kruger Effect is essentially being too stupid to appreciate how stupid you are. That sounds like a pretty good description of the world to me. So what I began to wonder was this: What if we are all getting stupid at more or less the same rate and we don't realize it because we are all declining together? You might argue that we'd see a general fall in IQ scores, but what if it's not the kind of deterioration that shows up in IQ tests? What if it were reflected in just, say, poor judgment or diminished taste?

We all know that regular exposure to lead can seriously impair brain function, yet it took decades for scientists to figure that out. What if something even more insidious is poisoning our brains from some other part of our daily lives? The number of chemicals in use in the developed world was more than eighty-two thousand at the last count, and most of them—86 percent, according to one estimate—have never been tested for their effects on humans. Every day, to take just one example, we all consume or absorb substantial amounts of bisphenols and phthalates, which are found in food packaging. These may pass harmlessly through us or they may be doing to our brains what a microwave oven does to a tub of baked beans. We have no idea. But if you look at what's on TV on a typical weeknight, you have to wonder. That's all I'm saying.

Chapter 16

Oxford and About

I

I HAVE DECIDED AFTER considerable thought that the honors system in Britain—that is to say, the giving out of knighthoods, lordships, and the like—is not a good thing. I realize I can be accused of hypocrisy in this because I accepted a small honor myself a few years ago. But then I have always made it my practice to put vanity before principle.

My award was an honorary Order of the British Empire, or OBE, which, because it is honorary and not really real, is not presented by the Queen but by a minister of her government. Mine was given to me in a brief ceremony in her office by the Culture Secretary, Tessa Jowell, and jolly nice she was, too. According to the citation, the award was for services to literature, which is very kind and generous but what it really meant was that it was for services to myself, because I didn't do anything that I wasn't going to do anyway. That's the problem with honors, you see. On the whole, people are rewarded just for being themselves, which in a lot of cases frankly is quite enough already.

America has two principal ways to receive formal adulation. Either you single-handedly take out a German machine-gun nest while carrying a wounded buddy on your back at a place called

Porkchop Hill or Cemetery Ridge, in which case you get the Congressional Medal of Honor, or you buy society's admiration by paying for a hospital wing or a university library or something along those lines. You don't add something to your name, as in Britain, but rather add your name to something. The warm glow of unwarranted prestige is just the same in both cases. The difference is that in America the system produces a hospital wing; in Britain, you just get a knobhead in ermine.

I bring this up here because I was on my way to see one of the supreme seats of privilege, Blenheim Palace, home of the Dukes of Marlborough, whose achievements over the last eleven generations could be inscribed with a Sharpie on the side of a peanut. Blenheim was also, of course, the birthplace of Winston Churchill, so it must be said that occasionally aristocrats do produce something worthwhile. Anyway, someone had very kindly bought me, as a present, afternoon tea and a tour of the palace, and the voucher was about to expire, so I had hastily made a booking as I was going to be in the area.

Blenheim is a most remarkable house, no doubt about that, and I was looking forward to seeing it. I don't know what went wrong exactly—whether I entered through the wrong door, stood in the wrong queue, or whether my ticket was restricted, but I was placed in a group of fourteen other slightly bewildered people and herded into something called "Blenheim: The Untold Story." This turned out to be an audiovisual adventure that took us through seven upstairs rooms. A lady gave us a short introductory spiel and then we were left in a small room and watched in quiet horror as an automatic door closed behind us. Everything from this point on was automated. In each room there was a recorded commentary and an animatronic figure or two—a duke sitting at a desk writing jerkily with a quill pen that didn't quite touch the paper and that sort of thing. We were treated to about two minutes of diversion in each chamber and then a new door swung open and we were instructed to move on to the next space. We weren't visitors so much as prisoners.

The rooms each covered a different period in the palace's history, with the idea, I gathered, that collectively these were to provide us with a moving appreciation of Blenheim Palace's role in the history and heart of the nation. But in fact the presentation was mostly incoherent. In two of the rooms it was simply not possible to know what was going on. One was about a plan to put on a play in the palace in the nineteenth century—the relevance of this to anything was never clear—and the other, even more confusing, was a meeting in 1939 between an eighteenth-century time-traveling servant and Consuelo Vanderbilt, who was then mistress of Blenheim. No part of the experience conveyed meaningful information or provided real entertainment. The rooms were small, airless, and cramped. To make matters worse, somebody in our group was making the most dreadful silent farts. Fortunately, it was me, so I wasn't nearly as bothered as the others. After twenty minutes or so of this audiovisual extravaganza, we were decanted into a gift shop, where our attention was drawn to the many other places on the estate where we could spend our money—on tea and scones, on bedding plants and designer trowels from the garden center, on rides on a little train. It was shit.

I had a reservation for a champagne tea in something called the Indian Room. It was very nice, with a flute of champagne, a big pot of tea, and a selection of little cakes and delicate sandwiches, but what I mostly enjoyed about it was that I wasn't paying the £35 that it cost.

Afterward, I strolled around the grounds, which are splendid, and then into the stately village of Woodstock, just outside the palace gates. When I came to Woodstock for *Notes for a Small Island*, it had a full range of shops, including a glover's, a gentlemen's hair stylist, a family butcher's, a secondhand bookshop, and lots of antique shops. Many of those have now gone, alas, though there is still a good bookshop and a popular delicatessen that didn't use to be there. But the overwhelming theme to Woodstock now is cars. They were parked everywhere, jimmied into every possible cranny and so thick on the high street that it was hard to cross on foot. Many of the houses had signs in their windows expressing alarm at proposals to build fifteen hundred homes on the edge of the village. As Woodstock has only thirteen hundred homes now, that didn't seem to me an unreasonable objection, particularly as the designated land is part of Oxford's green belt. The land is owned by Blenheim Palace, which said it needed to sell it to fund £40 million of palace repairs.

The problem with building big housing estates in places like this isn't just the loss of land, but that the new places overwhelm what exists already. Woodstock won't continue to be Woodstock if you put a new town with a shiny new supermarket and business park on its outskirts. I've no doubt that there is a powerful case for more housing for Oxford, but surely there are more sensitive and intelligent solutions than just plonking down fifteen hundred new houses in one giant field and hoping that the roads and doctors' surgeries and middle schools and everything else can handle an instant doubling of local burdens. Perhaps it would be an idea to require developers to live on their own estates for five years, as a demonstration of their superb livability. Just a thought.

I spent the night in Woodstock and in the morning rode a smart and stylish double-decker bus to Oxford. The bus was very blue inside and out, and very clean, too. This was the bus I had expected on my journey from Bognor Regis to Hove. The seats were exceedingly comfy, in a deep blue leatherette finish. I sat upstairs and enjoyed the views. The bus was popular, though not nearly as popular as the private car. All roads into Oxford were choked with traffic— backed up at roundabouts, queuing at petrol stations, creeping into town in barely moving lines. I don't mean to bang on, but am I the only one to wonder if the best solution to Oxford's problems is to make it more suburban?

Oxford is a victim of its own attractiveness. More people want to live there than it can comfortably accommodate, and you can't blame them. Traffic aside, I am prepared to nominate Oxford as the most pleasant and improved city in Britain. In *Notes from a Small Island*, I was hard on the dear old place, not because it was so sensationally bad but because it wasn't good enough. My feeling is that certain cities that are beautiful and historic—Oxford, Cambridge, Bath, Edinburgh, to name four—have a particular duty to remain so, and Oxford for quite a long time didn't seem to understand that.

Throughout the sixties and seventies, it put up an extraordinary number of ugly buildings. The main offices of Oxford University, mercifully tucked away on a side street, could win almost any ugliness competition.

Well, how all that has changed. New buildings have been going up all over the place in recent years, and nearly all have been innovative, striking, and sympathetic to their surroundings. The high street has been closed to through traffic and so is much more agreeable to stroll along, and it has some smart shops and restaurants and a chic hotel in a converted bank building. Millions of pounds have been lavished on improving the university's excellent stock of museums, notably the great and stately Ashmolean. Just outside the train station, some grand new scheme was being developed. At the time I passed it seemed to be concentrating on taking down healthy-looking trees and disrupting traffic, but I trust those are both temporary shortcomings. The idea, I gather, is to provide Oxford with a grand new concourse to welcome people emerging from the giant bike rack that is its rail station, which can only be a good thing.

When I came to Oxford in 1995 for my book, I was particularly scathing about the Merton College Warden's Lodgings, which I believe I likened to an electrical substation. Well, a couple of years ago they rebuilt the lodgings in a more discreet and sensitive style. Now it is a thing of quiet beauty, modern but respectful, and in perfect harmony with the medieval street on which it stands. Sir Martin Taylor, the kindly warden (which is to say head of the college), invited me to cut the ribbon at a small ceremony. It may have been the proudest moment of my life. I walked up Merton Street now and looked at the lodgings with admiration and a kind of proprietorial affection, then went for a good walk around the city, through smart neighborhoods and shabby ones, occasionally looking in shopwindows, once plunging deep into Blackwell's, the beloved and enormous bookshop on Broad Street, but otherwise just wandering.

Late in the morning, I did a circuit of the University Parks, which is really just one park but so good that it has evidently awarded itself a plural, and emerged in the university's science district and found myself outside the Natural History and Pitt Rivers museums, which are two museums in one building.

Both were already great museums, but in recent years they have been elevated to a state that is very near perfection through generous and ingenious restorations. The building—a Victorian gothic hulk with a distinctly oppressive air—had just reopened after a fourteen-month overhaul, which included cleaning and resealing eighty-five hundred panes of glass in the roof, so that today light floats in from above, giving the interior a fresh, gleaming airiness that it hasn't had in any living human's lifetime. The museum is not just interesting and informative, but imaginative and good-natured and fun—all the things museums ought to be and so often aren't. And its collections are fabulous. Every glass case was a little island of wonder.

The museum—its formal name is the Oxford University Museum of Natural History—was built in 1860. Charles Dodgson was a frequent visitor and based a number of the characters in his Alice stories on its collections, not least a painting of a dodo by the Dutch artist Jan Savery. Dodgson is of course something of a dual figure. Today we remember him as Lewis Carroll, beloved creator of children's stories, but to his contemporaries at Oxford he was known only as a shy and stammering mathematician, author of *An Elementary Treatise on Determinants in the Formulae of Plane Trigonometry*, and for dating children. Few if any of his colleagues had any idea that in his spare time he was writing memorable lines like:

I dreamt I dwelt in marble halls
And each damp thing that creeps and crawls
Went wobble-wobble on the walls

The display case dealing with Dodgson and Alice Liddell (who was the daughter of the head of his college, Christ Church) contains a very striking, very lifelike dodo, but it is in fact just a model since there are no real dodos left in the world, not even stuffed ones. In 1755, the very last dodo on earth, stuffed or otherwise, was thrown on a bonfire by the director of the Ashmolean Museum because he thought it was getting musty, thus proving that idiots are not just an invention of our own era. Another museum employee tried to pull the bird from the bonfire, but only managed to save its scorched head and part of a foot. These are in the display case, too, and are all that remains of earth's last dodo.

The Natural History Museum leads to the Pitt Rivers Museum, which specializes in anthropology, and is packed beautifully, and practically to the rafters, with the most wonderful array of ethnographic objects, all soothingly lit and artistically arrayed. It was built later, in 1884, and also has undergone a recent restoration.

The museum is named for Augustus Henry Lane Fox Pitt Rivers, a wealthy landowner who was also one of the nastiest, most mean-spirited men in history. He beat his children, including his grown daughters, and mistreated his estate workers. Once, he evicted a couple in their eighties from an estate cottage even though he knew they had nowhere to go, then left the cottage permanently empty. Once his wife arranged a Christmas party for all the local villagers and was devastated when no one turned up. What she didn't realize was that Augustus, learning of the party, had gone out and padlocked all the estate gates. But when he wasn't being a giant prick, Pitt Rivers was a considerable scholar, and amassed a notable collection of treasures, which he passed on to Oxford University. The result today is one of the great anthropological museums in the world.

I intended to have only a quick look around both museums, but stayed for nearly three hours and still hadn't seen half of what I wanted to see. It wasn't just that both are endlessly interesting, but that they are also actually useful. On a mezzanine upstairs in the Natural History Museum, a series of glass cases along one wall contain a more or less complete set of stuffed British birds, but with each case devoted to a specific habitat—meadow, woodland, coastal strand, farmland—so you can look at each bird closely and in the environment in which you are most likely to encounter it. Beside each bird was a little symbol indicating whether that bird's species population in Britain was rising, falling, or holding steady. (An alarming number were falling.) I have never learned so much so quickly and so painlessly. I have always wondered what exactly are the differences between all the various kinds of British black birds—rooks, crows, ravens, and so on—and here it was all set out for me. I don't remember any of that now, of course (I'm sixty-three years old), but for a minute I knew and was enchanted. And the new little café was excellent, too.

—

Emerging from the museum, I decided to round off this splendid day with a walk out to Iffley. I had just read *Unwrecked Britain* by the late architectural historian and writer Candida Lycett Green in which she declared Iffley one of her favorite of all places in Britain, so I thought it must be worth checking out. A walk to Iffley had the additional advantage of taking me down the Iffley Road and past something I have been mildly curious to see for some years: the track where Roger Bannister ran the first sub-four-minute mile in the spring of 1954.

It's a terrific story. Bannister was a young doctor in London. He had no coach or manager. He trained for just half an hour a day. On the day of the race, he went to work in the morning, then traveled up from London by train. He walked to a friend's house in north Oxford—that's at least two miles from the station—for a lunch of a ham salad, before accepting a lift to the track in the late afternoon. It would be hard to imagine circumstances less likely to produce a world-class result. The track was made of cinders, an impossibly awkward surface for running. It was Bannister's first race in eight months. Until fairly recently, runners trying for world records had been permitted a large measure of latitude to help them get the best possible outcome. When the British runner Sydney Wooderson had set the world mile record of 4 minutes 6 seconds sixteen years earlier, one of the other runners was given a 250-yard head start so that he could serve as a pacemaker. But such help was no longer countenanced. Bannister would enjoy no special assistance.

Bannister achieved his record time by pushing himself to the very limit of human capability. The photograph of him collapsing into the tape at the finish line was one of the iconic images of my childhood. Apart from the photographer and a few officials, hardly anyone saw the race. His winning time was 3 minutes 59.4 seconds.

He was so spent at the finish that he was "almost unconscious," as he notes in his autobiography.

The track, renamed the Sir Roger Bannister Track, is still there, though much modernized and surrounded by fencing that keeps you from seeing anything much. It occurred to me as I stood there that it was almost exactly sixty years—to the season, if not the day—since Bannister had run his great race. Something that almost no one remembers now is that his record only lasted a few weeks. An Australian named John Landy broke it in Finland the following month.

Iffley Road is a busy thoroughfare and not particularly delightful, and it seemed to grow progressively worse as I walked along it, to the extent that I wondered if this whole little adventure was a mistake. But then, taking a fork at a spot called Iffley Turn, I found myself magically transported to a Cotswold village, or something awfully like it, in the very midst of Oxford. A village within the city, Iffley was stood mostly along a single road, lined with cottages and a pub or two, leading to an old stone church with a square tower. The church, called St. Mary's, was built in the late twelfth century and from 1232 to 1241 was the home of a famous anchoress—a kind of pious female hermit—named Annora, who lived in a cell attached to the side of the church, with a window cut in the church wall so that she could watch services. An anchoress was in effect a voluntary prisoner. She could not leave her cell, but she could converse with visitors through a window and she had a servant to look after her, so in terms of hardship it was on the mild side. The cell itself is long gone.

I am grateful also to Candida Lycett Green for introducing me to the poet Keith Douglas, who knew Iffley well because the young woman he loved lived there. During the Second World War, while serving in the army, Douglas wrote these haunting lines to his beloved:

Whistle and I will hear
and come another evening, when this boat
travels with you alone towards Iffley;
as you lie looking up for thunder again,
this cool touch does not betoken rain;
it is my spirit that kisses your mouth lightly.

Douglas was killed at Saint-Pierre, near Bayeux, a few days after the Normandy landings in 1944, and is one of those crosses you see in straight rows in military cemeteries. He was twenty-four.

I walked back to Oxford on a footpath along the river and didn't see a soul.

II

The next morning I was at the Ashmolean when it opened. It, too, is a superlative museum that has recently been given a splashy overhaul—£61 million worth in this case. Outside, it looks as it always has—regal and severe, like the British Museum—but into this forbidding edifice they have ingeniously inserted a clean and friendly new building with double the previous exhibition space. Every room is now a zone of softly lit enchantment, of wonderful things exquisitely displayed.

The Ashmolean dates from 1683 and is the oldest public museum in Europe. It is named for Elias Ashmole even though most of the original collection was assembled by the Tradescant family. Ashmole merely inherited it, but he had the good sense to pass it on to Oxford with some stipulations about its upkeep and so it is his name on the building. The natural history collections were hived off in the nineteenth century—that's the stuff I was looking at across town the day before—and the Ashmolean focused thereafter on art and archaeology. It is just about the most beguiling museum there is. I spent almost an hour in a gallery of classical statuary comprising the Arundel collection. I have no special interest in statues, but the story of the assembling and near loss of the collection, told in a series of panels, is so absorbing that I found myself reading each and then studying the statues in between. And the next thing I knew an hour had gone.

The person most closely associated with the Ashmolean in modern times is Sir Arthur Evans, who was appointed keeper in 1884 and rejuvenated the place after years of neglect. Evans ran the museum for twenty-four years, though sometimes from afar. In 1900, he made a prolonged trip to Crete, where he discovered the Palace of Knossos and the ancient Minoan civilization that went with it. At Knossos, Evans found hundreds of clay tablets that bore two different types of mysterious inscription which he dubbed Linear A and Linear B. No one anywhere could decipher either script, and many tried. In 1932, Evans met a fourteen-year-old schoolboy named Michael Ventris and showed him some of the tablets. Ventris became fixated with this undeciphered script, and spent all his spare time, first as a student and then as a young architect, trying to crack the texts. In 1952, twenty years after he first saw the texts, he announced that he had deciphered Linear B. It was an astonishing achievement, particularly bearing in mind that he had no training in cryptology or ancient languages and had a full-time job elsewhere. Very shortly afterward he got into his car late one night in London and drove at high speed into the back of a parked lorry on the Barnet bypass. He was thirty-four years old and had no known reason to kill himself. Linear A has still never been deciphered.

A selection of tablets with Linear B script are displayed at the Ashmolean, along with an excellent account of how they were deciphered, plus a great deal more from Knossos. I lost nearly another hour at a single display case in the Minoan section, and realized I was not going to live long enough at this rate to reach the top floor, so I picked up my pace. But it still took another three hours to see the museum even briskly. It is just the most wonderful place.

Afterward, I had an urge for fresh air and decided to stroll out to a place called Wytham Woods, on a hilly site a little beyond the western edges of the city. Wytham Woods is almost certainly now the most studied woodland in the world. It was donated to the university in 1942 and has been used ever since for botanical, environmental, and zoological studies of every possible type. Its study of bird populations, begun in 1947, is the longest-running biological survey anywhere on Earth, and other parts of the woods have been used for the study of bats, deer, insects, trees, mosses, rodents, and almost everything else that lives and breeds in a temperate climate.

Wytham Woods (it's pronounced *wite-hum*, by the way) is just three or four miles from central Oxford, but it takes a little getting to on foot because you have to cross the Thames and get past the very busy A34 western bypass, neither of which is exactly replete with crossing places. The most congenial walk appeared to be across Port Meadow, a vast open flood plain beside the river, but I had a strangely difficult time finding it. I walked some of the time on residential streets near Port Meadow, some of the time on residential streets not near Port Meadow, some of the time in what seemed to be a nature reserve not too far but definitely separate from Port Meadow, and some of the time through a kind of swamp that could have been anywhere, before I could confidently pronounce myself actually on Port Meadow, and even here I seemed to be in its most remote and least visited corner. The route took me across a large stretch of open ground generously strewn with horses, some of them frisky in a way that wasn't necessarily friendly. Thoughts of animal tramplings running through my head, I walked briskly, but happily they paid me no heed.

I emerged to find myself in Wolvercote, considerably adrift of where I hoped to be by now, and followed the road toward the village of Wytham, at the base of Wytham Woods. It was an agreeable walk that took me past the Trout Inn, a famous riverside pub which appeared in about a thousand *Inspector Morse* episodes on television, and the remains of Godstow Abbey. Consulting my map, I found I was still quite a distance short of Wytham village. This was turning out to be much more of an undertaking than I had expected.

Wytham is a sweet little village, with a pub, a village shop, and a church, and not much else. The one thing it didn't have was any indication of how to get to Wytham Woods. Down whichever lane I ventured, I came across stern signs telling me to go away: "Private Residence. No Trespassing," "Private Road. No Thoroughfare," "Private—Authorized Vehicles Only." My Ordnance Survey map showed the woods as being laced with tracks, but there was no indication of how to get up to them. I couldn't find a single footpath sign anywhere, nor anyone to ask.

A sign on a side lane pointed to a field station, which sounded promising, and I walked a half mile down the lane but found neither station nor footpaths, and the woods, visible on the neighboring hillside, were growing more distant rather than less. I had already walked quite a distance and still had to get back to Oxford, so the idea of walking another mile or two up a big hill into woods was less enthralling than it had been two or three hours before. This is the problem with walking—that you can consume so much time and energy getting to your destination that you don't always have a great deal in reserve when you reach it.

I found my way back to the village. The shop was closed for the afternoon and there was no one around to ask for guidance. According to an information board nearby, the village was mostly owned by Oxford University and the villagers were mostly tenants, so all this seemed a little unnecessarily unfriendly, I have to say. Later I learned from an acquaintance who lives in Oxford that Wytham Woods isn't really open to the public. They might not Taser you, as they might in California, but they don't exactly welcome you with open arms onto the land. Then it occurred to me that if they are doing careful studies in the woods, if they have nesting boxes and traps and the like scattered about, they can't really have people up there with their dogs and mountain bikes disturbing things, so I forgave them in the name of science.

Besides, it was half-past five, nearly cocktail hour, so I strolled back to Wolvercote, and had a drink at the Trout Inn, the pub where the fictional Inspector Morse and his trusty sidekick Lewis often went for alcoholic refreshment and inspiration while solving one of Oxford's many murders. I once met Colin Dexter, the donnish creator of the *Morse* series, and asked him how many murders he was personally responsible for.

"Sixty-eight!" he answered proudly. He also told me that the number of murders that he had contrived for a dozen mystery novels was several times greater than the number of actual murders in Oxford in the same period. The pleasant fact is that the British are not much good at violent crime except in fiction, which is of course as it should be. I looked into this once and found that statistically a Briton is more likely to die by almost any other means—including accidentally walking into a wall—than to be murdered.

And if that's not a happy thought, I don't know what is.

Chapter 17

The Midlands

I

I RECENTLY BOUGHT A new laptop. It came loaded with some
software—I think it is called Microsoft Gestapo—that lets them
enter the computer at any time of the day or night, line everyone
up against the wall, and install some new software. I don't know
what this new software does or why they didn't think to put it in
in the factory, but it sure is important to them to get it in there now.
About every second time I fire up the computer, I get a message
that says: "Updates are ready for your computer. Would you like
to install now (now is recommended) or be reminded every fifteen
seconds for the rest of eternity?"

At first I submitted, but the updates took forever to load and
they didn't make any detectable difference to the quality of my life,
so eventually I tried to subvert the process by switching my computer off and then on again. Take it from me right now, you should
never do that. The next message I got said:

"Resuming installation process. Do not ever try anything like
that again. Remember: we know that you spent a whole afternoon
on March 10 watching Paris Hilton home videos. We'll tell your
wife. We're Microsoft. Don't fuck with us. Download will be complete in 14 hours."

So when I got an update notification now, as I sat on a train from London to Birmingham, I just stoically accepted and gave up the hope of doing any work for a while. Instead I had a look at the three strangers sitting with me at a snug little table. They were all dressed for work, but none of them were working either, as far as I could tell. The man beside me was watching a movie, and it wasn't even a good movie. I could tell because it had lots of explosions and starred Liam Neeson. The two people opposite held smartphones like little prayer books, transfixed by what they found on their screens. Nearly everyone else within sight was holding a phone and doing rapid things with their thumbs. Two young men who had not evidently mastered the use of their thumbs were asleep with earphones in. Only one man with a laptop and a document seemed to be engaged in paid labor.

All this was of interest to me because this was the very train line that the government wanted to replace with a new high-speed operation known as HS2, in an effort to make the nation more economically vibrant. (HS stands for "high speed"; there's already an HS1, for trains to the Channel Tunnel from London.) The idea was that by getting people to Birmingham twenty minutes quicker, they could get more work done and all those extra twenty minutes would collectively translate into gazillions of extra pounds for the economy. I am a little dubious about this myself because I think that if you give anyone anywhere an extra twenty minutes, they will just have a cup of coffee. It's what you and I would do. It's what anyone does with twenty minutes.

The people who are opposed to HS2 argue that there is no need to get people to Birmingham quicker anyway because they can work on the train—that thanks to laptops and tablets and cell phones people can be as productive now while traveling as in the office. In principle perhaps, but as my carriage mates were demonstrating, people don't actually work on trains. In fact, I am not sure they work at all anymore.

Not long before this, my wife and I ordered a sofa from a shop on the Fulham Road in London, and on a Saturday in May, just before the May Day bank holiday, we traveled all the way into London from Hampshire to complete the paperwork. When we got to the shop, we found three other couples standing outside. The door was locked and the interior in darkness. This was at 10 a.m. on a Saturday morning, thirty minutes after the posted opening time. We all took turns peering through the glass door, as if one of us might spot something that the others had missed. There was no sign in the window to indicate why the shop was shut. People with smartphones activated their thumbs and reported that the shop's website gave no clues. One man dialed the shop number, and we could hear the ringing inside, but obviously there was no one there to answer it. After about twenty minutes, we all gave up and wandered off. Three days later, curious as to what had happened, I called the shop for an explanation.

"Oh, yah," said a young woman with a posh voice, "we shut for the bank holiday."

"But Saturday wasn't a bank holiday. The bank holiday was Monday."

"Yah, we shut for the weekend."

"But you didn't put a sign in the window or a notice on your website. You just left a bunch of people standing there like idiots."

"Oom, yah," she said as if that were an interesting but pointless observation, and I realized that she was almost certainly doing her nails or reading e-mails.

"Well, you know what, you are a spoiled, brainless fuckhead," I said. Actually I didn't say that at all. I just thought it. Instead I muttered some pathetic lamentation, in the British style, and hung up. In the end, you just give up or move to another country.

I truly don't understand how Britain does it. Great Britain has the world's sixth largest economy, but as far as I can see it doesn't make much of anything anymore. So few industrial companies are left that the *Financial Times,* the British equivalent of *The Wall Street Journal,* had to take the word "industrial" out of the Financial Times Industrial Average, its principal measure of corporate well-being. Only five of Britain's largest companies manufacture any products at all in the UK now. When I was a child, Britain made a quarter of all that was produced in the world (though, to be fair, my being a child had very little to do with it); now the figure is 2.9 percent and falling. These days, Britain makes Rolls-Royce jet engines and all the little pots of marmalade in the world, but that's about it, as far as I can tell.

Nearly everything that's left seems to be owned by foreigners. French companies own Hamley's toy store, Glenmorangie whisky, Orange mobile phones, Fisons pharmaceuticals, and EDF, one of the country's main utilities. Two other leading utilities are German-owned; another is owned by a Spanish company. Jaguar, Blue Circle Cement, British Steel, Harrods, Bass breweries, most of the main airports, a number of the top soccer teams, and much else besides are all foreign-owned. Fewer than half of Britain's largest companies even have a British-born chairman.

HP and Daddies sauces are made in Holland. Smarties are made in Germany. Raleigh bicycles are made in Denmark. In 2010, RBS, a failed Scottish bank owned by the British government, lent the money to the American food conglomerate Kraft to buy Cadbury's, Britain's most venerable chocolate maker. As part of the deal Kraft promised to keep open a Cadbury factory near Bristol, but it was just fooling. As soon as the deal was complete, Kraft closed the factory and shipped its machinery to Poland.

I think these things matter. People used to be proud of what Britain gave the world, but now they can't even be sure of what it gives itself. If you sell out to outsiders, you must accept that it will be people from other lands who decide what snacks you eat and where your sauces are concocted.

And yet the country thrives. It's a miracle. How does it do it?

I have no idea. All I can say is that it isn't by working hard on trains.

I am fascinated by HS2. The whole idea is so mad that you have to, as it were, step back and walk all the way around it to take it in. To begin with, there is the projected cost. It began at about £17 billion, I believe, and the last I saw was up to £42 billion, but I am sure it is much higher now, because the costs of these big projects always inflate faster than anyone can type the numbers. The only certainty with large infrastructure projects is that no one can ever predict anything about them with certainty. The Channel Tunnel cost twice as much to build as expected and attracted half as many people as predicted. HS1, older sibling to HS2, was confidently forecast to carry 25 million passengers by 2006. In fact, it has never reached half that number.

Whatever the final cost of HS2, all those tens of billions could clearly buy lots of things more generally useful to society than a quicker ride to Birmingham. Then there is all the destruction to the countryside. There is nothing charming about a high-speed rail line. It would create a permanent very noisy, hyper-visible scar across a great deal of classic British countryside, and disrupt and make miserable the lives of hundreds of thousands of people throughout its years of construction. If the outcome were something truly marvelous, then perhaps that would be a justifiable price to pay, but a fast train to Birmingham is never going to be marvelous. The best it can ever be is a fast train to Birmingham.

Remarkably, the new line doesn't hook up to most of the places people might reasonably want to go. Passengers from the north of England who need to get to Heathrow Airport will have to change trains at a place called Old Oak Common, with all their luggage, and travel the last twelve miles on another service. Getting to Gatwick will be even harder. If they want to catch a train to continental

Europe, they will have to get off at Euston station in London and make their way half a mile along the Euston Road to St. Pancras station. It has actually been suggested that travelators could be installed for that journey. Can you imagine traveling half a mile on travelators? Somebody find me the person who came up with that idea. I'll get the horsewhip.

Now here's my thought. Why not keep the journey times the same but make the trains so comfortable and relaxing that people won't want the trip to end? Instead, they could pass the time staring out the window at all the gleaming hospitals, schools, playing fields, and gorgeously maintained countryside that the billions of saved pounds had paid for. Alternatively, you could just put a steam locomotive on front of the train, make all the seats inside wooden, and have it run entirely by volunteers. People would come from all over the country to ride on it.

In either case, if any money was left over, perhaps a little of it could be used to fit trains with toilets that don't flush directly onto the tracks, so that when I sit on a platform at a place like Cambridge or Oxford glumly eating a WHSmith sandwich I don't have to watch blackbirds fighting over tattered fragments of human waste and toilet paper. It is, let's face it, hard enough to eat a WHSmith sandwich as it is.

The last time I was in Birmingham was in 2008 when CPRE launched an anti-litter campaign called Stop the Drop and sent me to all three main political parties' annual conferences to try to drum up support. It was a strange experience. I went first to Bournemouth and talked to a small group of delegates from the Liberal Democrats Party. It was so small a group, in fact, that we could have held the meeting in the hotel elevator and still had room for the sandwich cart.

Then I went to Manchester for a breakfast with Labour Party

members, but nobody turned up—honestly, not one person—so that was a magnificent failure, although we did get to take a lot of doughnuts home.

That left just the Conservatives in Birmingham. They gave us a slot in the conference hall itself, which seemed much more encouraging. This was my chance not only to address the Tory faithful, but the whole nation on television, so I worked really hard on my speech. On the day itself, I went to the conference center in Birmingham, was dusted lavishly with makeup, and positioned in the wings. When I was introduced, I strode onto the stage to the lightest applause ever heard in a public place. There were only about thirty people in the auditorium. Six were conspicuously asleep and the rest, I think, were dead. I was sorely tempted to say: "Shall I start now or shall we wait for the body bags to get here?" I gave my speech and departed without disturbing any of those who were still breathing. I learned later that that's the way party conferences always are. The only time the seats fill is when the leader speaks.

Afterward I walked back to the station through Victoria Square and up New Street, all now cozily pedestrianized. I couldn't believe how improved the city was. It occurred to me then that I should come back one day and have a better look. Now was that day.

The first time I came to Birmingham, I had never seen a city that was this ugly on purpose. Where I came from there was plenty of ugliness, but it was mostly accidental. Birmingham seemed designed to be ugly. The chief culprit was a man named Sir Herbert Manzoni, city engineer from 1935 to 1963, who thought old buildings "more sentimental than valuable," and wanted to build an entirely new Birmingham. He is the man who filled the city with inner-ring roads, dank pedestrian tunnels, massive transportation interchanges, and brutalist tower blocks—in short, made Birmingham as soulless and dispiriting a place as you could find.

The Birmingham Museum and Art Gallery has a fascinating room devoted to Manzoni's vision. It contains a giant scale model of a proposed civic quarter in a style that might be called Canberra Meets Nazi Nuremberg. On the walls overlooking the model are visionary drawings, beautifully drafted, showing parklike expressways cutting through the city, lined on both sides with avenues of high-rise public housing, all surrounded by lots of greenery. A good deal of it actually looks quite exciting. The problem is that most of it was never built and the parts that were built didn't gleam for long. Within twenty-five years more than two hundred council-owned tower blocks had serious structural problems, and most have since been torn down.

In the process of making a new Birmingham, Manzoni demolished many of the city's best buildings, but mercifully he spared the Museum and Art Gallery. Built in 1885, it remains a magnificent institution, with room after room of treasures, including the largest collection of pre-Raphaelite paintings of any museum in the world. It also now includes the recently discovered Staffordshire Hoard, an Anglo-Saxon haul found buried just inches beneath the surface on a farm near Lichfield in 2009. And it has the best and most stylish museum café in the universe. I spent a happy couple of hours prowling through its many galleries, then went out and had a good tramp through the city, impressed by its improvements.

Birmingham really has made great strides in restoring itself to agreeableness, but I am afraid those days are coming to an end. Just after my visit, the Age of Austerity caught up with the city in a big way as the council announced massive spending cuts. Under the new plans, two-thirds of city employees will be made redundant. The new £189 million central library, opened in 2013, will have its staffing levels halved and its opening hours reduced from seventy-three a week to forty. Across the city, football fields and play areas will be closed. CCTV cameras will no longer be monitored continuously. Birmingham, instead of becoming a greener, cleaner, more congenial place, will be dowdier, dirtier, and more unsafe. I love a city with vision.

All of this is being done to save £338 million over four years. That sounds like an enormous and urgent sum, but in fact it is a saving of about £1.40 per week per citizen. I wonder what all those lucky people of Birmingham will do with that extra £1.40 flowing into their pockets every week. Perhaps they can use it to enjoy those extra twenty minutes their faster train journeys will bring them.

Oh, thank you, Government of Britain, thank you for enriching us all.

II

I went to Ironbridge, a village in Shropshire so proud of its most prominent structure that it named itself after it. And it is a very fine structure, it must be said. It was the first iron bridge in the world—the first substantial iron anything.

The bridge and the iron industry that made it possible were the work of three generations of men all named Abraham Darby. The first Abraham Darby was a Quaker businessman who came to Coalbrookdale, as Ironbridge was then known, in about 1706 with a plan to make better cooking pots. He had devised a way to smelt iron with coke instead of charcoal, which gave a hotter flame and produced a better product. His son and grandson, Abrahams II and III, extended the business, built several powerful blast furnaces, made enormous volumes of cast iron, and were generally the fathers of England's industrial revolution. It was Abraham III who built the iron bridge as a way of demonstrating the firm's ingenuity and promise. So the Darbys not only gave the world the age of iron and steel, but also modern marketing.

For the design of the bridge, Abraham Darby III turned to a local man named Thomas Pritchard, who was a decidedly curious choice. Pritchard had no training in engineering or architecture. He was a joiner by trade, though in recent years he had started to do a little conceptual work as well. He had designed and built a couple of churches and even one bridge, albeit comparatively small and made of wood. He had never done anything monumental with cast iron, but then of course no one had. Pritchard proved an inspired choice—in fact, much more than that, for his bridge is one of the great structures of the age. It is at once elegant and decorous, yet wholly utilitarian. Every bit of it has a purpose and yet it is endlessly agreeable to look at, too. Indeed, as I learned now, you simply can't take your eyes off it. It is nearly impossible, I think, to resist the urge to walk over it and around it and to view it from as many angles as you can contrive. It is, in short, gloriously, uniquely arresting. Poor Pritchard never got to see it at all. He died of some sudden but unrecorded misfortune two days before Christmas 1777, only a month after work started and nearly four years before the bridge was finished. He was fifty-four years old.

Ironbridge is an unexpectedly serene and pretty village on the side of a steep, wooded ravine above the River Severn. Though it clearly exists these days to serve tourists, it does so rather more stylishly than it has any need to. The shops are interesting and attractive, and the cafés and guesthouses looked pretty good, too. I had an excellent cup of coffee (with a free small biscuit—always much appreciated), then strode around the shops and looked in a few windows. I might well have bought a sofa cushion or lap rug were it not that Mrs. Bryson already has very substantial collections of each. I have on occasion been astonished to discover in our house that if you dig through piles of cushions and blankets you sometimes find a sofa or bed underneath. At the bottom of the village was a pub called the White Hart Inn, which had a signboard out front stating that you could come in and use the toilets without buying anything—a statement so kind and agreeable and unique that I instantly made it my favorite pub in Shropshire, and Ironbridge my favorite community.

A mile or so along the valley from the bridge is the spot where the Darby furnaces formerly blazed—where the industrial revolution began really. This district, once a permanently glowing hellhole, is now a picturesque cluster of preserved buildings, dominated by a large brick factory that is now a museum. Entrance was £9.25, but I got a pound off, to my quiet satisfaction, for being a qualified elderly person. I was further gratified to discover that the ticket also included admission to the "Darby homes," whatever exactly they were. The ticket man suggested that I should start there because the museum had just admitted three busloads of schoolchildren who would spend the next twenty or thirty minutes racing everywhere before being rounded up by harried teachers, and guided into a special area where they would eat their packed lunches.

I thanked the man for this consideration and strolled across the grounds to the Darby homes a couple of hundred yards away. These proved to be a pair of eighteenth-century houses built by the Darby family so that they could keep an eye on the factories outside the windows. The houses were pleasantly furnished and gave a reasonable idea of what life must have been like for the original inhabitants, minus the smoke and soot and earth-shaking vibrations that they must have lived with when this was a factory site. On a table in a parlor, left for the casual perusal of visitors, was a book by Arthur Raistrick called *Quakers in Science and Industry* and I glanced through it for a few minutes, then carried it to a nearby chair and sat reading for about half an hour, so unexpectedly absorbed did I become. I hadn't realized it, but Quakers in the Darbys' day were a bullied and downtrodden minority in Britain. Excluded from conventional pursuits like politics and academia, they became big in industry and commerce, particularly, for some reason, in banking and the manufacture of chocolate. The Barclays and Lloyds banking families and the Cadburys, Frys, and Rown-trees of chocolate renown were all Quakers. They and many others made Britain a more dynamic and wealthy place entirely as a consequence of being treated shabbily by it. It had never occurred to me to be unkind to a Quaker, but if that's what it takes to get the country back on its feet again, I am prepared to consider it.

Between the Darby houses and the museum stands the Old Furnace, as it is known—the spot where the very first spark of the industrial revolution was struck. As recently as the 1950s, the importance of the Darby works was almost forgotten. The Old Furnace lay hidden under decades of accumulated soil and rubble, and had to be excavated, with brush and trowel, like a Roman villa. Today things couldn't be more different. The furnace is sheltered from the elements inside a stylish glass-fronted structure. Inside, a guide was conducting a party of a dozen or so people around. It has become a treasured shrine, though I have to say to me it just looked like any old furnace. I eavesdropped on the guide's lecture as closely as I could while of course pretending not to—I affected a close interest in some loose pointing just beside him—but the talk was way too technical for me.

Realizing I required more knowledge if I was ever going to appreciate the steel industry, I went across to the museum proper, and there I learned a great deal about wet puddling, dry puddling, smelting, and Bessemer processes, all of which went into my head and straight out again, like water through a pipe, so that although I learned nothing at all from the experience I felt strangely cleansed by it. The museum also contained a large collection of cast-iron objects—dining chairs, garden furniture, decorative tables, stoves, kitchen equipment, even serving bowls. Much of it was really quite splendid.

Content with what I had seen, I went off to the men's room to do a little puddling of my own. Then I walked to the bus stop and waited for a bus to take me back to the twenty-first century.

Chapter 18

It's So Bracing!

I

EVERYONE IN BRITAIN KNOWS one thing about Skegness, a coastal resort in Lincolnshire, and that is that it is bracing. That understanding dates back to a 1908 poster by the illustrator John Hassall, which shows a cheerful and portly fisherman skipping along a beach above the caption "Skegness is SO bracing." Called the Jolly Fisherman, it is a splendid illustration, but what is especially interesting, I think, is that it gives no hint of sunshine, frolicking swimmers, donkey rides, deck chairs, or any other traditional seaside divertissements. The man is dressed for foul weather and is quite alone, yet that one image and four simple words have made Skegness famous in England—indeed, have persuaded hundreds of thousands of people to go there. Hassall was paid twelve guineas for the work. (A guinea was one pound and a shilling.) The original hangs in Skegness Town Hall. I would love to have seen it, but the building was closed as it was the weekend.

It was the most miserably rainy weekend of the summer. I drove the two-hundred-odd miles to Skegness from Hampshire on lightly puddled roads, tires swishing, to the steady metronome of the windscreen wipers flapping until I was so half-mad with boredom that I began to fantasize about trying to jump the car over the roadside ditch and see if I could land upright in a potato field. I figured the worst possible outcome was death, which didn't seem so bad compared with continuing on to Skegness. Lincolnshire is a big, flat, boring, empty country a long way from anywhere, and Skegness is about as far into Lincolnshire as you can get.

When at last I got there, I checked into a B&B, dropped my bags, and went out. Hunched beneath the drumming rain, I had a look around. Skegness was the most traditional of any English seaside resort I had seen so far. It offered lots of bright neon and noisily chiming arcades and a sickly smell of spun sugar which even the rain could not suppress. The seafront was dominated by a handsome clock tower, with a good-looking park called the Tower Gardens standing nearby. People everywhere were sheltering in doorways or under awnings. A few were eating fish and chips, but most just stood staring at the bleak, wet world. It wasn't in the least bit bracing.

I walked up and down the high street, Lumley Road. At one end was an old-fashioned store called Allison's, where you could buy the kinds of clothes your grandparents used to wear, and beyond it was a selection of charity shops selling the actual clothes your grandparents used to wear. Farther along was a pub called the Stumble Inn. Outside it was a man who looked as if he had spent the last twenty-five years doing little else. Beyond this, downtown Skegness was just a couple of streets bearing the usual mix of cut-price shops, mobile phone dispensaries, betting parlors, and cafés. On a side street an establishment called Hydro Health and Beauty advertised an impressive array of treatments, most of which I didn't know were desirable or even necessarily legal: glycolic peels, thread vein removal, Botox injections, dermal fillers, colonic hydrotherapy, and more. Skegness was clearly a full-service community. Call me fussy, but if I ever decide to turn my colon over to someone for sluicing, it won't be at a beautician's in Skegness, but in this, as in so much in life, I seemed to be in the minority because the shop was clearly prospering, unlike many of its neighbors.

And that pretty largely exhausted central Skegness. My initial reconnoiter completed, I turned north along the seafront and followed a sign pointing to Butlin's holiday camp—a place I had been quietly longing to see since my first summer in England a million years ago. It was all to do with several large boxes of a magazine called *Woman's Own*.

When I started work at Holloway Sanatorium, you see, I was assigned to a place called Tuke Ward, high up in the garret level of the main building. It was there that I enjoyed the view across the cricket pitch that I mentioned earlier. The patients on Tuke Ward were a pleasant and tractable bunch and practiced insanity with a certain élan. They existed in a permanent medicated serenity, requiring only the lightest supervision. They dressed themselves (by and large in the right clothes), were well mannered and obedient, and never late for a meal. They even made their own beds after a fashion.

Every morning after breakfast a head nurse named Mr. Jolly would blow through the ward like a north wind, rousing the inmates from chairs and toilet stalls, and dispatch them to their duties on gardening detail or to pass a few hours in light occupational therapy. Then he would clear off himself, to points unknown, not to return until teatime. "Don't let anyone back on anything less than a stretcher," he would call to me upon departing, leaving me in sole charge for the next six or seven hours.

I had never been put in charge of anything in the adult world before, and I took the responsibility seriously, and spent the first morning marching around the ward like Captain Bligh patrolling the deck of the *Bounty*. But gradually it dawned on me that there wasn't a great deal of prestige or reward in being in charge of forty empty beds and a communal bathroom, so I began to look for diversions. Tuke offered precious little. The dayroom contained a small selection of games and jigsaw puzzles, but the puzzles were either mixed up or conspicuously incomplete and the games required a second player. The ward's numerous cupboards yielded nothing but cleaning materials, a stepladder, and an artificial Christmas tree with several branches missing. But then at the very back of one cupboard I found five or six boxes of the aforesaid *Woman's Own*, a weekly magazine full of cheerful advice and enlightenment for the homemaker, representing a more or less complete set of issues from about 1950 to nearly the present, and these I hauled out one box at a time and carried to the ward office.

And so began my education in the life and culture of Great Britain. For the rest of that long and tranquil late summer and early autumn, I sat at Mr. Jolly's desk, feet perched on an open drawer, reaching from time to time into a box of *Woman's Own*s, as if into a box of very special chocolates, for instruction in the ways of British life. I read every word with interest and profit. I read profiles of Hattie Jacques, Adam Faith, Douglas Bader, Tommy Steele, and Alma Cogan, among many other personalities I had never heard of before, and in many cases have not heard of since. I learned about the tears behind the smiles for Princess Margaret and how we were all going to have to knuckle down and get to grips with the vexing new decimal currency. I learned how cheddar cheese could be made into an exciting treat by cutting it into cubes and sticking toothpicks into them. (From subsequent issues I learned that nearly all foods could be made exciting by sticking them with toothpicks.) I learned how to make my own swimming jacket and to build a garden pond. I learned that there wasn't any edible substance that the British wouldn't put into a baked potato. I learned that it was possible to conquer the world and still bring home just one salad dressing.

Every single thing was new to me, every turned page a revelation. Here was a car with three wheels. How splendid! How wondrously ill advised! Here was a town where once a year the people chased a rolling cheese down a hill. Well, why not! Here was something you could eat called blancmange, a pastime called Morris dancing, a drink called barley water. I learned more in that one summer than in all my previous summers put together.

It was while wallowing in this endless sea of fascination that I first heard the names Skegness and Billy Butlin and of the rise of the British holiday camp. Butlin grew up in Canada, but came to Britain as a young man and grew wealthy as the European agent for Dodgem cars. Through the Dodgem business, he met Harry Warner, a retired army captain, who owned an amusement park and restaurant at Hayling Island, on the Hampshire coast (not far from Bognor Regis). Butlin took over the running of the amusement park in 1928, then got the idea of the holiday camp—a place where people could come and spend a week in a giant compound beside the sea for an affordable all-inclusive price. On the site of a former turnip field just outside Skegness, he opened the first Butlin's Holiday Camp in 1936. It had six hundred tiny cabins rather grandly known as chalets, and was a success from the start. Soon Butlin was opening camps across the country and others were following. Church groups, youth clubs, and trade unions all opened camps. The British Union of Fascists had two. Butlin's old associate Captain Warner opened several camps of his own, as did a businessman named Fred Pontin.

I can't tell you how much this fascinated me. It seemed extraordinary to me—barely within the limits of credibility—that people paid to go to them. Campers were awakened by a loudspeaker in their room, which they could neither turn off nor turn down, summoned to meals in communal dining halls, harried into taking part in humiliating beauty contests and other competitions, and ordered back to their chalets to be locked in for the night at 11 p.m. Butlin had invented the prisoner-of-war camp as holiday, and, this being Britain, people loved it.

The chalets were tiny but had carpet, an electric light, running water, and maid service. These were luxuries most customers had never before enjoyed, often even in their own homes. Outside there was one bathroom for every four campers. For an all-inclusive price of £3 a week, patrons got three square meals a day, evening entertainment, which could range from ballroom dancing to plays by Shakespeare, and activities like swimming, archery, lawn bowling, and pony rides. It sounded pleasant enough, but I didn't altogether understand the appeal until, just before this present trip, I read *Holiday Camps in Twentieth-Century Britain* by Sandra Trudgen Dawson, a historian at Northern Illinois University, where I learned that mostly what the patrons of holiday camps got was sex. "Many of the waitresses," she writes, "were prostitutes"—giving new meaning to the slogan "Butlin's—where you will meet the kind of people you'd like to meet." Sex of a nonfiduciary nature was equally rampant. Employees carnally embraced other employees and as many of the guests as they could. At some camps, Dawson reports, employees had a secret scoring system: five points for sleeping with a female guest, ten for a beauty contest winner, fifteen for the camp manager's wife. Groups of unchaperoned teenagers came purely for the prospect of sex with other unchaperoned teenagers.

The postwar years were a golden age for the camps. At Skegness, Butlin's boasted a monorail and its own small airport. By the early 1960s, two and a half million people a year were staying at holiday camps. Conventional seaside hotels and guesthouses watched helplessly as their business dwindled. In a desperate attempt to compete, a hotel proprietor named J. E. Cracknell came up with the idea of "Sel-Tels"—short for Self-Service Hotels, where there would be no staff to provide services, but guests would have free run of the facilities, provided they brought their own provisions. Mum could cook an evening meal in the hotel kitchen, then carry the food through to her waiting family in the dining room, and wash up afterward—all at no extra charge to the family. Not surprisingly, Sel-Tels never caught on. Neither did anything else independent hoteliers tried.

The holiday camp phenomenon seemed set to go on forever. But just as it reached its peak it all began to fall apart. The advent of cheap package holidays meant people could go to the sunny Mediterranean for less than they paid to shiver for a week at Butlin's. For older people and those with families, the teenage clientele became a disincentive because of their tendency to fight and vomit copiously. Under pressure to keep costs down, the holiday camps skimped on maintenance and grew increasingly threadbare. At one camp on the Isle of Wight—not a Butlin's, it must be said—conditions were so appalling that four hundred holidaymakers revolted and refused to pay their bills. But all the camps got pretty shabby. Many years ago, when I was away working, my wife took our children to the Butlin's at Pwllheli, in Wales. They were booked to stay for four nights, but by the second afternoon the children were begging to be taken somewhere where the pillows didn't stick to their faces and they weren't mugged for their sweets by feral children wedged into a bend on the helter-skelter (a kind of enclosed slide). One of my children swore that if you sat quietly in the bathroom, you could hear the fungus breeding.

Through the seventies and eighties the three main holiday companies, Butlin's, Warner's, and Pontin's, were sold over and over, to companies that should have known better. The Rank Organisation, Scottish and Newcastle Breweries, Coral Leisure, and Grand Metropolitan Hotels all bought into the business in the belief that they could turn it around. They were all wrong. Most of the camps were shut. Just when it seemed that all the camps were doomed, a family firm called Bourne Leisure bought up what was left, smartened up and modernized three camps—in Skegness, Bognor Regis, and Minehead—and appears to be doing pretty well out of it.

At Skegness, I had read, they have preserved one of the original 1936 chalets, so that people can appreciate how far the camps have come, and I was eager to see it. So I set off along the sodden seafront in the direction of Butlin's, and walked for quite a distance, but I didn't encounter anything but a lot of rain and duney spaciousness. I stopped a youth on a bike and asked him how far it was to Butlin's. "Oh, miles," he said, and kept going. Butlin's Skegness, it turns out, is not in Skegness at all, but in Ingoldmells, nearly four miles away up the A52. I peered into the murk through glasses that were like windows in a steam room and decided that I would try again in the morning.

Soaked, I returned to my room to change into dry clothes. Out of idle curiosity, I looked up some figures on the Internet from VisitEngland, as the English Tourist Board has restyled itself in the evident belief that if you fuse two words in a title it makes you look stylish and forward-thinking instead of just slightly desperate and in need of new management, and these were frankly astounding to me. Skegness, it turns out, receives 537,000 visitors a year, making it the ninth-most-visited place in Britain. Among seaside resorts, only Scarborough and Blackpool are more popular. Measured by spending, visitors to Skegness spent more than visitors to Bath, Birmingham, or Newcastle upon Tyne. Perhaps they come for the colonic hydrotherapy. Who could possibly say?

When enough time had mercifully passed to consider it the evening, I went to a large, popular, characterless pub for a pint before dinner, then dined in a quiet Indian restaurant called the Gandhi. The food was fine, but the Gandhi didn't seem to be doing a lot of business. Reluctant to return early to my lonely room, I dawdled over my jalfrezi and drank one giant bottle of Cobra beer too many, which left me ruminative but in good spirits. At the door, I spent quite some time stabbing unsuccessfully at the right armhole of my jacket, until a young employee stepped up and kindly sorted me out.

"Thank you," I said, then shared with him a sudden idea that I thought might perk up the place. "You should make this into an Elvis-themed restaurant," I said. "You could call it Love Me Tandoor."

Leaving him with that thought, I toddled off, just a touch unsteadily, into the night.

II

In the morning, I drove north to Ingoldmells and found Butlin's. It wasn't hard as it was an enormous compound that looked like a prison camp. Lethal-looking fencing with lacerating tops surrounded the entire camp and gave every appearance that it was trying to keep people in at least as much as it was trying to keep the rest of us out. The front entrance had barriers and a security booth. I told the security man that I just wanted to look at the original chalet, but he said, and seemed genuinely regretful, that he couldn't let me in. I would have to buy a day ticket to the camp when the office opened, but that wasn't for another two hours. A day ticket would cost £20. We agreed that that was a lot of money just to look at an eighty-year-old chalet, and on that note we parted.

I should say that I had thought already of booking into the camp as a staying guest, but the idea of a man on his own hanging around in a Butlin's just watching people seemed a little bit creepy, even to me. What if I was challenged or, worse, recognized? Come to that, what if I was mugged by feral children? The consequences hardly bore thinking about. ("Bryson was taken into custody after he was seen giving sweets to children by the helter-skelter.") So, disappointed, I returned to the car and headed north to Grimsby.

Grimsby in the early twentieth century was the largest fishing port in the world. Not in Britain, not in northern Europe, but in the *world*. I have seen photographs of giant stacks of ling, a large cod-like fish that once abounded in British waters, piled higher than a man's head on the Grimsby dockside. Each ling was about six feet long. No fisherman alive today has seen a ling that big. In 1950, Grimsby's fleet brought in 1,100 tonnes of ling. Today the annual haul is eight tonnes. And ling was only ever a small part of the overall catch. Cod, halibut, haddock, skate, wolffish, and other species most of us have never heard of were heaped on the docks in staggering, but unsustainable, volumes. In a generation, beam trawlers scraped the seabed bare, turning much of the North Sea floor into a marine desert. In 1950, Grimsby landed over 100,000 tonnes of cod. Today it brings in under 300. Altogether Grimsby's annual wetfish catch has fallen from nearly 200,000 tonnes to just 658 tonnes—and even those paltry numbers, according to the York University oceanographer Callum Roberts, are more than the denuded North Sea can sustain. In a riveting book called *Ocean of Life*, Roberts notes that every year the fisheries ministers of Europe agree quotas that are on average one-third higher than the levels recommended by their own scientists.

But compared with much of the rest of the world, Europe is a beacon of enlightenment. Among the many amazing and depressing facts in his book, Roberts gives a list of all the aquatic life incidentally killed—the bycatch, as it is known—by a fishing boat in the Pacific Ocean in the process of legally catching 211 mahi-mahi. Among the aquatic animals hauled aboard and tossed back dead after a single sweep were:

488 turtles
455 stingrays and devil rays
460 sharks
68 sailfish
34 marlin
32 tuna
11 wahoo

8 swordfish

4 giant sunfish

This was legal under international protocols. The hooks on the longlines were certified as "turtle friendly." All this was to give 211 people a dinner of mahi-mahi.

Grimsby was not at all what I expected. I had imagined it to be a compact city, at its heart a network of narrow lanes, built around a stone-walled harbor—like a Cornish fishing village but on a somewhat grander scale. In fact Grimsby's port was huge and industrial and far removed from the town. The town center wasn't compact and charming and townlike, but grubbily urban, with busy roads that were difficult to cross on foot. Between the center of town and the port was a soulless zone of box stores, none of which seemed to be doing terribly well. The chain-link fence outside a large home-decorating store called Homebase bore a strangely festive banner announcing that it was closing down imminently. Several other businesses were gone, their perimeters ankle deep or worse in blown litter and illicitly dumped rubbish. I passed the police station, which had a rather nice lawn out front, but it was strewn with beer cans and other detritus. What kind of community is it where people can throw litter on the lawn of a police station with impunity? What kind of police force doesn't tidy up its own grounds?

There were a few nice places here and there. John Pettit and Sons, an old-fashioned butcher's on Bethlehem Street, which has been there since 1892, according to its sign, was busy with loyal customers and looked splendid. I wish it every success. I was also rather taken with a hairdresser's called Curl Up and Dye. But that pretty well summarizes the high spots of Grimsby.

Victoria Mills, an enormous brick heap, a former flour mill, loomed above the box stores. It is a fantastic building, but it seemed largely derelict. Later I learned that half the building has been converted into apartments—very nice ones, too, it seems—but the other, forlorn half was owned by a company that had repeatedly failed orders to carry out conservation work. According to the *Grimsby Telegraph* it had been fined £5,000 in the local magistrates' court in June 2013 for failing to undertake necessary maintenance. The company didn't represent itself at the hearing. A fair-sized shrub could be seen growing out of a window eight floors up. This did not give the appearance of a building that was loved and cared for.

Nearby, on a stretch of quayside overlooking the broad River Freshney, was a large, rather stylish building called the Fishing Heritage Center. This turned out to be a museum, which was delightful and fascinating and about much more than just fishing. On the ground floor were several re-created interiors, including those of a local pub and a fish-and-chips shop as they were in the twenties or thirties. I was particularly interested to note that people in Grimsby used to bring their own fish and have the shop fry it for a penny. The best display of all was one showing what the interior of a ship's galley was like in rough seas. The display was built on a steep slant so that everything was caught in a frozen moment of slopping, the harried chef desperately trying to keep things under control. This was everything a museum should be—fun, imaginative, thoroughly absorbing, wonderfully instructive.

Elsewhere there was lots of interesting stuff about fish and fishing—that a single turbot can produce 14 million eggs, for instance. I know that sounds a trifle dull out of context, but three of us reading the label simultaneously made an appreciative, slightly camp "Oooh," sound, and meant it sincerely. Everywhere the displays were thoughtful, intelligent, and carefully spelled and punctuated. Someone needs to go and get the Natural History Museum people in London and bring them here. Then it needs to leave them here and take the Grimsby museum people back with them.

In the gift shop, I spent some time looking at a fascinating book called *Grimsby: The Story of the World's Greatest Fishing Port*, which surveyed the rise and tragic fall of this once-great place. Grimsby's problems, I learned, were mostly self-inflicted. While fishermen cleared the seas of almost everything that swam or rested on the sandy bottom, the town fathers were tearing down nearly all of Grimsby's finest buildings and monuments. Doughty Park cemetery was swept away, as were the town's many theaters and grand hotels, and many of its finest houses, too. The Corn Exchange, a nineteenth-century landmark that looked rather like a prototype rocket ship, was first turned into a public lavatory, as a kind of preliminary insult, then demolished altogether. It was as if Grimsby was trying to obliterate every reminder that it had ever known greatness. It succeeded. You have to conclude that Grimsby today is about what it deserves to be.

And with that gloomy thought to mull over, I collected my car and drove on to a very much nicer place: elsewhere.

Chapter 19

The Peak District

I

FOR YEARS WHEN I was growing up, I often walked on Sunday afternoons to the Ingersoll movie theater, a mile or so from my home in Des Moines, and took in a matinee. It was a single-screen theater (they nearly all were then) and I watched whatever was showing. The Ingersoll clearly didn't get the first pick of pictures. Mostly it showed small, little-noted movies, often European. Frequently I was one of just two or three people in the audience. The result of this is that I have seen, and can often still fondly recall, movies that I suspect even their stars have forgotten: *Woman of Straw* with Sean Connery and Gina Lollobrigida; the chilling *Unman, Wittering and Zigo* with David Hemmings; *Laughter in the Dark* with Nicol Williamson and the sultry Anna Karina. How we could have done with a few like her at Roosevelt High School, I used to think.

I enjoyed these movies often as much for their locations as for their plots—the sooty buildings of London, the mad traffic of Rome, the sunny villas and twisting corniches of the Mediterranean—and of none was this more true than a slow but lustrous feature called *The Virgin and the Gypsy,* based on the D. H. Lawrence novella and starring Joanna Shimkus and Franco Nero. It was a languorous piece of work, with lots of moody shots across moorland. In one scene, a camera panned across an enormous stone dam and reservoir, which stood in a silent landscape of wooded hills and heath. The dam was made of great blocks of stone and rose like a mountain from the green water. At each end it had a decorative castellated tower. It was, at the very least, intensely picturesque, and I couldn't understand why it wasn't better known. It would be famous in Iowa, believe me. When the movie finished, I walked home and never thought another thing about it.

Thirty years later, while walking in the Peak District with my friends Andrew and John, we came down a wooded slope at a place called Howden Moor and there, abruptly filling my view, was the castellated dam from the movie. I recognized it at once. It was a little smaller than I would have expected, but otherwise was just as splendid, just as commanding and beautiful, as I remembered it. It's called the Derwent Reservoir and it was built in the early years of the twentieth century to supply water to Sheffield, Derby, Chesterfield, and the other old industrial towns that border the Peak District. I understand now, having lived in Britain for a long time, why it isn't better known. Britain is packed so solid with good stuff—with castles, stately homes, hill forts, stone circles, medieval churches, giant figures carved in hillsides, you name it—that a good deal of it gets lost. It is a permanent astonishment to me how casually strewn with glory Britain is. If the Derwent dam were in Iowa, it would be on the state's license plates. There would be campgrounds, an RV park, probably a large outlet center. Here it is anonymous and forgotten, a momentary diversion on a countryside amble.

Let me take just a moment to say some numbers. Britain has 450,000 listed buildings, 20,000 scheduled ancient monuments, twenty-six World Heritage Sites, 1,624 registered parks and gardens (that is, gardens and parks of historic significance), 600,000 known archaeological sites (and more being found every day),

3,500 historic cemeteries, 70,000 war memorials, 4,000 sites of special scientific interest, 18,500 medieval churches, and 2,500 museums containing 170 million objects. Having such a fund of richness means that it can sometimes be taken for granted to a shocking degree, but it also means that very often you find you have something quite wonderful pretty much to yourself, as I did with Derwent Reservoir today.

It is managed by Severn Trent Water, a utility, which provides a little visitor center with a tea counter and a small parking lot, which was mostly empty when I arrived. A lovely walk goes around the lake, and connects with two nearby reservoirs, Howden and Ladybower, both also very fetching.

Derwent Reservoir is notable for one other thing. It was here that they practiced for the famous dam-busters raids of the Second World War when the British engineer Barnes Wallis invented his celebrated bouncing bombs. These were designed to skip across water, like a stone across a pond, until they hit a dam wall, at which point, it was proposed, they would explode with devastating consequences. In practice, the scheme didn't really work. The low-flying planes were easy targets for German gunners—40 percent of the squadron didn't return from the first mission—and many bombs exploded spectacularly but harmlessly in the water or bounced straight over the dam walls and detonated in neighboring fields. Only one dam was seriously breached. The floodwaters from it killed 1,700 people, but those were mostly Allied prisoners, so in fact Barnes Wallis killed more people on his own side than on the German one. But never mind. It was one of those feats of wartime ingenuity that could be set alongside radar and the Enigma machine as evincing Britain's indomitable spirit and ingenuity. In 1955, the bouncing bombs story was made into a film much beloved by the people who program daytime movies on television. I don't believe I have ever had the flu without watching *Dam Busters* at some point.

I had a good walk along the Derwent and Howden reservoirs, enjoying the combination of shady woodland and sun-splashed water, amazed that I could have this much splendor to myself. On the way back to the parking lot, I passed an imposing stone monument to a sheepdog named Tip, which, according to the inscription, "stayed by the body of his dead master, Mr. Joseph Tagg, on the Howden Moors for fifteen weeks." That's a very long time. Mind you, Tagg was lying on the dog's lead. Actually, I don't know what the story was, but I do know that personally I would be more inclined to pay for a monument that said, "In memory of Tip, who went for help when I needed it."

It was interesting, I thought, that the memorial to Tip was grander than the memorial to the men who took part in the dambusters raids, but then I remembered that this was England and Tip was a dog.

The Peak District is 550 square miles of big skies and hilly beauty in the middle of the country where the Midlands and North subtly merge. The highest point in the Peak District at 2,100 feet is Kinder Scout, which stands just a few miles west of the Derwent Valley. Kinder Scout was the site of a celebrated act of civil disobedience in 1932 when workers from nearby factory towns defiantly walked across the Duke of Devonshire's grouse moors. Their actions that day had much to do with the subsequent opening of much of the countryside to walkers, so I thought I would pay my respects as I was in the neighborhood. I parked in the pretty village of Hayfield and walked the mile or so to the trespass site at Bowden Bridge and was glad I had. Along the way I passed a terraced cottage with a blue plaque on it noting that this was the birthplace of the great character actor Arthur Lowe—Captain Mainwaring in the television series *Dad's Army*. And there you have a perfect demonstration of the merits of foot travel over motorized travel, for if I had driven I would never have noticed the plaque, thus proving that a walker's life is not only healthier but richer.

Kinder (it rhymes with "cinder") Scout isn't a peak, but a grassy plateau, visible in clear weather from Manchester and Sheffield, both about twenty miles away. That was the root of the problem, it seems. Workers in Manchester and Sheffield gazed dreamily upon Kinder Scout from their gritty neighborhoods and thought of it as their hill, the place where they could go for fresh air and spiritual refreshment at weekends, and for years they did. But in the 1920s, the Duke of Devonshire closed Kinder Scout to the public for the sake of his grouse shooting. This naturally bred resentment, and in April 1932 five hundred people, mostly factory workers, gathered at Bowden Bridge to undertake a protest walk across the duke's land.

Tipped off about the hike, the duke's gamekeepers were waiting and ordered the hikers to turn back. The result was a brief and rather endearingly ineffectual scuffle. One gamekeeper was knocked unconscious, probably accidentally, but there were no other injuries and the walkers swept past the gamekeepers and completed their march to the summit. The authorities, overreacting, arrested the group's leaders and charged them with criminal trespass. Five men were sent to prison for up to five months—an outrageously disproportionate punishment. The result was a wave of anger and resentment that went well beyond Derbyshire. The Mass Trespass (as it is now invariably written) became an iconic moment in the history of both class struggle and the British countryside. In other countries they fight over politics and religion. In Britain, it is over who gets to walk on a windswept moor. I think that's rather splendid.

The trespassers' efforts were not in vain. Four years later, Parliament set up a committee to consider creating national parks across England. The Second World War intervened, but in 1951 the Peak District became England's first national park. Considering the symbolic importance of the Mass Trespass, the memorial is modest nearly to the point of invisibility. It's just a small plaque at the back of a parking lot, hanging about eight or ten feet up a quarry wall and half obscured by vegetation. If I hadn't known to look for the plaque, I never would have noticed it. The words on it say simply: "The mass trespass onto Kinder Scout started from this quarry, 24th April 1932." Across the road, a narrow lane beside a stream led up to the start of the footpath to Kinder Scout. It was a lovely day and wonderful countryside, but Kinder Scout was a taxing, three-hour hike from here. I still had to get to Buxton, at the other end of the Peak District, where I had a room booked, so I walked for only a mile or so toward Kinder Scout, just enough to get something of a view, then turned reluctantly and walked back to the car. Once again, I didn't see a soul.

Buxton is an old spa town, mostly built of stone, mostly in the eighteenth century. The Pavilion Gardens, covering twenty-three acres in the very heart of the town, must be the most delightful town park in the country. Buxton has a striking opera house, a couple of grand hotels, and an outsized building with an impressive dome that was once a hospital and is now an outpost of the University of Derby. Near the gardens is a crescent-shaped building vaguely reminiscent of the famous Royal Crescent at Bath, but with the difference that this one has been derelict for years since structural problems were found in it. Plans exist to turn it into a hotel, but at the time of my visit it was still boarded up and surrounded by worksite fencing—a sad fate for a Grade I–listed building. (Grade I buildings are those of special architectural significance.) The problem is that the East Midlands Development Agency, which had promised £5 million of funding, was closed by the government in 2012 before the money could be paid over, so now this rare and lovely building, which ought to be contributing to the economy, sits quietly deteriorating as part of a national economy drive. The madness of modern life sometimes seems boundless.

I had a walk around the town, browsing in shopwindows. I was particularly taken with Potter's, a men's outfitters that has been in Buxton since 1860 and looks to be still going strong, which these days seems not so much an achievement as a miracle. I was immediately attracted to some shirts in the window, entirely because of the name: Seidensticker Splendestos. I know I am on the record as saying that I don't need another thing, but who could resist that name? I am prepared to wear a shirt sight unseen if it's called a Splendesto. It's so good a name it ought to be a word in its own right, denoting a higher level of excellence beyond splendid. I even thought of a slogan for the company: "Splendesto—when splendid isn't good enough."

I grew up in an age when people valued good names. It was a time when washing machines had Luxe-o-Matic spin cycles, lawn mowers had Trigger-Torque starter buttons, record players had Vibro-Sonic speakers. Even clothing was exciting. My father once owned a McGregor Glen Plaid Visa-Versa Reversible Jacket and got real pleasure from showing people, including total strangers, how you could turn it inside out and have a second, bonus jacket. "That's why it's called Visa-Versa," he would explain, as if revealing one of the secrets of the universe. He never called it "my jacket" or "the jacket." It was always "my Visa-Versa Reversible." Just saying the name gave him pleasure. I understand that.

All that is gone. Nowadays we have nothing but meaningless names. Look at Starbucks and their cup sizes—Venti, Trenta, and Wanko Grande or whatever. Giant corporations everywhere have names that mean nothing—Diageo, Lucent, Accenture, Aviva. I used to have an insurance policy with Windsor Life, but now the company is called ReAssure. That is a fabulous name if they ever decide to make incontinence pants for the elderly, but it is a terrible name for an insurer.

I miss having exciting product names in my life and felt a genuine pang of envy, as I stood looking in Potter's windows, for the people who get to shop in such lovely old preserves. As I walked on, I fell into a little fantasy in which I saw myself calling in at Potter's from time to time, for the linguistic pleasure of it as much as anything else.

"Good afternoon," I say in my fantasy. "I special ordered a couple of Splendestos a week or two ago and I wonder if they are in yet."

"Let me just check the book, Mr. Bryson," says the manager and runs a finger down the page of an enormous leather-bound ledger. "They should be in on Wednesday," he tells me.

"And what about my Lloyd, Attree & Smith brown Donegal-style tweed sports coat with faux suede elbow patches?"

"Let me look. Yes, that's due on Wednesday, too."

"Excellent. I'll call back on Wednesday. For now I'll just take these Sloggi Shur-Fit Boxer Shorts in mint green with cranberry piping."

"Of course. Shall I wrap them for you?"

"No, I'll wear them now."

In the evening, comfortable in my new Sloggis ("So stylish you'll want to wear them outside your trousers"), I would stroll to a public house for an aperitif and afterward I would dine at some nice little bistro near the gardens. That is in fact precisely what I did now, except that I wasn't wearing Sloggi Shur-Fits outside my trousers, regrettably.

I had an excellent evening. When the waitress cleared my plate she asked me how my meal was.

"Oh, splendesto," I said and meant it most sincerely.

In the morning, I woke keen and eager, for the sun was shining and I was to walk the Monsal Trail, which runs for eight and a half miles between Buxton and Bakewell, through tunnels and gorges and views of sumptuous beauty. This was originally part of the Midland Railway line from Manchester to Derby, but that closed in 1968. The route never made much economic sense since it ran through lightly populated countryside. One of its principal stations, Hassop, was built more or less for the private use of the Duke of Devonshire's estate at Chatsworth. Today, restored as a roomy, level cycling route and footpath, it brings pleasure to far more people than ever it did when trains ran over it. It is a wonderful walk.

The moment of supreme glory is the crossing of Monsal Dale on the majestic Headstone Viaduct. Monsal Dale is a place of great natural beauty already, but the viaduct, three hundred feet long and standing high above green meadows and the little River Wye, raises it to an even more transfixing level. When the viaduct was built in 1863, the art critic John Ruskin famously raged against it, saying that a setting of tranquillity and beauty had been cruelly sacrificed just so that "every fool in Buxton can be in Bakewell in half an hour and every fool at Bakewell in Buxton." Headstone Viaduct is often used as an example of how things that are hated when new later become treasured. Well, sure, that sometimes happens. But there is a difference here in that the Headstone Viaduct was from the start a thing of actual beauty, carefully built, which is rarely the case with intrusions on the landscape today.

Not far from Monsal Dale is a view nearly as good as, and even more historic than, the one that so exercised Ruskin, where the trail emerges from a long tunnel into a green valley. Holding a commanding position at the valley head is a white Georgian building that looks at first sight like a stately home. In fact, it is Cressbrook Mill, built by Richard Arkwright in 1779 (and rebuilt six years later after a fire) to spin cotton. It is quite the most handsome factory you will ever see and possibly the most important, for it changed the world. Along with Cromford Mill, built a few miles away near Matlock, this was where the factory system started. Everything that is manufactured on Earth today traces its beginnings back to this tranquil corner of rural Derbyshire. Arkwright built his mills in the narrow valleys of Derbyshire because they had plenty of water to power his machines and because the remote location made it less likely that they would be besieged by angry spinners put out of work by his new methods. It also made it easier for him to exploit his workers. Cressbrook Mill was operated mostly by orphans who were treated worse than abysmally.

Within half a century, the cotton industry employed over four hundred thousand people. Nearly everything that followed and made Britain great—shipbuilding, finance, the building of canals and railways, the growth of empire—had its foundations here. It is interesting to think that Britain's commercial supremacy was built on a product, cotton, that Britain couldn't grow and came from the one part of the empire it had lost and didn't control. Derbyshire's spell at the center of all this didn't last terribly long. As the cotton industry grew, larger factories and bigger rivers were required, and the work moved to more urban places like Manchester and Bradford. Derbyshire sank back into a picturesque oblivion. Today Cressbrook Mill is upmarket apartments.

I finished the day in Ashbourne, another very agreeable little town, with the kinds of shops that you hardly see these days: a cheese shop, a sweet shop, a shoe repair shop, at least two butchers, a greengrocer's, an old-fashioned toy shop, several pubs, and some good-looking antique shops. At one end of town are the Memorial Gardens, which are pleasant if nowhere near as splendid as Buxton's Pavilion Gardens, and at the other end stands the magnificent Church of St. Oswald's, with a tall, graceful spire that brings to mind Salisbury Cathedral on a slightly smaller scale.

I went in a snug-looking pub and noticed that one of the guest bitters was from the Ringwood Brewery in my part of the country.

"They do a very nice lager, too," I said to the bartender, just making conversation.

"We do very nice lagers ourselves," he responded defensively as if I had just told him his wife was ugly.

I was taken aback. "I wasn't suggesting anything about your lagers. I just thought this was a good one you might not have heard of."

"As I say, we have very good lagers already," he said, a touch frostily, and handed me my change.

"And you're a bit of a jackass," I thought, and went with my beer to a corner table, where I sat under a framed newspaper photograph from the time when a lorry with failed brakes had gone through the pub's front wall. I was kind of sorry now that I had missed that.

Just before leaving home, I had stuck a bundle of forwarded correspondence from a publisher into my rucksack and I pulled it out now. When you write books for a living, you come to realize that while not all people who write to authors are strange, all people who are strange write to authors. Recently a man in Huddersfield wrote to tell me that he quite liked some of my books and thought it would be an idea if we swapped houses for a couple of weeks so that he could get to know me through my possessions and I could keep his tropical fish fed. "I haven't told the wife yet, in anticipation of a positive reply," he wrote. Another wanted to do a book called *The Great British Breakfast* but wasn't good at writing, so he proposed that we travel around Britain together; he would eat the breakfasts and describe them to me and I would put the experience into words. He proposed a 70/30 split of the proceeds in his favor since it was his idea and I was quite well off already. Another man wrote saying that in 1974 he was working as a bush pilot in Canada and he gave a lift from Goose Bay, Newfoundland, to Halifax, Nova Scotia, to a young man with a reddish beard. The thing he particularly remembered was that the young man was wearing a kilt, and he wondered if I'd ever worn a kilt while traveling in Newfoundland.

Occasionally the mail includes some good surprises, and I was treated to one now. From a padded envelope, I pulled an advance copy of a book called *Maphead* by Ken Jennings, about one man's passion for geography. It didn't look my kind of thing at all, but I glanced through it and was immediately hooked. It was ostensibly about the joys of geography, but mostly it was about how uninformed Americans have become with respect to the world.

Jennings relates the story of an assistant professor at the University of Miami named David Helgren who had given freshman students a blank map of the world and asked them to locate thirty well-known places. He expected mixed results, but what he found was that the students mostly couldn't do any of it. Eleven who were from Miami couldn't even locate Miami. The *Miami Herald* picked up the story and then it became national news. Helgren was interviewed by lots of newspapers and film crews. And how did the University of Miami respond to this? It fired Helgren. When a colleague spoke up in Helgren's behalf, it fired him, too.

Other findings have shown that about 10 percent of university students can't find California or Texas on a map and about a fifth of Americans overall can't even find the United States on a map. How can you not find your own country on a map? Jennings quotes the response of a contestant in the Miss Teen USA competition when asked to explain why so many Americans couldn't even find their own country on a map. With solemnity and conviction she responded:

> I personally believe that U.S. Americans are unable to do so because some people out there in our nation don't have maps, and I believe that our education like such as in South Africa and, uh, the Iraq, everywhere like such as, and I believe that they should, our education over here in the U.S. should help

the U.S, uh, should help South Africa and should help the Iraq and the Asian countries so we will be able to build up our future, for our children.

Well, thank God at least we haven't lost our articulacy. I hadn't intended to have another pint, but I was having such a good time with the book that I went back to the bar and ordered another, so that I could read even more, though this time prudently I didn't mention to the barman any other beers I had ever had in case he took it personally.

Returning to my book, I learned that Sarah Palin thought Africa was a country. It was a wonderful evening.

II

The British are sometimes magnificently sensible. In 1980, the government established the National Heritage Memorial Fund, to provide money to save things that might otherwise be lost, but nowhere did it define what heritage was. So the trustees of the fund are free to save anything they choose as long as money is available and they consider it as coming under the general category of heritage. You couldn't devise a system more open to foolishness and abuse, yet it has worked brilliantly. It has helped to save everything from works of art to threatened species of birds, but I don't think the money has ever been better spent than on saving Calke Abbey, my next port of call.

Calke Abbey has never been an abbey—the family that owned it just called it that to make it sound more interesting—but it was once a very substantial estate, spread over some thirty thousand acres in southern Derbyshire. For four hundred years it was the home of the Harpur Crewe family whose defining characteristic was "congenital unsociability," as the house guidebook nicely puts it. For the last 150 years of their reign, most members of the family barely left the property or let anyone onto it. A visitors' book from the nineteenth century was found to contain not a single entry. The first automobile wasn't allowed up the drive until 1949 and electricity wasn't installed until 1962.

Before the First World War, Calke employed sixty staff, but then the estate fell into decline and by the end it employed no one. When Charles Harpur Crewe died in 1981—amazingly, not to say moronically, intestate—his brother Henry was confronted with an inheritance tax bill so large that the interest alone increased by £1,500 every day. Unable to pay, Henry gave the house to the National Trust. Brilliantly, the Trust decided to keep the house just as it found it. They call it "the un-stately home," and that couldn't be more enchantingly correct.

The property had not been improved or substantially decorated since the early 1840s. After Vauncey Harpur Crewe, the tenth baronet, died in 1924, the family retreated to one small corner of the house. When the National Trust arrived in 1985, it opened doors on rooms that hadn't been entered in more than fifty years. The whole place was a musty time warp.

I was put on a tour with seventeen other people, and it was superb. It lasted a very generous ninety minutes and was led by a well-spoken, good-natured, admirably well-informed lady. The trust has done a superb job of halting the deterioration without losing an air of neglect and decline. Everywhere the paint was peeling or the plaster was rough. I leaned against a wall at one point and one of my fellow tour members whispered to me with great pleasure and many eager nods that the back of my jacket was now absolutely filthy. I took it off to look and he was right, and we both nodded vigorously. As well as the furnishings and a great deal of taxidermy, the house also contains an outstanding collection of archaeological treasures, most of which were found on the grounds by our old friend Basil Brown of Sutton Hoo, I was pleased to learn.

I was so delighted with the whole thing that I decided to make my peace with the National Trust and went straight back to the ticket office and took out membership. I hadn't realized quite what a big deal it was—I had to provide two sets of fingerprints, a chest X-ray, and swear an oath promising to buy a Volvo and a wax jacket—but I did get my admission to Calke refunded as part of the deal, and I appreciated that very much, as you can imagine.

I was on my way to Rutland to visit my son and his family, who live near Oakham. It was a grandchild's birthday and I seldom miss a family occasion where cake is involved. But I wasn't expected until teatime and I was pleased to have a day to just pootle around in this most delightful corner of England. The green and rolling countryside shared between Leicestershire, Northamptonshire, and Nottinghamshire is quite distinctively lovely and hardly anyone outside those counties knows it.

Not far from Calke Abbey is the hamlet of Coton in the Elms, which has the distinction of being the furthest place in Britain from the sea, and I couldn't resist that. The specific site is Church Flatts Farm, which is officially 70.21 miles from the nearest patch of coastline. Some passerby had marked the spot with a roll of old carpet heaved into the hedge. I pulled over by the farm drive and got out and just stood there, quietly proud to be the least salty person in Britain. About fifteen or twenty seconds into the experience, I realized that it wasn't going to get any better than this no matter how long I stood there, so I got back in the car and drove on, but with a lasting sense of satisfaction and a profound readiness for a party tea.

Chapter 20

Wales

I HAD TO GO to America for a while to give some talks. Going to America always does me good. It's where I'm from, after all. There's baseball on the TV, people are friendly and upbeat, they don't obsess about the weather except when there is weather worth obsessing about, you can have all the ice cubes you want. Above all, visiting America gives me perspective.

Consider two small experiences I had upon arriving at a hotel in downtown Austin, Texas. When I checked in, the clerk needed to record my details, naturally enough, and asked for my home address. Our house doesn't have a street number, just a name, and I have found in the past that that is more deviance than an American computer can sometimes cope with, so I gave our London address. The girl typed in the building number and street name, then said: "City?"

I replied: "London."

"Can you spell that please?"

I looked at her and saw that she wasn't joking. "L-O-N-D-O-N," I said.

"Country?"

"England."

"Can you spell that?"

I spelled England.

She typed for a moment and said: "The computer won't accept England. Is that a real country?"

I assured her it was. "Try Britain," I suggested.

I spelled that, too—twice (we got the wrong number of T's the first time)—and the computer wouldn't take that either. So I suggested Great Britain, United Kingdom, UK, and GB, but those were all rejected, too. I couldn't think of anything else to suggest.

"It'll take France," the girl said after a minute.

"I beg your pardon?"

"You can have 'London, France.'"

"Seriously?"

She nodded.

"Well, why not?"

So she typed "London, France," and the system was happy. I finished the check-in process and went with my bag and plastic room key to a bank of elevators a few paces away. When the elevator arrived, a young woman was in it already, which I thought a little strange because the elevator had come from one of the upper floors and now we were going back up there again. About five seconds into the ascent, she said to me in a suddenly alert tone: "Excuse me, was that the *lobby* back there?"

"That big room with a check-in desk and revolving doors to the street? Why, yes, it was."

"Shoot," she said and looked chagrined.

Now I am not for a moment suggesting that these incidents typify Austin, Texas, or America generally or anything like that. But it did get me to thinking that our problems are more serious than I had supposed. When functioning adults can't identify London, England, or a hotel lobby, I think it is time to be concerned. This is clearly a global problem and it's spreading. I am not at all sure how we should tackle such a crisis, but on the basis of what we know so far, I would suggest, as a start, quarantining Texas.

I was thinking about all this as I sat now in a motorway services area on the M4 near Bristol. I was on my way to the far west of Wales, and was very much looking forward to it, let me tell you, but it's a long drive and I was hungry, so I thought I would treat myself to breakfast. I had rather touchingly supposed that I would be strolling with a tray through a brightly lit cafeteria called the Granary, with booths and shiny cutlery and a hearty if not hugely attractive choice of cooked foods, but it turns out that all the Granaries and other motorway restaurants are gone now. Today all you get are food courts served by fast food chains. I ended up with a biscuit filled with whatever they could find that was foodlike and bright yellow—I think it was called a Breakfast Crudwich— accompanied by a little bag of Potato Greasies and watery coffee in a paper cup.

As I sat nibbling my crudwich and worrying about the deterioration of the modern human mind, I pulled from my rucksack a document titled "Unskilled and Unaware of It: How Difficulties in Recognizing One's Own Incompetence Lead to Inflated Self-Assessments." This is the famous study by David Dunning and Justin Kruger of Cornell University in New York mentioned a few chapters ago that launched the new science of what we might call Stupidology.

It is an academic paper, so it comes with some impenetrable jargon—"metacognitive skills," "interrater correlation analysis," and so on—but its basic premise appears to be that if you are truly stupid you not only do things stupidly but are in all likelihood too stupid to realize how stupidly you are doing them. I can't pretend that I understood it all, which is worrying in a paper on stupidity, but some of it was a little technical. Consider this sentence: "Top-quartile participants did not, however, underestimate their raw score on the test, M = 16.9 (perceived) versus 16.4 (actual), t(18) = 1.37, ns." I read that eight or ten times, and all the sentences just before and after it, and I still cannot understand any of it beyond about the fourth word. However, I am at least aware that I don't understand it, which I gather indicates that I am just averagely stupid and not dangerously stupid.

Dunning and Kruger have unquestionably done groundbreaking work, but their paper was written in 1999 and world stupidity has raced ahead in the years since, as we have just seen in Texas. One clear shortcoming of the Dunning-Kruger study is that it gives no guidance on how to assess one's own mental acuity. This troubled me greatly, so as I returned to the open road and headed west into Wales, in a spirit of public service I constructed a checklist of ways to tell if you are becoming dangerously stupid yourself. This list isn't comprehensive by any means, but it should help you to decide whether your own situation is worrisome. Here are some questions to ask yourself:

In a Thai restaurant when your plate comes garnished with a decorative flower carved from a carrot, do you believe that yours is the only plate that flower has been on this week?

Do you think that if you pat your pockets enough times it will make a missing object reappear?

If someone wearing oven mitts brings food to the table and says, "Careful, the dish is very hot," do you touch it anyway, just to see if it is?

If you have been to a tanning parlor, do you think that because you cannot see that your eyelids are white no one else can?

If you are at a sporting event and you think a camera is trained on you, do you wave excitedly and call someone on your cell phone?

If you are waiting for an elevator that's slow to come, do you push the button again and again in the belief that that will speed things up?

In hotels, do you think you can operate the shower without experiencing the full range of temperature possibilities?

Do you sometimes spend $90 on a shirt with a little polo pony on it in the belief that that will somehow bring you a more rewarding sex life? (The people who sold you the shirt for $90 are having the rewarding sex life.)

Do you think that you can feed five or six coins into a vending machine without the last one always being rejected? Do you keep putting the rejected coin back in anyway?

Do you think you can write down a list of questions in a notebook balanced on your thigh while driving on a busy four-lane highway without drifting dangerously across one or sometimes two other lanes?

That's as far as I got, but I hope it is some help. We shall return to this subject when we get to Tenby, but for the moment let's leave all these angry motorists and turn onto the quiet and winding A4066 and follow it through the valley of the River Taf to the comely village of Laugharne.

The poet Dylan Thomas lived in Laugharne (pronounced *larn*) from 1949 to 1953 in a cottage called the Boathouse and did some of his best, and ultimately final, work there. I parked beneath the stately ruins of Laugharne Castle, and followed a helpful directional sign to a paved path along the broad, tidal estuary of the Taf and up onto a wooded hill. Here I came upon Thomas's famous writing hut, perched on the cliff edge. The hut is permanently locked, but you can look through the window. Inside, it is as if Thomas has just toddled off to Brown's Hotel in the village for a lunchtime refresher but will be back soon. It has a couple of wooden chairs, a table strewn with work, some shelves of books, wadded paper balls on the floor. The hut doesn't look very comfortable, but the setting is sublime. It was here, according to the

Boathouse website, that Thomas wrote *Under Milk Wood* and "Do Not Go Gentle into That Good Night" (though actually I think he wrote the poem earlier).

A short way beyond and no less beautifully situated is the Boathouse, where Thomas lived with his wife, Caitlin, and children after his friend and patron Margaret Taylor (wife of the historian A. J. P. Taylor) bought it for them, an act of startling generosity. Today it is a museum with lots of interesting Thomas memorabilia. It is very small, but snug and cheery. I thought it would be busy— 2014 was the centenary of Thomas's birth—but I was one of just three visitors.

On a wall upstairs was a front page from the *South Wales Argus* for November 10, 1953, reporting the death of Thomas in New York after a spectacular bender (though actually his whole life was a spectacular bender). The main story, however, concerned the mysterious disappearance of a farm couple, John and Phoebe Harries, from their eleven-acre holding just down the road in Pendine. Their bodies were found a week or so later in a shallow grave. They had been bludgeoned to death. A young but distant relative named Ronald Harries was subsequently tried and found guilty, and hanged the following spring, one of the last criminals to be executed in Wales. I thought it was interesting that all this got much more play in the *Argus* than the death of a drunken poet.

Seventeen miles around Carmarthen Bay from Laugharne is the old resort of Tenby. I had heard that it is a charming place, but in fact it is exquisite—full of pastel-colored houses, sweet-looking hotels and guesthouses, characterful pubs and cafés, glorious beaches and gorgeous views. It is everything you could want in a coastal retreat. How had this escaped me for so long?

Tenby stands on a steep-sided promontory high above its many beaches, which are reached by fetching zigzag paths, and seems bounded everywhere by water. The beaches are long and broad and, at the time of my visit, quite empty. I am not a beach person, as I think we have established, but these beckoned even for me.

The artist Augustus John was born in Tenby and spent a miserable childhood in a house on Victoria Street, just off the cliff-top Esplanade. John's mother died of rheumatic gout when he was just six (I have gout; nobody ever told me it was lethal) and he grew up in a house that was silent and gloomy, presided over by a grieving and unfeeling father. It is said that the young Augustus never showed any talent for art until at the age of seventeen while diving off some rocks at Tenby he smashed his head and emerged from the water "a bloody genius." That seems a little improbable—I have hit my head a lot and it has never improved anything—but in any case he cultivated drawing from that point and became so skilled that John Singer Sargent declared him the best draftsman since the Renaissance.

I walked up and down practically every street in Tenby and I don't think I passed a house or cottage that I wouldn't have been happy to own. I strolled the beaches and admired the boats in the harbor and the views to Caldey Island, two miles offshore.

Speaking of islands, here is an interesting fact. Nobody knows how many islands there are in the British Isles (an interesting vagueness given the name). The numbers have been variously put at anywhere between one thousand and four thousand or so. Partly it is a question of deciding where to draw the line between a large rock and a small island, and partly it is a question of tides (depending on when you look, you can find fifteen Farne Islands or twenty-six Farne Islands), and partly there is the problem that quite a number of islands are only kind of British. The Channel Islands, for instance, have a measure of autonomy that makes them quite separate from the rest of Britain. They have their own courts and postage stamps and set their own tax rates (at about the same level you or I would choose if we set our own tax rates). The citizens carry British passports but have no representation in Parliament and are not officially part of the United Kingdom. They are a "Peculiar of the British Crown." The same is true of the Isle of Man.

Once, for a magazine article, I asked the chief information officer at Ordnance Survey, the government department responsible for whatever geographical certainty Britain can muster, for a definitive figure for the number of British islands and he disappeared for several days. Eventually, after much hunting around, he told me that the closest he could find to an official figure was 1,330, but he frankly doubted that that was anywhere near right. I think it's rather charming that Britain doesn't quite know how much of itself there is.

Just after I was in Tenby, incidentally, Caldey Island made a rare appearance in the news when two visitors from my own dear native land decided to visit the island, and asked the satellite navigation system in their rental car to give them directions from Tenby. The sat-nav guided them down a boat ramp, onto the beach, and thence into the great zone of blue that lay beyond, and it seems they dutifully followed. I'd love to have heard the conversation inside the car as they made their way toward two miles of open sea. As it turned out, their car got bogged down in sand halfway across the beach, robbing them of the opportunity to become the first motorists in history to reach Caldey Island from underwater. The visitors declined to give their name to the local paper, though they did say they were from Illinois.

I trust you see what I'm saying. Matters are getting worse and they have spread beyond Texas.

In the morning, I drove on to St. David's, on the westernmost point of the Welsh mainland, above the rolling surf and crashing waves of St. Brides Bay. St. David's boast is that it is Britain's smallest city, which is really just another way of saying that it is the smallest place that has a cathedral. By any other measure, it's a village, but an adorable one, on a hill a little inland from the sea. It is very pretty and prosperous, with a butcher's, a National Trust shop, a tiny bookshop, several cafés.

The town and cathedral are named for the patron saint of Wales who was resident here a very long time ago. I knew nothing about him, so I looked him up in the *Oxford Dictionary of National Biography* before leaving home. I defy anyone to read the *Oxford DNB* entry on St. David and not lose consciousness by about a third of the way through. Here is a typical sentence: "Yet the declaration that David was predestined to sanctity was also designed to confirm the Augustinian orthodoxy of the hagiographer, Rhigyfarch, and to foreshadow the culmination of David's career at the Synod of Llanddewibrefi (second 7), when he preached against the Pelaginian heresy." What I was able to gather is that David lived in the sixth century and that the only interesting things about him were that he liked to stand up to his neck in cold water and that he was said to live to 147.

The cathedral is terrific and interesting. I was one of only two people there. The most striking thing to me was that the floor slopes quite conspicuously. If you put a marble down near the altar, it would roll pretty quickly into the northwest corner. I asked a steward, a genial and impressively well-informed gentleman named Philip Brenan, about this. "Yes, it is quite a slope," he agreed with enthusiasm, "and the interesting thing is that it must have been built that way intentionally because all the lintels and windowsills and so on are still perfectly horizontal. If the slope was from subsidence, they would have tilted too. So happily the slope doesn't indicate structural problems. But it is indeed strange."

He showed me some other oddities. The nave is bounded on both sides by arches, which are rounded and neatly symmetrical in the Romanesque style until you get to the very end when the last arch on either side abruptly takes on a pointed but clumsily asymmetrical gothic shape. He also indicated how the outer walls, when looked at closely, seem to be falling outward. "All this was done on purpose but no one knows why," he said.

The greatest curiosity of all is where the cathedral is built. It's at the bottom of a steep hill, in a depression, so that it is almost invisible till you get right upon it. The village, which came later, stands on the hillside above. It is as if the builders didn't want anyone to find them.

I spent a very happy morning exploring St. David's and the bewitching peninsula on which it stands. Nearly everywhere in Pembrokeshire the land ends in rounded cliffs, like the backs of whales, which provide the most striking and memorable views. It is about as lovely as a coast can get.

In the afternoon, I drove on to Fishguard, the place that I was most eager to see. I have a very fond memory of Fishguard, which is a little strange because I was only there for eight or nine hours forty years ago and I spent most of that time asleep. In the summer of 1973 when I was hitchhiking around Europe and was on my way to Ireland, some kindly truck driver dropped me in the town very late at night. I remember that I was by a little park opposite a row of shops, all with awnings. The streetlamp cast a stark light distinctly reminiscent of an Edward Hopper painting. It seemed a little corner of perfection. I looked around the upper town, but, finding nowhere better, I returned to the compact park, spread my sleeping bag, and slept on the dewy grass. In the morning, I woke very early, with Fishguard still asleep, and walked down a steep curving road to the harbor and caught the first ferry to Rosslare, in Ireland.

That was the entirety of my experience, but I was so curious to see it again now that I parked off the high street and went for a walk around the town before checking in to my guesthouse. Fishguard was an oddity, I have to say. Three large pubs on the main square were closed down—the Abergwaun Hotel, Farmers Arms, and Royal Oak—as was the Ship and Anchor up the road. Several shop premises were empty, yet Fishguard still had a bookshop, a florist, a craft-shop-and-café—the very kinds of places you would expect to be first to go when a town is not doing well. I found my sleeping place with difficulty. The little park I recalled was really just a patch of grass. The shops across the road were still there, but weren't in any way special. The awnings were long gone.

I stayed in the Manor Town House, a stylish guesthouse with entrancing sea views from all the back windows—quite the nicest guesthouse I stayed in on the trip. It was run by a friendly couple named Chris and Helen Sheldon. I chatted to Chris for quite a long time about Fishguard and west Wales generally. This part of Wales has a lot of economic problems—its GDP is just two-thirds the EU average, which is not all that spectacular in its own right since it includes places like Bulgaria and Romania—and yet it is a popular tourist area because of the beauty of the Pembrokeshire coast. So some places like Tenby and St. David's are prosperous and lovely, and some like Milford Haven and Haverfordwest are struggling, and a few like Fishguard don't quite know which camp they fall into.

Chris told me that the three pubs on the square had all failed recently, but that about half a dozen others had preceded them. Fortunately, one that survived was the tiny and exquisite Fishguard Arms, across the street. Five locals lounged comfortably in the front bar when I called in about half-past six. They looked surprised to find a stranger in their midst, but gave me amiable nods.

I retired with a beer to a small table in the corner. As I sat there, watching the golden bubbles of happiness rising in my glass, feeling awfully contented, I became aware that a man at the bar was looking at me in a not unfriendly way.

"You look like Bill Bryson," he said.

I never know quite how to answer that.

"Do I?" I said stupidly.

"I saw Bill Bryson at the Hay Festival two years ago and you do look quite like him."

You can see how powerfully I sear myself into people's consciousnesses. The man had spent ninety minutes in my company at a literary festival and still wasn't sure he recognized me.

The upshot is that I was outed, and I had to explain to them why I was in their fair little town, which elicited much interest. My new acquaintances couldn't have been more welcoming. From them I learned all about Fishguard and its history—people in pubs always know everything—including that it was the last place in Britain invaded by a foreign army. That was in 1797 when a large French force led by a seventy-year-old American named William Tate came ashore in the harbor below, hoping that the Welsh would join them in revolt. In fact, the people of Wales didn't like being invaded and fired guns at them. Since Tate's army was made up of criminals and men who had been pressed into service—and since, let's be frank, they were French—they surrendered more or less at once. Twelve invaders dropped their weapons and put their hands up when a farmer's wife pointed a musket at them. All the invaders, including apparently Tate, were sent back to France and told never to do anything like that again, and they didn't.

With warm feelings for Fishguard and the Fishguard Arms, and with one pint too many sloshing in my stomach, I bade my new friends farewell and toddled off in search of dinner.

In the morning, I drove down to the ferry terminal and had a look. It's rather a forlorn place now. When I sailed from there in the 1970s, nearly a million people a year passed through Fishguard's terminal. Today the number is 350,000 and falling. Now just two ferries a day go to Ireland and one of them leaves at two thirty in the morning. The other departs at two thirty in the afternoon. In between times, it seems, the place is dead.

I continued north to Aberystwyth, the main town along this stretch of coast, on a road between the sea and the Preseli Mountains. The hills were big and bleak, made bleaker by a sudden squally rain, which fell in sheets across the bare slopes. Somewhere in the crags above, now lost in gray swirl, was the outcrop from which the bluestones of Stonehenge came. It seemed to me beyond extraordinary that the people of Salisbury Plain would even know about stones high up in these remote hills, never mind decide to haul eighty of them home with them. There isn't anything about that ancient world that doesn't stagger.

Aberystwyth squatted, grim and gray, beneath a steady rain around a crescent bay. It is both an old seaside resort and a university town—one of several outposts of the University of Wales—which I thought might give it a certain perkiness, and perhaps it does in fine weather, but on this day of falling rain it was never going to be anything but miserable. There were no students on the streets—indeed, almost no people. I parked on the seafront and walked along its long, curving, lavishly puddled promenade. The prom had been battered by storms the previous winter and was being extensively reconstructed, but there were no workers visible, just idle machinery. At one end of the prom was a strikingly ugly pier. Photographs show that it was once quite lovely, but it has since been boxed in with what looked like painted plywood. How do people get permission to do these things? Beyond the pier was a headland with a big war memorial featuring a female figure with a curiously erotic air. I studied that for a minute, rain running down my neck, then went and had a cup of coffee. Then I shuffled around the town center pretending to look with interest in shopwindows, until I realized that this was ridiculous, so I squelched back to the car and returned to the road.

I drove inland past Devil's Bridge, a beauty spot, and on through two attractive old spa towns, Llandrindod Wells and Builth Wells, stopping from time to time to have a look around and get wet all over again, and finally in midafternoon headed for the Brecon Beacons. This is an area of big hills and lush valleys of an intense and celebrated beauty, though I could see hardly any of it because of the clinging mists and drifting rain. It was an altogether wretched day.

The radio was full of talk of the upcoming Scottish referendum, in which the Scots were to decide whether they wished to remain in the United Kingdom or not, and I wondered idly why the Welsh weren't more restive, too. They seem at least as marginalized as their Scottish cousins, and even more visibly a separate nation because of the Welsh language, whose wondrous agglomerations of consonants[*] are visible everywhere—in street signs, house names, and in Welsh programs on the radio and television. You even quite often hear people speaking Welsh, whereas in Scotland the number of people who seriously speak Gaelic would barely fill a shower stall.

Not so long ago, Wales was the more conspicuously disgruntled member of the British tribe. Between 1979 and 1993, some two hundred English-owned second homes in Wales were burned down or seriously damaged in politically motivated arson attacks. Only one man was ever held accountable, a fellow named Sion Roberts, who was sent to prison for seven years in 1993, but he could hardly have been the only one doing it since he was only seven years old when the attacks began. After Roberts's jailing the attacks abruptly ceased, and Wales returned to being tranquilly beautiful and entirely peaceful.

The Welsh had a referendum of their own in 1997 to decide on self-rule. It didn't exactly electrify the nation. Voter turnout was

---

[*] Just to give you an idea, the Welsh for "What's your name?" is "Be' ydy'ch enw chi?" and "Do you speak English?" is "Ydych chi'n siarad Saesneg?"

barely 50 percent, and the vote to create a semi-autonomous Welsh Assembly passed by just 6,700 votes, out of 1,116,000 votes cast.

The weather cleared as I headed through the big valleys to my final destination, the little town of Crickhowell. The mists thinned and vanished, the sky filled with a fleet of puffy clouds, and the sun poured golden light across the hillsides. In the west, a nearly perfect rainbow shimmered above the hills. Wales was glorious.

Crickhowell is a perfect community, charming, prosperous, well preserved, with good shops and streets of pretty cottages. I checked into my hotel, the Bear, an old coaching inn, then went straight out to stretch my legs and enjoy being dry. The one problem with Crickhowell is that it is bombarded with traffic. All the routes out of the village seemed to turn into busy highways, unpleasant and difficult to stroll along, but at length I found my way down to the little River Usk and followed a path along the north bank through the valley. It was intensely beautiful.

Looking at my trusty Ordnance Survey map, I was slightly shocked to realize that just over the hills before me was the Rhondda Valley, once home of the greatest concentration of coal mines in the world. Among the communities was the famously tragic Aberfan, cruelly devastated by a landslide in 1966. I remember very clearly sitting at a kitchen table three thousand miles away, reading with horror about the sudden death of teachers and schoolchildren. I was fourteen years old and I think it may have been the only time in my adolescence that I interrupted my own enormous self-absorption to think about others.

I couldn't remember many of the details now, but later back in my room I looked on the Internet. The story is simply told: one morning in October 1966, the people of Aberfan heard a terrible rumbling and looked up to see tens of thousands of tons of mining waste crashing down upon them. Years of mining spoil, casually heaped on a slope above the village, had broken loose. It wiped out the local school and much of the neighborhood around. One hundred and sixteen children and twenty-eight adults perished. Had the landslide happened a half hour earlier, the school would have been empty and nearly all those lives would have been spared. Had it happened the following day, the children would have been on half-term holiday and no one at all would have been hurt. They couldn't have been unluckier.

Lord Robens, head of the National Coal Board, didn't go to Aberfan at once, but instead stopped at the University of Surrey to receive an honor, an act of callous indifference. He refused to accept any blame, personal or collective, for the disaster. People from all over the world sent money to help Aberfan rebuild, but the NCB gave only £500 from the disaster fund to each family that lost a child, and only after making them prove that they were actually close to their children. At the same time, the NCB secretly appropriated £150,000 from the fund to clean up the mess that its own negligence had created. An inquiry later found the NCB wholly responsible for the landslide, and it paid the money back. No one was ever punished for all those deaths.

And with that melancholy thought floating through my head, I went to the hotel bar and had a very quiet beer before dinner.

Chapter 21

The North

ONE OF THE THINGS I noticed almost at once when I first came to Britain was how quiet it was. The United States, for all its other virtues, exists in a permanent din. It is a noisy country. We are noisy people. Our voices carry. You can sit in a crowded restaurant in America and follow every conversation in the room. If a guy fifty feet away has hemorrhoids, you're going to know about it. You're probably going to know what kind of unguent he is using and whether he applies it with two fingers or three. (We are medically candid as well.)

Noise is everywhere in America. Waitresses shout orders to the cook. Bus drivers shout at passengers. Check-in clerks bark: "Next in line!" Baristas at Starbucks shout: "Conchita, your order's ready!" (I prefer not to give them my real name.) Disembodied voices in big stores ceaselessly hector you to take up their special offers or fill the air with thinly coded messages that someone's having a heart attack in housewares. ("Attention: horizontal event in aisle seven.") Moving walkways tell you over and over again that you are coming to the end and need to prepare yourself for independent locomotion.

England was so quiet in comparison. The whole country was like a big library. Even airport announcements were preceded by a gentle *bing-bong* sound, soothing in itself, followed by a soft female voice telling you that the 15:34 to Kuala Lumpur was now boarding. And there was such politeness, too. The voices in England didn't order you to do something. They invited you to make your way.

All that is gone now. Today Britain is noisy, too, thanks mostly to cell phones. It's a strange thing, but people in Britain still whisper when sharing a confidence face to face, but give them a cell phone, a seat in a railway car, and a sexually transmitted disease and they'll share the news with everyone. I was on a packed rush-hour train from Swindon to London a while back when some idiot farther down the car put a conversation on speakerphone. The whole car could hear every word loud and clear. It was actually quite fascinating. You don't usually get to hear both ends of a conversation, particularly when both parties are cretins. The man at our end was evidently seated with colleagues—they appeared to be returning from a regional meeting—and was speaking to another colleague back at the office. The banter between them was excruciating. I can't remember anything at all of the conversation except that at one point the man back at the office said, in a hearty voice, "So how's the fat slag?" and suddenly the speakerphone was switched off and the conversation became much quieter. It appeared that the man in the office didn't know he was on speakerphone. All of us in my area beamed happily and returned to our reading. Nothing brings the English together like witnessing a deserving humiliation.

I was thinking about this now because I was on a train from London to Liverpool and I was surrounded by people on cell phones. Behind me, unseen but nearby, a young woman was holding an intense and apparently endless conversation with a friend that appeared to involve saying everything three times: "He's a knob. He's a total knob. I've told you a million times, Amber, he's a total knob . . . I told her, but she wouldn't listen. She never listens. She never listens to anything . . . But then that's just Derek, isn't it? That's Derek all over. Derek's never going to change. He's a knob . . ."

Across the aisle, a young woman was having exactly the same conversation but in a Slavic language. Once, I would have been helplessly trapped with these people, but now I can do something about it. I rooted in my rucksack and pulled out a small zippered case containing noise-reduction headphones—the very model I had played with at John Lewis in Cambridge recently. I had told my wife about them and she had bought me a pair as a surprise, as an anniversary present. I really wanted a red sports car, but that's OK. The headphones are miraculous. It's like being back in the Britain I used to know. I don't listen to music or anything recorded. I just enjoy the silence. It's lovely—like being adrift in outer space.

The woman across the aisle was still talking away but now I saw only silently moving lips. Looking around, I noticed that nearly everyone around me had wires dangling from their ears.

I turned on my laptop. "Installing update 911 of 19,267," it told me.

So instead I closed my eyes and just drifted through space, like Sandra Bullock in *Gravity*, but calmer. The next thing I knew we were in Liverpool and my installation was nearly complete.

I was in Liverpool for a soccer match: Everton v. Manchester City. I can't pretend that this was an event of huge moment to me, or even necessarily to many people who follow English soccer, but it was a big deal for my son-in-law Chris, who lives and dies for Everton. This is a trifle odd as he grew up two hundred miles away in Somerset. He became an Everton supporter simply because Everton (which I should note is an area of Liverpool) won the first match he ever watched on TV and because he quite liked their blue uniform. (He was ten years old.) I find that endearing and pathetic in roughly equal measure. In all his years of support, he had never seen Everton play at home, so for his birthday his dear wife, my dear daughter, had bought him four tickets to today's match: for him, his two little boys, and for me. It was going to be a guys' day out. I was very excited.

Chris and his boys—Finn, aged eight, and Jesse, six—had traveled up from London the day before, so we had arranged to meet in the city center for lunch. I spied them walking toward me up Chapel Street, all three of them dressed, without embarrassment, as if for a competition called "How Many Things Can You Wear That Say 'Everton' on Them?" They would easily have won for they were the only people in the center of Liverpool wearing anything at all with "Everton" written on it. You soon discover that Everton Football Club is something of a secret even in its own city.

We had lunch, then took a cab to the grounds, or at least to within about half a mile of the grounds, which is as close as it could get on a match day. Here there were tens of thousands of people dressed in Everton jerseys, scarves, hats, and other tribal regalia—a sight that staggered my two grandsons. These boys live in outer London, more than two hundred miles from Liverpool. Every one of their friends supports a London team like Chelsea or Arsenal. They had never seen another Everton fan before, and now here were forty thousand of them. It was as if they had died and gone to heaven, albeit a heaven populated largely by people with enormous bellies and neck tattoos.

Everton Football Club isn't actually in Everton. It's in Walton, a neighboring district full of boarded-up pubs, mean-terraced houses, and vacant lots filled with builders' rubble. If you do an Internet search for "Walton, Liverpool," what comes up is a succession of entries like "Two men arrested after stabbing in Walton," "Off-license in Walton targeted by ram-raiders," and "Walton burglary gang jailed." I had never seen an area quite this rough at first hand in Britain. I stayed close to Chris. He's a London policeman and, more to the point, retired Metropolitan Police Force middle-weight boxing champion. The boys and I held his jacket.

Everton's ground is Goodison Park, which is not merely the most venerable stadium in English soccer, but in the world. It was built in 1892 and is evidently the oldest surviving purpose-built soccer ground anywhere. This sounds charming but what it means in practice is that even places like Liberia and Burkina Faso have more modern, up-to-date stadiums. Still, because of its cherished history, we assumed reverential countenances as we entered the stadium and found our way to the tiny vise-like numbered spaces that are called seats. They were unbelievably uncomfortable and so narrow that I could sit on only one buttock at a time, but eventually both cheeks became so numb that I lost any active awareness of discomfort.

And so the match began. I do love a live sporting match. I had brought some small binoculars and I spent much of the first half looking at all the peripheral things that aren't shown to you when you watch on television, like what the goalkeepers do when play is at the other end of the field (stand there with their hands at their sides and occasionally jump up and down once or twice, then do some neck rolls, then stand some more) or what the players do when the ball is nowhere near them. I particularly liked watching the linesmen run sideways up and down the sidelines, as if imitating a giraffe.

I noticed, as I have often noticed at English soccer matches, that I was the only person in the stadium enjoying himself. The rest of the spectators, on both sides, were perpetually stressed and dismayed. A man behind me was simply full of despair.

"Now why did he do that?" he would say. "What was he *thinking*? Why didn't he *pass* it?"

His companion seemed to have some issues with eighteenth-century German metaphysics because he kept saying over and over, "Fucking Kant." I am not quite sure how he was relating this to the actions before us, but every time Everton failed to score he called them a "load of fucking Kants."

"Oh, now why did they do that?" said the despairing man.

"Because they're fucking Kants," replied his partner bitterly.

At halftime the score was 0–0. Naively I said to Chris, "Well, you must be reasonably happy with that," for Everton was the underdog, and he said: "Are you kidding? We had *so* many missed chances. We were just rubbish." He looked wretched.

In the second half, Manchester City scored a goal, leaving us sitting in suicidal silence, but then Everton came back and drew level and it was like Mardi Gras. When the referee blew the final whistle with the score 1–1, I thought honor had been satisfied, but we were gloomy once more at our end of the pitch.

I chose to look on the bright side.

"It is, after all, just a game," I pointed out philosophically.

"Fucking Kant," said the man behind me, still philosophical himself.

In the evening, Chris and the boys and I walked around the city center and were dazzled, as all visitors to Liverpool are these days, for the whole place has been practically rebuilt. At the heart of the city now is the Liverpool One development—forty-two acres of stylish new apartments, restaurants, cinemas, hotels, department stores, and shops. It is like a new city. We dined at a Pizza Express restaurant and generally partied wildly, as four guys on the town do, until about 8:30 p.m., when we returned to the hotel and called it a night.

After breakfast the next morning, I walked with Chris and the boys to Lime Street station, where they were catching a train back to London. I had more of Liverpool I wished to see and walked out past the Anglican cathedral to a neighborhood known as the Welsh Streets.

John Prescott, a voluble and mystifyingly successful politician who was elected deputy leader during the last Labour government, had a mad plan, called the Pathfinder Initiative, to tear down four hundred thousand homes, mostly Victorian and Edwardian terraced houses, in the North of England. Prescott claimed, on no evidence, that house prices there were too low because of an oversupply of stock. Mercifully, Prescott didn't have the brains or focus to complete the plan, but he still managed to spend £2.2 billion of public money and bulldoze thirty thousand houses before he was stopped. So at precisely the time that one part of the government was talking about the need to build hundreds of thousands of new homes, another part of the same government was trying to tear down as many of them as it could. You simply can't get madder than that.

Nowhere were Prescott's demented ambitions more keenly pursued than on Merseyside where forty-five hundred houses, nearly all comfortably lived in and doing no harm, were compulsorily purchased and swept away. Amazingly, the local council is still trying to tear down homes, mostly in the Welsh Streets district (so called because the streets have Welsh names) on the edge of Princes Park. It is a neighborhood of snug and settled terraced houses of the sort that people pay fortunes for in Fulham or Clapham in London. But here the houses are empty, their doors and windows blanked off with metal plates, as they await a needless destruction. It is a seriously dispiriting sight. So I strolled back to town through the university quarter, where the housing is pleasant and appreciated, and Liverpool doesn't seem like a city run by idiots.

I returned to Lime Street station to catch a train to Birkenhead Park, across the Mersey. I couldn't see from the departures board how to get there, so I asked at the information desk and the young man who served me was an American, which fairly astounded me.

We ended up talking about the Chicago White Sox, which I believe may be a first at a British Rail information booth. He pointed me in the right direction, and twenty minutes later I was at the main entrance to Birkenhead Park.

It is a typical large Victorian city park, with playgrounds and playing fields, some woodlands, a picturesque lake with a boat-house and rustic bridge. Couples walked, dogs and children scampered, men in shorts chased after a rolling ball on a soccer field. It was a pleasant, wholly conventional urban park on a Sunday morning, but Birkenhead has one special feature: it is the oldest city park in the world.

It was designed by the great Joseph Paxton, former head gardener at Chatsworth, and laid out to resemble the grounds of a stately home. It opened in 1847 on 125 acres of former wasteland. It is almost impossible to imagine now what a novelty this was. There were parks of a sort already, mostly in London, mostly on royal land like Kensington Gardens and Regent's Park, but admission was limited, tacitly or even sometimes explicitly, to people of an elevated class. Birkenhead was purpose-built for the amusement of all people, and it was an immediate success.

Four years after it opened, Frederick Law Olmsted, an American journalist, was on a walking tour of the north of England when he stopped at a Birkenhead bakery and the proprietor urged him to go and have a look at their new park. Olmsted was so taken with what he found that he went back to America and became a landscape architect. He designed Central Park in New York City, then went on to build more than a hundred other parks all over North America. So this was the template from which all other public parks are descended, rather a remarkable thought.

Back at Lime Street station, I boarded a train for Manchester. We trundled through a featureless landscape of boggy-looking farms and worn-out suburbs. You would never think it (I was having a day of "you would never think its") but this was perhaps the most historic stretch of railway on the planet, where the very first passenger trains ever ran, on thirty-three miles of track linking Liverpool with Manchester.

My interest was to do with a forgotten nineteenth-century politician named William Huskisson, who was once widely esteemed—at one point he was even tipped to be prime minister—but is remembered now chiefly for being the first person in history killed by a train. The occasion for this emphatic milestone was the official opening of the Liverpool and Manchester Railway, the line I was on right now, on September 15, 1830. Eight hundred of the most eminent people in Europe, led by Britain's prime minister, the Duke of Wellington, came to Liverpool for the entirely novel experience of riding a man-made conveyance at speed. They were loaded, chattering, onto eight separate trains.

Near the halfway point, at Newton-le-Willows, Huskisson's train stopped to take on water. Most of the passengers got off to stretch their legs and chat. As they stood alongside the tracks, George Stephenson's *Rocket*, the fastest and most famous train of its day, came hurtling toward them on a parallel line at twenty miles an hour. It takes a little imagination now to conceive of people being confused and put to flight by the approach of a train at twenty miles an hour, but of course they had never seen a machine moving laterally and it left them a touch disoriented, Huskisson most of all. He moved about in contrary directions, and somehow managed to get himself between the train and where it was going, with predictably grisly consequences.

Dreadfully mangled, he was lifted onto the train that had just struck him and rushed to Eccles, the nearest town. As the *Rocket* sped onward, Huskisson had the satisfaction, if he could feel any, of knowing that he and his fellow passengers were now traveling faster than any humans had ever gone before—thirty-five miles an hour. Huskisson was taken to the vicarage at Eccles, where he was attended by a local doctor, but his injuries were too severe and he died that evening.

A few hundred yards beyond Newton-le-Willows station, on the right-hand side as you travel toward Manchester, is a memorial to Huskisson, fixed to the wall of a little service building, at the spot where he met his tragic fate. The memorial is only visible from a passing train, and you have to look out carefully for it. I watched as the monument flashed past—much too fast to read—very possibly the only person on the train who knew the history of this line, even more possibly the only one who cared, very certainly the only one who wasn't listening to music or shouting at a child.

Fifty thousand people lined the funeral route for Huskisson in Liverpool, and the city's shops and factories shut for the day as a mark of respect. Seventeen years after his death, his widow commissioned a statue of Huskisson, incongruously dressed in a Roman toga, and presented it to Lloyd's of London, the insurance market. Lloyd's didn't really want it and, once Mrs. Huskisson was safely dead, gave it to the London County Council, which didn't want it either, but found a home for it in Pimlico Gardens, one of the smallest and least visited parks in London, where for the past one hundred years it has been prized as a lavatory by pigeons but otherwise not noticed much at all. And that, I think, is as it should be.

At Manchester Piccadilly station, I went to the men's room for a pee (it's what I generally do first upon arriving anywhere these days) and discovered that it now costs 30p to wee in Manchester. Even more annoyingly, the turnstiles into the men's room don't give change and only accept 10p and 20p coins. How hard can it be to make a machine that gives back 20p if you put in 50p? Really, how hard?

Sighing, I went to the food court area to buy a cup of tea in order to acquire the proper assortment of small coins, and as I was hungry I bought a sandwich, too. I paid takeaway prices even though I took the food to a seat just ten feet away, a shorter journey than I often take when dining in. It seems a little strange to be taxed on the basis of whether you have passed through a door or not. I have to say I have never understood the concept of Value Added Tax anyway. Consider my sandwich. Where's the added value? I'm certainly not adding any. With every bite I take, I must be reducing its value, until finally there is no sandwich at all and no value either. Clearly, any added value is coming from the sandwich vendor. So why am I paying their tax? You see why I'm confused?

The idea of charging tax on food eaten in a restaurant but not on food taken away from it is completely backward, if you ask me. It rewards people for taking packaging out into the wider world where much of it ends up as litter, and imposes a surcharge on those whose leftovers are responsibly disposed of indoors and whose plates and silverware are more likely to be washed and reused. That seems the wrong way around to me. Altogether, Britons spend £12 billion a year on takeaway food. VAT on that would raise £2.4 billion. You could build a lot of schools and hospitals with that, or just sweep up streets more effectively. Perhaps you could use it to buy some litter bins. There is no country in the developed world—not one—that has fewer litter bins on its streets than Great Britain. And there is not one country in the developed world—again, not one—that has more litter on the ground than Great Britain. Does anyone here see a relationship?

VAT on food would be just the first of many new taxes I would bring in. I would also introduce male jewelry tax, stupid ponytail tax, carrying an open umbrella even though it's stopped raining tax, texting while walking tax, earphone music leakage tax, walking much too slowly in crowded places tax, tattoos on knuckles tax, dribbled paint on the pavement tax, answering a question by

305

saying "how long is a piece of string?" tax, having an irritatingly small dog tax, and vending machines that don't give change tax. Taken together, I believe these would erase the national deficit within months.

As I sat eating my sandwich, I watched people coming and going through the 30p toilet turnstiles across the way. All three turnstiles were constantly engaged. I estimated that one person went through each turnstile every ten seconds. That's £5.40 a minute, over £3,000 a day. If you figure, conservatively, that the turnstiles are active for ten hours a day, six days a week, that comes to roughly £1 million a year, just to let people pee, giving a whole new meaning to the expression "income stream." I wouldn't tax that money. I would appropriate it.

I had decided already not to stay in Manchester. It was a Sunday and I couldn't face spending a Sunday evening wandering around a dead city center. I wrote about Manchester at some length in *Notes from a Small Island*, and I have been back many times since, and I am happy to state here for the record that Manchester is vastly improved from what it used to be. You should go and see it yourself. Just don't go on a Sunday.

I had somewhere else I wanted to be: Alderley Edge. I had read in *The Economist* that Alderley Edge is one of the ten richest towns in England, with seven hundred high-net-worth individuals (which is another way of saying millionaires) in a population of forty-six hundred. Alderley Edge is in pretty countryside fifteen miles south of Manchester and is famous as the home of many famous soccer players. Among those who live or have lived there are Cristiano Ronaldo, Rio Ferdinand, Carlos Tevez, David Beckham, and Wayne Rooney. If a Google news search is any guide, many of them seem to spend their time crashing Ferraris, collecting speeding fines, or doing something to their houses that their neighbors don't want them to do. But many of them live quietly, too. I once met someone who lived in Alderley Edge at the same time the Beckhams did, and she told me that they often saw them in the local supermarket or on the high street, just going about their business. This was in the days when David Beckham couldn't step out of a limousine anywhere in the world without being mobbed, but at home in Alderley Edge he could walk around just like a normal person. I thought that was grand.

I was delighted to find that Alderley Edge is a very attractive place, with a handsome, well-maintained high street. It doesn't have a bookshop or a huge amount in the way of practical businesses like ironmongers or butchers, but it was dazzlingly well provisioned with cafés, bistros, and wine bars. I thought it would be like Beverly Hills, filled with overwrought houses with high walls and automated gates, but there wasn't much of that at all. Most of the houses were big, but not ostentatious, and on the whole seemed reasonably restrained and tasteful. In a strange way, it was disappointing and comforting at the same time.

In the evening, I called in at a pub called the De Trafford and was pleased to find a table with some discarded sections of weekend newspapers on it. I don't usually read English newspapers anymore, so it was a bit of a treat.

I decided to give up newspapers a few years ago after reading a long news story in *The Times* about a journalism student at a college in Cornwall who had come up with an idea to go to the United States and challenge all those zany laws that we all know exist there. The article helpfully gave thirteen examples of these amusing laws—that it is illegal to fall asleep in a cheese factory in South Dakota; that it is illegal to say "Oh, boy," in Jonesborough, Georgia; that it is illegal in Carmel, New York, for a man to go outside wearing a jacket and trousers that do not match; that it is against the law to take a lion to the movies in Baltimore, Maryland; and so on. The idea, *The Times* reported, was that the student would travel all across America, get himself arrested repeatedly for breaking the laws, then come home and write a book about it.

It happened that at this time I had been invited by a friend at City University in London to deliver their annual lecture on the practice of journalism, so I decided to look into this particular article as a way of discussing the commitment to accuracy of the British press. I got in touch with twelve of the thirteen places cited by *The Times* and inquired about their odd laws. I couldn't find anyone to contact in Jonesborough, Georgia, because there is no Jonesborough, Georgia. For the others, I phoned or wrote to the police chief or mayor or whoever else seemed most likely to have an answer. In two cases, I couldn't get a response from anybody. In all the others, the local officials assured me that there was no such law and never had been. As someone from the Baltimore mayor's office explained, if you take a lion into a movie theater there you can expect to be arrested, but they have never enacted a statute for that specific offense for the obvious reason that it is unnecessary. All the laws, in short, were made up.

So if we consider the article again, the situation we have is that a young journalism student who hadn't gone to America, hadn't written the book, hadn't been arrested, and hadn't gotten a single one of his facts right still managed to get almost a full page of coverage in *The Times* of London. I would give that boy an A. As for the *Times* news editors, I think somebody should sit down and have a little chat with them.

Now I am not quite so shallow that I would stop reading newspapers over one foolish article, but I did stop reading them regularly and quickly discovered that I didn't miss them very much at all. There was a time when the highlight of my week was coming home with the *Sunday Times* and *Observer* and sitting down to read amusing reports from far-flung places by Clive James or television reviews by Julian Barnes or long essays by Martin Amis. In those days, the most gifted scribblers in Britain worked for the newspapers. I don't want to be dismissive of a whole generation's journalistic endeavors, but, well, just look at the weekend papers now. I picked up one of the magazines.

"If yellow is good enough for Amal Clooney, it's good enough for Anna Murphy," read the strapline on the lead article. Now I have nothing whatever against either of these people. I don't know anything about them and hope they have nothing but happiness in their lives. But with respect to what color clothing they'll be wearing this summer, I don't give a paramecium's shit.

"I learned early on never to wear yellow," confided Ms. Murphy in the opening sentence of her report, then with candor added: "Which just goes to show how much I used to know." That was too overpowering a thought for me to try to assimilate, so I turned the page and found an article suggesting sixteen ways to "pimp up" my salads. I took a moment to wonder what my wife would say if I suggested to her that we should pimp up our salads. Elsewhere I found guidance on what to look for in facial serums (a very big price tag apparently), how to acquire a sexy pout, a solemn report on transgender issues which was really an excuse to run some new pictures of Bruce Jenner in drag, and much more in similar vein. Is it really just me getting old or is it actually the case that all people under the age of thirty are basically now about ten years old? I looked at a couple of other weekend sections and they were much the same, so I put the papers to one side and pulled a book from my bag and read it instead.

I do have a little David Beckham story, by the way. It involves my publisher and friend Larry Finlay, whom we last encountered, eyes pulsating, in the prologue. Well, one day not long ago, Larry had been to the London Book Fair and stopped for a drink on his way home at a pub in Maida Vale. He was sitting at a table reading a manuscript when somebody said:

"Do you mind if we sit here with you, Larry?"

Larry looked up and it was David Beckham with another man.

"Of course," said Larry in amazement and moved his papers to give them some space.

"Thanks, Larry," said David Beckham.

"How do you know my name?" asked Larry, mystified but proud to be recognized.

"Because it says 'Larry' on your name badge, Larry," David Beckham said brightly.

They had a nice chat and Larry told me that David Beckham was an extremely nice man. And I can tell you sincerely that I was very, very pleased to hear that.

I thought about that happy story now as I sat with my book and my pint, secretly hoping that somebody famous would come in and sit near me, until gradually it dawned on me that I wouldn't actually recognize them because I don't read newspapers any-more.

Chapter 22

Lancashire

I

I TRAVELED BY TRAIN to Preston, then transferred to another so rattling and threadbare that I think it may have begun its life in a coal mine.

Outside, an endless run of industrial estates and general cruddiness flashed past and then suddenly we were in a little oasis of comeliness: Lytham. I disembarked to find myself at a strikingly handsome station—actually a former station, now converted into a bistro, but with a still-functioning platform. Just beyond, leading into the town, was a small park.

Lytham is a neat little town of rosy red brick: prosperous, neat as a pin, comfortably Victorian, with a great sward of lawn standing between the town and the estuary of the River Ribble on which sits a picturesque white windmill with black blades. Beyond, across the shiny mudflats, were hazy views to the town of Southport, ten miles or so to the south.

I dropped my bags at the Clifton Park Hotel overlooking the sward, and immediately set off on foot for Blackpool, the most celebrated and traditionally raucous of English seaside resorts, eight miles along the coast. It was a trek, but splendid. The seafront was lined with a paved promenade all the way to St. Anne's, another little outpost of coastal elegance. The sky was gray and heavy, like a pile of wet towels, but the day was dry and the sea air felt great. I was very happy.

You see Blackpool long before you reach it, thanks to the distant eminence of Blackpool Tower, Lancashire's answer to (and near replica of) the Eiffel Tower. Blackpool Tower is actually only about half the height of the original, but it seems as big because it is so solitary and striking, and it is nearly as venerable. It was built just five years after the Eiffel Tower went up.

Blackpool has a spanking new promenade. The town spent £100 million upgrading it in recent years, mostly to improve sea defenses, but the exercise also gave the town two miles of broad, artfully sinuous, thoroughly pleasing walkway. It isn't so much a promenade as a piece of sculpture that you walk on. It curves and dips, divides into multiple levels, incorporates ramps that must be wonderful for skateboarding, and steps that can serve as seats. It is the nicest promenade in the world, as long as you keep your gaze fixed firmly out to sea and don't look over your shoulder at the town facing it, for poor old Blackpool isn't much to look at these days.

When I first came to Britain, 20 million people—equivalent to a third of the national population—visited Blackpool each year. Now it is fewer than half that. Blackpool has always been cheerfully downmarket, but in those days it was good-natured and fun. Today it is depressed and half derelict, its streets empty by day and intimidating by night.

According to the *Blackpool Gazette*, more than a hundred business premises in the middle of town were empty. One hundred and fifty hotels were for sale. A short while before, the *Guardian* had declared the New Kimberley Hotel, a once-proud establishment on the seafront, the worst hotel in Britain. The owner, Peter Metcalf, had just been jailed for eighteen months for a string of serious safety breaches, including having no fire alarms, nailing shut fire-escape doors, and supplying water to only half the hotel's ninety rooms. This followed an earlier conviction for twenty food hygiene offenses.

All the statistics for Blackpool are depressing. It lost almost 11 percent of its jobs between 2004 and 2013, making it one of the three worst-performing towns in the country. In 2013 it was declared the unhealthiest community in Britain. It has the highest proportion of alcohol-related deaths. Forty percent of pregnant women in Blackpool smoke. Men die five years earlier than they do elsewhere in Britain. Like many other seaside towns it has become a sink for deprived people. The patrons of the New Kimberley Hotel weren't holidaymakers. Those people stopped coming long ago. They were the indigent and semi-homeless who stayed in a squalid, dangerous fleapit because it was all they could afford. At the rate Blackpool is going, soon that is all there will be.

That is a pity because Blackpool should be a pleasure. The air is invigorating, the views lovely, the beaches vast. Blackpool Tower remains one of the jauntiest structures in Britain. The town has two piers, the world's most ornate and luscious ballroom, its venerable amusement park, some good theaters, and a lot of fine Victorian architecture.

All Blackpool needs is to make itself safe and wholesome again, and give people worthwhile things to spend their money on—some decent shops, amusing shows, a selection of clean and inviting restaurants. Here is a really zany idea. Why not have the government get involved? The things Blackpool needs to do—smarten itself up, create decent jobs, improve its facilities, make itself appealing to respectable visitors—are things that are clearly best achieved with a big, well-directed master plan involving grants and incentives and targeted investment. What is actually happening? Well, according to a *Guardian* report, Blackpool's principal recent big idea for regeneration is to introduce an improved park-and-ride scheme and to provide charging points for electric cars in its main parking lots. Somehow I don't think that is going to swing it.

The first thing I would do if I were put in charge of Blackpool (and I am not saying I want to be put in charge of a place where the number one activity is drinking a lot of beer and the number two activity is throwing it up again) would be to bring back the traditional seaside shows. These have changed in a most dismaying way. All along the front were advertisements for shows that featured either Elvis or Queen tribute acts or comedy revues with names like Cirque du Hilarious starring people that no one has ever heard of (almost certainly for a reason). Something very important has been lost.

Years ago, I spent a month in Blackpool for a *National Geographic* assignment, and I made a point to take in all the shows. I particularly remember a popular comedy duo called Little and Large, who at the time were big television stars. They were splendid: quick-witted, likable, and absolutely expert at engaging with the audience, with a quip for every person's profession or hometown or spouse or style of dress. I have never had so much fun in a theater. Afterward I interviewed them backstage and was taken aback by how drained they looked. Eddie Large (who had a heart transplant soon afterward—no wonder he looked tired) made the point that there was no one coming up behind them, that they were in effect the last music-hall performers. I didn't think much of it at the time, but he was of course right.

After that, I took our younger children to seaside shows from time to time, and they were always great. We saw a children's act called the Krankies at the Pavilion Theatre in Bournemouth, for instance, and it was delightful. The music was loud and infectious, the jokes broad but enjoyable, the support acts deft and accomplished. The whole thing moved along at a noisy, lively clip and was done with considerable polish. It was something the British did superlatively well, and now it is all gone. I find that very sad.

I walked quite some distance along the front, past one dying hotel after another. It would soon be time for the curious spectacle known as the Illuminations. This consists simply of the town switching on a zillion strings of colored lightbulbs all along the seafront early every autumn as a way of extending the summer season a little. The Illuminations date from a time when electricity was exciting, but somehow the tradition has survived and remains an attraction. But this innocent pastime of yore has come increasingly to clash with the new Blackpool tradition of drinking and being menacing. Three days after my visit some five hundred youths gathered in the center of town and began to destroy property at random. Loose objects were picked up and hurled at the police. What exactly provoked this outburst of high spirits wasn't specified in the press, but presumably it involved the volatile chemical reaction you get when you combine strong beer with small brains. Three policemen were hurt and twelve youths aged thirteen to twenty-two were arrested. And Blackpool took another step toward suicide.

I retraced my route to Lytham. When I reached the end of the Promenade, I turned and had a last look. The lights in the seafront amusements were just coming on. The Tower stood grandly above the town. From a distance, Blackpool looked great.

It was quite late, getting on toward evening, when I shuffled back into Lytham, and I was tired, but fortunately there was an excellent and restorative pub called the Taps just behind my hotel and an Indian restaurant called Moshina's (hygiene rating of five—well done, fellows) a door or two down from it, and the combination of these two left me with warm feelings toward Lytham and the world for some distance beyond. I had a little stroll through the town after dinner and was delighted to find that Lytham on close inspection was even better than on my earlier flying appraisal. It had terrific old-fashioned shops. I was particularly taken with a menswear palace called George Ripley's. It was gloriously of another age—the kind of place that sold cardigans with stripes and chevrons, sweaters with zippered pockets, ties with patterns that look like champagne bubbles on hallucinogens, jackets with pointed collars that could be used as weapons in a street fight. I didn't wish to own any of these clothes—I am a Splendesto man myself, as we know—but I was very pleased to find that there are evidently still people in the world who do want them. Long may Mr. Ripley prosper, say I.

Nearby was "Tom Towers' Tasty Cheese Shop, est. 1949," which I thought was impressively venerable until I came across Whelan's Fish and Chips, "est. 1937." They both looked awfully nice. The town also boasted an old-fashioned department store called Stringers and a good-looking bookshop, Plackitt and Booth.

On the basis of all this, I nominated Lytham as best small town in the north of England, and in a spirit of celebration I wheeled into a cheery-looking establishment called the Ship and Royal for a quick one before bedtime.

II

One of the things that impresses me about Belgium—and we are of course dealing here with a very short list—is how reliable the train timetables are. You can be confident not only that the 14:02 to Ghent will be on time, but that it will always arrive at and depart from platform two, and no other. The platform numbers are printed on the timetables; that's how confident they are.

The people who run Britain's rail network take a slightly more relaxed approach to getting people from place to place. I remember one day at King's Cross station in London, not long after we moved to Norfolk in 2003, I found that the ticket machines wouldn't give me a ticket to Wymondham, my nearest station, so I went and stood in a long line and explained the problem to a man who had once answered a British Rail ad that said: "Wanted: cheerless bastard to deal with public."

"You have to go to Liverpool Street for trains to Wye-mund-ham," he said flatly, mispronouncing the name. (It's pronounced *win-dum*.) "Trains from Wye-mund-ham don't go from here."

"Well, for the past month I have been going to Wymondham from here via Cambridge," I replied.

"Can't do that," he said.

"Do you mean I physically can't do it or that it isn't permitted?"

"Both."

"But I have been doing it. Look," I said and dug out an old ticket that stated clearly: "Wymondham to London stations via Cambridge."

He studied the ticket but refused to allow it to be entered into evidence.

"So what's it going to be?" he said. "People are waiting."

I sighed and told him just to give me a ticket to Cambridge.

"You won't get to Wye-mund-ham from there," he promised darkly.

"I'll take my chances," I answered, and he shrugged and gave me a ticket. At Cambridge, I bought another ticket on to Wymondham but missed the connection because I was standing in a ticket line when the Wymondham train left. I wrote a letter of complaint and the next time I went to the ticket machines at King's Cross, they allowed me to buy a ticket to Wymondham. So now thanks to me you can travel from King's Cross to Wymondham, though I wouldn't actually recommend it as there is bugger all there. In that respect, it is rather like Belgium.

—

I had reason to reflect on all this the next morning when I bounded cheerfully off a morning train from Lytham to Preston, intending to transfer to the 10:45 to Kendal. I clutched a sheet of printed instructions that made this seem a reasonable ambition, but there was no 10:45 train listed, to Kendal or anywhere, on the television screens or on the printed timetables on the wall. So I walked to an information desk and asked the man there about it.

"Ah," he said as if I had touched on an exceedingly interesting point. "The 10:45 to Kendal is actually listed as the 10:35 to Blackpool North."

I stared at him for a long moment. A voice in my head said, "If you are expecting the 10:45 train to Kendal but are told it is the 10:35 to Blackpool North, you could be having A STROKE."

"But why?" I asked.

"Well, you see, the train divides here. Half of it goes to Blackpool North. That's the 10:35. At that point the remaining part of the train becomes the 10:45 Windermere train, which calls at Kendal en route. But there isn't enough room on the television screens to put all that, so we don't put anything, to avoid confusion."

"But I am confused."

"That's the problem!" he agreed enthusiastically. "In trying to avoid confusion, we seem to have created even more. People come up to me almost every day asking where the 10:45 is. Shall I show you where to stand?"

"That would be very kind."

He walked me to platform three and positioned me very specifically. "The train will arrive at 10:28. On no account get on the front four coaches or you'll end up in Blackpool."

"I've just come from there."

He nodded significantly. "Quite. Be sure to get on the rear four coaches only."

"So this is where I stand?" I said, pointing to the ground directly under my feet, as if a move a few inches to the right or left might spell catastrophe.

"Right there, and don't get on the next train or the one after that, but the one after *that*." He looked slightly concerned about me. "All right?"

I nodded without confidence, then stood and waited. Across the way, on the facing platform, a small group of hobbyists known as trainspotters stood with clipboards and notebooks. These are people who stand on rail-station platforms and jot down the engine numbers of the trains that pass. They collect as many numbers as they can, and then presumably go to a café and sit around talking about which numbers they are still hoping to find one day. They all looked like the sort of people who had never had sex with anything they couldn't put in a closet afterward. I tried to imagine what the rest of their lives was like if this was the fun part, but couldn't.

Two more trains came in, and then the flickering screen confirmed that the 10:35 to Blackpool North was the next train due, but was running a bit late and was expected at 10:37. More people came along, many of them accompanied by a station employee, and were positioned on an exact spot, with considerable pointing at feet. Well, you can imagine the frisson of consternation that swept along the platform when a train pulled in unexpectedly at 10:29. Was this the 10:35 arriving early or another train altogether? Who could tell? There were no railway employees to be seen now. I was reluctant to move from my spot, having been told on no account to leave it, but the man beside me volunteered to go and find out. He left and never came back. After a few minutes, I boarded the train and an older couple sitting at a table asked me anxiously if this was the Windermere train.

"I *think* so," I said, sliding in opposite them, "but we should be ready to jump off at a moment's notice."

They nodded and clutched their things tight in readiness.

A moment later an announcement told us that this was indeed the Windermere train and that those wanting to travel to Blackpool North should get off now and join the other four coaches. At this, a man at the back of the car got up and hurriedly left.

My new friends were a couple from Widnes having a day out to Windermere. They had brought a picnic made up entirely of things that needed a lot of careful attention—little bottles with caps to take off, Tupperware containers that had to be opened in a particular sequence, a miniature pot of jam whose lid came off with a satisfying *pock*. They had two hardboiled eggs with shells that they picked off with great care, collecting the fragments on an open napkin with forensic attention, as if they thought they might have to reassemble them later. I suppose this was how they filled their days.

We got on very well. They gave me a chocolate digestive biscuit and I told them how on my last visit to the Lake District I traveled to Windermere from Wymondham, which meant that the station abbreviations printed on my ticket showed me traveling from "WDM" to "WMD." I wondered if I was the first person ever to have done that.

"Oh, I shouldn't wonder," said the woman admiringly.

"Not long after that, I went from Diss to Liss," I added.

"Oh," said the woman, still full of admiration.

"I don't suppose many people do that either."

"No. I don't suppose."

"It was a wonderful time for me," I said, and we all fell into a dreamy silence.

I bade farewell to my new friends in Kendal, where I had arranged to pick up a rental car, public transport being pretty well impossible in the Lake District. When the railway age came along, William Wordsworth and others of a refined and romantic disposition ferociously opposed the spread of the railways' noise and smoke and low-class day-trippers into their cherished valleys, so the railway only goes to the edge of the Lake District and stops there. It means the Lakes never got giant factories and suburban sprawl, but it also means that the modern traveler has little option but to visit by car.

I decided to go up the outside of the Lakes, around the western, seaward edge, a much quieter way in than through Windermere and Ambleside, and so twenty minutes later I was heading toward the pleasant old resort of Grange-over-Sands, on the northern side of Morecambe Bay. We used to go to Grange a lot when my children were small. Grange was a place of simple amusements—miniature golf, swings, a lovely little park with a lake with ducks to feed, a nice tearoom to which we were partial. I hadn't been to Grange for many years, and I was pleased to see that it was still handsome, though quieter than I remembered and with more empty shops than can be good. On the plus side, Higginson's, the best butcher and pie maker you will find anywhere, was still there and crowded with customers. I bought a small pork pie and went with it to the park where I found a bench with views across the water to Morecambe. The pie was delicious. The British are surely the only people in the world who have made a culinary feature of boiled cartilage and phlegm.

Morecambe Bay may be the most beautiful bay in Britain. Thanks to the tides, it drains more or less completely twice a day. You can be standing on sand that a short while before was under thirty feet of water and vice versa. It's the vice versa that you have to worry about because the tide comes back in very quickly, though not in a line like an advancing army, but in fingerlets and channels that can easily surround you and catch you by surprise. People sometimes go for walks, then belatedly notice that they are on a giant, but steadily shrinking, sandbar. The worst incident was in February 2004 when at least twenty-one cockle pickers—nobody knows the actual number because they were all illegal, undocumented immigrants from China—were caught out in the bay and drowned when they misjudged or misunderstood the tides. They were paid 9p a pound for cockles.

Some years ago, I made a television series based on *Notes from a Small Island,* which necessitated traveling around the country for a couple of months with a film crew. One day we arrived in a place I didn't recognize.

"Where are we?" I asked.

"Barrow-in-Furness," replied my friend the producer Allan Sherwin in a sunny tone. Over the course of our weeks together, I learned that producers' minds don't work like normal people's minds.

"Why are we in Barrow-in-Furness, Allan?" I asked.

"Couldn't get Bolton, mate," he said.

"I beg your pardon?"

"We couldn't get permission to film in Bolton."

"So you chose Barrow-in-Furness instead?"

He frowned thoughtfully, then counted off his reasons on the fingers of one hand. "It's a northern town. It's industrial. It's depressed. It starts with a B. That ticks the boxes, doesn't it?"

"I've never been here, you know. I didn't write about it in my book."

"Yeah, but they'll let us film here," he explained patiently, and gave my arm a friendly squeeze. "You'll think of something to say. It'll be great."

So we filmed for a day in Barrow-in-Furness, and I don't remember a single thing about it. I thought I would have a quick look around now, as I was in the neighborhood, to see if any of it came back to me.

Barrow is just about the most out-on-a-limb, end-of-the-line place in England. It inhabits its own peninsula and is miles from anywhere along slow roads. Once it was a seat of industry—for a while its steel mill, now long gone, was the biggest in the world—but these days it is famous for being forgotten and depressed. On a sunny morning, it didn't look so bad. I parked on the edge of the business district and had a walk around. The streets were broad and clean and lined with imposing red sandstone buildings, reminders of its age of greatness. At each corner was a roundabout with flower beds and a statue of some forgotten worthy, but I couldn't read the inscriptions from across the road and wasn't about to venture into the speeding traffic to get a closer look just to find that I was looking at a statue of Josiah Gubbins, inventor of the cat flap or flat cap or whatever. At all events, around the periphery, Barrow looked OK—clean, reasonably prosperous, respectful of its past. But as I penetrated farther into the center it became increasingly bleak.

The heart of the business district was a long, curving pedestrianized street, and it was fairly busy, though it seemed to be more a place for congregating than for shopping. Groups of men, nearly all tattooed and dangerous-looking, hung out in clusters of four or five, giving the area something of the air of a prison yard.

I stopped at a Costa coffee bar and suddenly, rather startlingly, I was in a world of well-dressed, employable people. I had a refreshing cup of coffee, then stepped back out into the prison yard, walked to the far end of the pedestrian precinct, into a kind of forest of "For Rent" signs and men with genetically fierce dogs straining on leashes, and concluded that I had pretty well exhausted the possibilities for amiable diversion in central Barrow-in-Furness. So I returned to the car and headed for the more familiar Cumbria, the one with sheep and green hills and dogs you can pet without losing a hand.

Chapter 23

The Lakes

IN 1957, BRITAIN WAS doing awfully well at a lot of things. It still produced about a fifth of all the world's manufactured goods. It owned the world's land, sea, and air speed records, and now once again held the record for the mile run: Derek Ibbotson won it back from the Australian John Landy with a time of 3:57.2 in July.

Britain's aviation industry was the greatest in the world outside the United States. The Atlas computer made by Ferranti, a British company, was the world's most powerful mainframe—more powerful than anything even IBM had. Britain had just built a hydrogen bomb—something beyond the fiendish wits of all other nations except the United States and USSR. And at Calder Hall at Sellafield, on the Cumbrian coast, it had installed the world's very first working nuclear power station.

I hadn't realized quite how extraordinary Britain's nuclear achievements were until I did a little reading before this leg of the trip. It turns out that in 1944, as the Second World War was winding down, Winston Churchill and Franklin Roosevelt signed an agreement pledging to share information on the development of nuclear weaponry and energy after the war. But then Roosevelt died, and two years later Congress passed the McMahon Act, making it a crime punishable by death to give any information on nuclear reactions, peaceable or otherwise, to any third party, including Britain. So Britain had to develop its nuclear industry and hydrogen bombs wholly independently. That it did so successfully and quickly was a signal achievement.

So as 1957 got under way Britain was on top of the world. But then it all fell apart, and it was at Sellafield (then known as Windscale) that the unraveling began. In October 1957, during routine maintenance, a reactor overheated and caught fire, and it quickly became evident that no one knew what to do. The reactor cores at Sellafield were air-cooled. That was supposed to ensure that they never overheated. Since overheating was not supposed to happen, no contingency plan had ever been considered. Cooling the reactor with air now would just fan the flames. The only possible alternative was to hose the core down, but nobody knew what would happen if water were poured onto a hot nuclear core—this was all new technology. The fear was that the water would cause a massive detonation—a nuclear explosion, in effect—sending radioactive material high into the stratosphere and causing chaos across Europe and the North Atlantic. At a minimum, the Lake District would need to be evacuated, and several hundred square miles of Cumbria would be placed off-limits to humans for years, if not decades. One of the loveliest landscapes in the world would be lost for at least a generation. The cost to Britain, in prestige, reparations, and lost earnings, would have been colossal.

In the event, the water solution worked, and there was no great disaster. Some churns of milk had to be poured away and sheep glowed for a few years, but all in all it was a lucky escape. But it was also a disastrous PR blow, and it meant that nuclear energy would never be trusted or embraced in Britain as it was in France.

I have to say I haven't trusted the nuclear industry one bit since I read an article in *The New Yorker* some years ago about the giant Hanford facility in Washington State. Hanford may be the single most irresponsible achievement of modern man. Between 1943 and 1980, Hanford released 6.3 trillion liters of liquid waste containing strontium, plutonium, cesium, and sixty-three other dangerously toxic substances into the groundwater of the Columbia River basin. Sometimes these releases were careless and accidental, but more often they were intentional. The Hanford engineers did this and then lied about it. They insisted that the Columbia River water was wholesome and clean, and cited tests on salmon as an example of how safe it was, arguing that a person would have to eat one hundred pounds of salmon at a single sitting to ingest enough radiation just to reach detectable levels. What they knew but didn't say was that salmon don't eat when they are in the Columbia River. They come there only to spawn, and salmon don't eat when spawning, and in any case are not there long enough to absorb significant quantities of radiation. However, as the scientists well knew but failed to say, other types of aquatic life—crustacea, plankton, algae, and all the permanent fish—had concentrations of radioactivity that were on average one hundred thousand times greater than natural levels. What a lovely bunch of people.

I read all this in pained astonishment—I honestly didn't know that Americans could be so deceitful to other Americans—and hoped the British example would be better. In fact, no. British nuclear authorities were perhaps less callous but no less hypocritical. In 1972, Britain joined the other nuclear powers of the world in signing up to something called the London Convention, which prohibited the dumping of high-level radioactive wastes at sea from ships. But the agreement didn't mention pipelines, so Britain built one and pumped unknown tons of dangerous wastes straight into the Irish Sea without any idea, or evident concern, as to the consequences. By the late 1980s, according to Jacob D. Hamblin, an environmental scientist at Oregon State University, the people at Sellafield had exposed the whole of Europe to more radiation than "the combined levels of exposure from . . . all other nuclear sites, weapons testing, the Chernobyl accident, and packaged solid wastes," all while claiming to be a virtuous adherent of the London agreement.

There is still a lot of other toxic stuff at Sellafield, including the world's largest stockpile of plutonium (28 tons of it), but nobody knows exactly what is lying around the place because record keeping was so poor. According to the *Observer* newspaper, Building B30 at Sellafield is the most hazardous building in Europe. The building next door is the second most hazardous. Both are filled with slowly decaying fuel rods and old, contaminated hunks of metal and machinery.

In June 2014, the UK Nuclear Decommissioning Authority, an ominous-sounding body if ever there was one, announced that the cost of cleaning up the nuclear waste at Sellafield would be £79.1 billion. John Clarke, the group's chief executive, told the *Financial Times*, "Now we have to figure out what's in these facilities and how to get it out."

I think I can help you there, Mr. Clarke. It's half a century's worth of lethal, irradiated gunk that should, at the very least, have been recorded as it was being deposited. Clarke described the process facing him as "a journey of discovery," which is not exactly what you want to hear with a nuclear cleanup operation.

The upshot is that whatever benefits Sellafield gave the nation during its relatively short working life, the economic costs have been vastly greater, with the additional consideration that we now have heaps of lethally polluted materials that will remain dangerous for, oh, millions of years. I am no expert, but it does seem on the face of it that human beings are not quite grown up enough yet to be entrusted with nuclear fuels.

When I filmed the *Notes from a Small Island* television series in the late 1990s, we went to the Sellafield visitor center. It was a smart, high-tech museum confidently extolling the safety, reliability, and excitement of atomic energy. I remember it as being a fun place, if a little heavy on the propaganda. It was perhaps the only place in the world where plutonium was portrayed as lovable. At the time of my visit, Sellafield received two hundred thousand visitors a year, but those numbers evidently dwindled away in the following years. When I drove up to Sellafield's main gate now, hoping to refresh myself on the wonders of atomic energy, the man in the booth told me that the visitor center closed in 2012.

Nonplussed, I drove on to St. Bees.

St. Bees is the name of both a village and a private school occupying handsome buildings on spacious grounds in the village. I had always envisioned St. Bees himself as a kindly soul in a beekeeper's veil—adored by his insects, the patron saint of honey—but in fact St. Bees was a woman, an Irish princess, who fled to this corner of Cumbria to escape an enforced marriage with a Viking. She had nothing to do with bees. Her name was really Bega, and it just became corrupted over time. Some authorities believe she didn't actually exist.

The village of St. Bees is the western end of the famous Coast-to-Coast Walk across the width of northern Britain from the Irish Sea in the west to the North Sea in the east, and so tends always to have at least a few hikers about, looking either fresh and keen or slightly shell-shocked, depending on whether they are beginning or ending their trek. The only other time I have been in St. Bees was in 2010 when I went on a charity hike across the Lake District organized by my friend Jon Davidson. Jon is a professor of geology at Durham University, but not at all boring about it. (Well, actually sometimes he is a little boring about it, when he spies a novel schist or something.) In 2006, Jon's son Max, who is my greatest hero on earth, got leukemia at the age of four. Not long afterward, Jon got leukemia, too. Jon didn't contract his leukemia from Max or anything like that—it was a different strain altogether—so it was just a magnificently unfortunate coincidence. How unlucky is that? Happily, and wonderfully, both have recovered and in 2010 Jon set up something called the Max Walk to raise funds for leukemia and lymphoma research. The idea was for Jon and his old friend Craig Wilson to do the 190 miles of the Coast-to-Coast Walk from west to east, and for other of their friends to join in for all or part of it. I could only fit in the first three days, but that took us right across the Lake District from St. Bees to Patterdale—42.4 miles. It was a murderous slog over craggy hills, but the weather was glorious and I don't think I have ever encountered so much continuous beauty while clutching my heart and begging for mercy.

I went to the sea now to revisit the setting-off point, and walked a way along the breezy headland toward an old lighthouse, but it was getting late and I was hungry, so I returned to my guesthouse and had a shower, then repaired to the Queens public house in search of refreshment. The Queens was agreeably quiet as it was a weeknight. A couple sat at a table with silverware, obviously waiting for food to come, and two men were perched at the bar, but that was about it. I ordered a beer and then asked if I could order food, too. The man behind the bar made a grave face. "It's going to be at least an hour. We're a bit stretched tonight."

"But there's nobody here," I said with a hint of sputter.

The man nodded grimly toward the kitchen. "Chef's on his own out there," he said as if he were crawling on his belly through enemy fire. Some other people came in and inquired about food but were sent away. What is it with pubs and food these days? I drank my beer, then went across the road to the Manor House Hotel, which was really a pub, but it was very busy and there didn't seem to be anywhere to sit. So I walked into the village where there was one other option, a bistro called Lulu's, and I dined there. I don't know quite what to say other than that the food was beautifully described on the menu and filled me up.

Afterward, reluctant to turn in, I went for another stroll and liked St. Bees no less by night than by day. Every little cottage emitted a cozy glow of light through drawn curtains. The one discordant note was that the village shop had heavy security shutters over the door and windows, as if they felt they might need to repel a raid by Rommel's tank corps. I gather shops are given a better insurance rate if they install shutters, whether they are really called for or not. It is a great shame because nothing gives a more crushing air of distrust and decline—of a place gone to the dogs—than a shop battened down under metal. It is bad enough seeing it on the streets of inner London or Liverpool, but it really shouldn't be allowed in a country village. It just shouldn't.

In the morning, I returned to the coast road, high above the Irish Sea. Few visitors to the Lake District bother to go to the coast, but it is an interesting experience. On one side, you have long views down to the sea; on the other, steep lakeland fells (as northern hills are known; it's an old Viking word) of immense and daunting beauty; and in between you have some of the most straggly and depressed-looking villages you have ever seen—like little fragments of Barrow-in-Furness that have somehow drifted off and washed ashore here. The problem is isolation. Apart from Sellafield, which is being wound down, work in the area is scarce. But on the plus side, if you are going to live a life of bleak prospects, you do at least get some stunning views.

I was bound for Keswick by way of Cockermouth when I came to a sign pointing down a side road to Loweswater. I thought I knew the Lake District pretty well, but here was a lake that I had never heard of, as far as I could recall, so I made a sharp turn and went to investigate. The road was cramped and slow but breathtakingly gorgeous. The Lake District, when it is fine, and it usually is at least that, is about as beautiful as Earth can get, and this was as sumptuous a corner as I had ever come across. I had it to myself.

Apart from a couple of farmhouses it felt as if no one had been here for years. The road was so narrow that I needed constant vigilance to avoid scraping the stone walls on either side. Eventually I abandoned the car altogether in a lay-by and walked about half a mile between the bottom of Loweswater and Crummock Water, a neighboring lake, through the most sumptuous valley, beneath towering hills, all bathed in sunshine. I never saw another soul. I could have left the car in the middle of the road.

I was now in the heart of the Lake District National Park. From an American perspective, a British national park is an oddity since it isn't really a park at all, but just an area of land deemed special because it is lovely to behold and has exceptional amenity value for Britain's three principal countryside activities: walking, cycling, and sitting in a parked car having a nap. Whereas American national parks are wilderness areas in which no one is allowed to live (apart from a few rangers), national parks in Britain are just normal chunks of countryside with farms and villages and market towns, but with the addition of large numbers of tourists—and in the case of the Lake District it is very large numbers.

In 1994, I did an article for *National Geographic* on the Lake District. Then, the Lake District received 12 million visitors a year. Now it is 16 million. Ambleside, one of the main towns, then received up to eleven thousand cars per day. Today the number can exceed nineteen thousand. All these people are packed into an area of exceedingly modest dimensions. The Lake District National Park is only thirty-nine miles long from top to bottom, and thirty-three miles across at its widest point. Put another way, the Lake District gets four times as many visitors as Yellowstone National Park in America in an area just a quarter the size. On the busiest days, a quarter of a million people pour in.

And yet it handles it remarkably well, on the whole. Most of the crowds go to just a few places—Ambleside, Grasmere, and Bowness primarily. If you walk just a couple of hundred yards up any path you can easily get a whole hillside to yourself. That's what I did now. Just beyond Buttermere, I came to a roadside parking lot with only two cars in it (in one of which, honestly, a couple were having a nap) and decided to park and go for a little walk. The landscape looked oddly familiar, then I realized from my map that I was on the lower slopes of Haystacks, a hill I had walked over with Jon Davidson and his friends in 2010. It looked positively enormous from below. The hills of the Lake District are not terribly high—the very highest, Scafell Pike, only a mile or so from where I stood now, is just over thirty-two hundred feet—but they are muscular and steep. If you climb a Lake District hill, you know it.

An old riddle is how many lakes are there in the Lake District? The answer is one because only Bassenthwaite Lake has "lake" in the title. All the other bodies of water use the terms "mere" (as in Windermere and Buttermere), "water" (as in Crummock Water and Coniston Water), and "tarn" (as in you get the idea). There are hundreds and hundreds of tarns, some not much bigger than puddles. So the answer is that there are sixteen lakes and hundreds of what any sensible person would call ponds. It is impossible to say which is the loveliest, but I do vividly recall once looking down on Derwent Water from the side of a rugged eminence called Skiddaw, and thinking that heaven really must look like this. I had never been to the lake itself. I decided to correct that deficiency now.

Keswick is the main community on Derwent Water and I think is the most pleasant town in the Lakes. The main street had been pedestrianized since I was last there, and was much improved for it. I was pleased to see that Bryson's Tea Room (est. 1947) is still going strong. I walked down to and then partway around the lake. It really is quite sensationally lovely, with clear, sparkling water spread beneath a backdrop of craggy mountains of stone and sheep-nibbled grass. A couple of hundred yards offshore is a wooded island, called Derwent Island, with a grand house on it.

An information board from the National Trust informed me that an eccentric eighteenth-century owner named Joseph Pocklington held a regatta every year "where he challenged the people of Keswick to attack the island while he shot at them with his cannons." They certainly know how to have a good time in the Lake District, it seems. I would love to have seen the island, even without cannon fire, but it is not generally open to the public, so I contented myself with an hour's ramble at the lake's edge, then went back to explore the town.

Part of the reason I like Keswick is that it is full of outdoor shops. This is a place for people who just can't get enough Gore-Tex into their lives. I went into an emporium called George Fisher's and was so enchanted with its range of packs and water bottles and rustly waterproofs that I felt moved to buy something. I picked up a smart metal clip that you could use to hold together two objects—a water bottle to a rucksack, say—and never mind that I didn't have two objects to hold together. One day I may, and when that day comes I will be ready. The man at the till gave me a nod of respect, recognizing me as a member of the fraternity, albeit one from the more waddly end of the spectrum.

"Doing some walking?" he said.

"Headed for Cape Wrath," I responded solemnly.

"Long way," he said, impressed.

"Yes," I agreed, still solemnly, hoping he would recognize me and that for the rest of the day he would be saying to people, "Bill Bryson was in today. He was stocking up for an expedition to Cape Wrath," and that they would reply, "Goodness. He's brave. I think I'll go and buy some of his books." But he didn't recognize me, so that fantasy was stillborn. On display by the till was a book called *Peter Livesey: Stories of a Rock-Climbing Legend*. I knew Pete Livesey. He lived a mile or so from us in Malhamdale, in North Yorkshire, when we were there in the 1980s and '90s. I knew that he was a dedicated rock climber, but I had no idea that he was a legend—

but then he was an admirably modest fellow. I bought the book and took it with me upstairs to a small café at the back of the shop, where I sat with a sandwich and read, impressed with Livesey's skill and courage. I hadn't realized, but he died of pancreatic cancer the year after we left Malhamdale. He was just fifty-four, poor man.

The café had one other group of customers, a party of four made up of two couples of early retirement age who seemed to be on holiday together. They were well dressed. Their accents were southern and educated. They each had coffee and cake, so their bill must have come to something like £20. When I got up to pay, a woman from their group got to the cash register just ahead of me. She received her change and dropped a tip into a bowl by the till labeled "Tips." The bowl was a little high for her to see into and I am guessing she assumed that it was full of coins already and that hers would disappear among many others, but when I stepped up I could see that the bowl had a solitary 10p coin in it.

Am I wrong or is this becoming a feature of British life—and I mean by that behaving in quietly disgraceful ways when you think no one is watching? I am not saying that this is exclusive to the British or that it is universal among them by any means. I am just saying that it barely used to exist at all and now you see it pretty regularly. The Britain I came to was predicated on the idea of doing the right thing most of the time whether anyone knew you were doing it or not. So you didn't drop litter or empty your paint can at the curb or let your dog shit on footpaths and willfully take two parking spaces and all that sort of thing. You might not leave a tip—you were British, after all—but you wouldn't pretend to leave a decent tip and then stick in a small coin. Slyness wasn't part of the culture. It didn't occur to you to be a dick. Now lots of people are governed not so much by whether something is right or wrong as by whether they think anyone's watching. Conscience only operates when there are witnesses. Where did that come from?

And what do you do about it when it infects even pleasant-looking ladies in Patagonia jackets?

I drove on to Bowness-on-Windermere, the Lake District's principal town and tourist center. Bowness is always described as bustling, which really means packed. It is perennially thronged with visitors, mostly white-haired, shuffling around, looking in windows, killing time between pots of tea, waiting for it to be time to go home. Since I came to the Lake District twenty years ago for my *National Geographic* article, the number of visitors has increased by eleven thousand a day on average, and most of them seem to end up in Bowness without any clear idea of why they are there.

Bowness does have a lovely lakefront, it must be said. Windermere is the largest of the Lake District lakes, though that isn't saying a great deal. It's only ten miles long, barely half a mile wide at its widest extent, and often only a few feet deep. It is one of the most intensively studied lakes in the world thanks in large part to the Freshwater Biological Association, which has its headquarters at Windermere and has been dipping nets and beakers into its waters since 1929, one of the longest stretches of freshwater monitoring anywhere.

The British, as you may have gathered by now, are the most devoted studiers of nature on the planet. If a thing breathes or twitches or even just sits like lichen doing nothing at all, they are all over it. There is a British Bryological Society, a British Myriapod and Isopod Group, a British Phycological Society, a Simuliidae Study Group, a Malacological Society of London, a Conchological Society, a Chironomid Study Group, and of course a British Lichen Society, plus several dozen more, all devoted to collecting, conserving, and studying tiny living things that most of us are barely aware of, if at all.

And when I say study, believe me I mean study. Between 1976

and 2012, volunteers with the United Kingdom Butterfly Monitoring Scheme walked 536,000 kilometers of "butterfly transacts"— which is to say, arbitrary squares of countryside—to record the state of the nation's butterflies. Other groups have just as devotedly counted moths, bats, frogs, caddis flies, dragonflies, fungus gnats, freshwater flatworms, and—well, everything. There is even a Slime Mold Recording Scheme, whose manager—I am so pleased to tell you this—lives in Mold. Some of what these people have found is more interesting than you might expect. A species of millipede was found in a domestic garden in Norfolk and has never been seen anywhere else on earth. A moss that had only ever been recorded on the campus of Stanford University in California was also found living beside a path in Cornwall. How it came to inhabit two such dispersed localities and no others is a question no one can answer, though you can be certain it is the kind of thing they talk about pretty avidly during cocktail hour at moss conferences.

For the *National Geographic* article, I spent a morning on the lake with a young scientist from the Freshwater Biological Association without for a moment understanding a single thing she told me. I found the file with my notes in it the other day and this is the sort of thing the notes say: "Biotic assessment—dichotomous? Rotifers, ostracods, fairy shrimps. V. difficult to measure. Outlook not good. Diptera pupae. V. alarming!"

Eventually I stopped taking notes, and then stopped listening altogether, and just enjoyed the scenery while she prattled away and dipped containers in the water. The man driving our boat was a park ranger named Steve Tatlock, and he told me that on a busy day you could have as many as sixteen hundred powerboats on Windermere, an amazing number for a lake of its size, all of them speeding wildly, many pulling water-skiers and slicing through flotillas of sailboats, rowboats, canoes, inflatable rafts, and even some hardy swimmers, filling the lake with noise and danger and irksome, bouncy waves. England doesn't have a lot of lakes, and most are closed to motorboats, so Windermere was a rare place where people could drop a boat in the water and let her rip.

Tatlock asked me if I wanted to experience the speed water-skiers went, and of course I did. He let the scientist stow her stuff, then threw open the throttle and we took off with a velocity normally only seen in cartoons. We bounced across the water, barely touching the surface. It seemed wildly reckless, but at least it was a quiet morning and we had a few acres of empty water to ourselves. "Imagine sixteen hundred other boats doing this," Tatlock shouted, "moving about in all directions at top speed. It's absolutely mad."

In 2005, after thirty years of arguing, a ten-mile-an-hour speed limit was introduced on Windermere, so the lake is much improved for those who value tranquillity. As for all the things that live in and around it, the news isn't so cheery. Algal blooms have become common and fish populations have been falling steadily for years. In the wider world of nature, things aren't so good either. In 2013, a consortium of wildlife organizations released a report called *State of Nature* which found that about two-thirds of all species in Britain, plant and animal, are in decline, in some cases perilously so. The number of breeding birds has fallen by 44 million since the late 1960s. Over a longer period, fourteen mosses and liverworts have vanished from the British landscape, as have twenty-three species of bees and wasps. Britain, it turns out, is outstanding at counting what it has, but not so good at holding on to it.

Still, I must say, on the day I was there it all looked lovely and healthy, too. The water by the shoreline was clear, and the insects that darted about near its surface seemed happy enough, insofar as I am capable of judging, which obviously isn't very far. I walked along the waterside to the landing stage for the ferry to Sawrey, across the lake, and peered over the edge there, too. An empty cig-arette pack sat in the water. I fished it out and gave it a shake and looked around for a litter bin, but there wasn't one, so I sighed, squeezed it more or less dry, and put it in my jacket pocket. Realizing that there wasn't much of anything else I could do about the state of nature at Windermere, or indeed most of the other matters troubling the planet, I wandered back to the car and moved on.

Chapter 24

Yorkshire

I STAYED THE NIGHT in Kirkby Lonsdale, unofficial capital of the Lune Valley. It is a region of great beauty that hardly anyone knows about, but then that can be said about a lot of this corner of England. The Lake District and Yorkshire Dales National Parks so dominate everyone's thinking that the rest of the region is blissfully overlooked. The Lune Valley is as fine as anything in the Lakes (though without a lake, it must be said) or the neighboring Dales, and yet who has ever heard of the Lune Valley?

Kirkby Lonsdale is a nice little town, compact and prosperous. It used to have shops selling sweaters made of local wool and little craft galleries and things like that, and those are mostly gone now, but there are more restaurants and cafés, which I suppose is what the world wants these days.

In the morning I drove to Sedbergh, an attractive town now in the county of Cumbria but historically in Yorkshire, in the area known as the West Riding. Sedbergh is best known as the home of an ancient public school, also called Sedbergh, dating from the fifteenth century, but it has been trying in recent years to become known also as "England's Book Town," based on the fact that it has one large and excellent bookshop selling mostly secondhand books and a couple of smaller ones. It has a good hiking shop, excellent hardware store, some cafés and delis—in short, more than you would expect to find in a small and fairly remote place.

I went into a café on the high street for a coffee. The café had clearly taken the Book Town boast to heart because it had a selection of books that customers could read while enjoying their refreshments. One that instantly caught my eye was a hardback called *You Only Live Once* by Britain's number one goddess, Katie Price. You may only live once, as Ms. Price so astutely observes (very little escapes her with regard to existential issues, I find), but clearly that needn't stop you from writing about it again and again. This, I was surprised to learn, was her fifth autobiography—quite an achievement considering that she is only about twenty-five years old, I think (though some parts of her may be somewhat older). As well as her compelling autobiographical offerings, Ms. Price has also written five novels. All this is in addition to running an international business empire and progressing through life with breasts that must weigh at least thirty kilos apiece.

You Only Live Once concerned only a fragment of Ms. Price's rich and eventful life, but appeared to involve two marriages, some children, and a number of relationships. Chapter One, entitled "Too Much in Love," rather seemed to say it all. Chapter Six more intriguingly was entitled "Pink Up My Pony." (I have no idea. I had only just had breakfast.) The book was primarily about her marriage to Alex Reid. They had met, I believe, in some antipodean jungle while taking part in a reality television program called *I'll Eat Bugs for Money*. (I'm guessing this from the pictures.) They were married in February 2010 and divorced eleven months later. I've had pimples last longer than that.

I looked to see who published this treasury of high-class reminiscence and it was Random House, my very own publisher. I was part of the Katie Price family. We were corporately conjoined. But have they ever invited me to a launch party? Have they fuck.

—

And so to Yorkshire. I love Yorkshire and Yorkshire people. I admire them for their bluntness. As I said in *Notes from a Small Island*, if you want to know your shortcomings you won't find more helpful people anywhere. I lived for eight years in Malhamdale, not far from where I was now, and hardly a day passed when some crusty Dalesman didn't take time to help me identify one or more of my deficiencies.

I love and miss Malhamdale, but decided now, for the sake of novelty, to visit some parts of the Dales I was less familiar with and so headed to Dentdale. Insofar as Dentdale is known at all, it is as one of the principal locations of the celebrated Settle-to-Carlisle railway line, which may be both the most picturesque and wonderfully unnecessary railway line ever built in England. It was conceived sometime in the 1860s by James Allport, general manager of the Midland Railway, who wanted a route to Scotland. East coast and west coast routes already existed, so Allport decided to go up the middle. The only possible way was through the bleakest, remotest, emptiest stretch of the Pennine Hills, through seventy-two miles of landscape so irregular and deeply folded as to be an engineer's nightmare. The project required fourteen tunnels, including one at Blea Moor that is almost a mile and a half long, and twenty-one viaducts, several of them quite enormous. None of this could ever be economic. Indeed, when it eventually dawned on Allport and his colleagues what a mad project it was, they applied to Parliament for an abandonment bill—which is to say, permission to pull out of the project—but Parliament cruelly refused to grant it.

Allport appointed a young engineer named Charles Sharland to get the line built. Almost nothing is known about Sharland other than that he came from Tasmania and was only in his early twenties. The immensity of the task confronting Sharland was almost unimaginable and made all the harder by the privations of laboring in a wilderness. He slept in a wagon and often worked for hours in drenching rains or driving snow. Even more remarkably, he did all this while suffering acutely from tuberculosis. Inevitably, it caught up with him and, with his work almost finished, he retired to Torquay at the age of just twenty-five. He died soon afterward, never having seen a train run on the line he helped to create. I had hoped to see his residence when I was in Torquay, but he was too obscure, it seems, for anyone to have noted where it was. But I could at least have a look at his line now.

It opened on May 1, 1876, and from its beginning it was a magnificent folly. For practical reasons it didn't even go terribly near many of the communities it was built to serve. Kirkby Stephen station is a mile and a half from the village of Kirkby Stephen. Dent station is four miles from, and a steep six hundred feet above, Dent village.

I have ridden the line several times and the views across this very austere end of the dales are sensational, but you can't really appreciate the engineering from the train. For that, you must stand alongside it. I stopped at Dent Head Viaduct now and got out to have a look. The viaduct is 199 yards long with ten arches, and rises a hundred feet above the valley floor. That doesn't sound spectacularly lofty when you just say it, but when you see it in three dimensions, it is stunning. I tilted my head so far back to take it in that I lost my balance and very nearly fell over backward.

British Rail spent years trying to close the line, and did succeed in running it down almost to nothing. Dent station was closed for sixteen years and many of the others received only minimal attention. Today, however, the line is a model of what you can do with a little intelligent management and marketing. Now seven trains a day run in each direction, and the number of passengers has soared from just 90,000 in 1983 to a staggering 1.2 million in 2013.

The most iconic structure on the Settle-to-Carlisle line is Ribble-head Viaduct, running a quarter of a mile across the rolling valley of the River Ribble. It has twenty-four arches and at its highest point stands 106 feet above the surrounding landscape. For years British Rail wanted to retire it, on grounds of cost, and build a modern steel bridge alongside. This of course would have ruined one of the classic views of Yorkshire. Fortunately sense prevailed, money was found, and the viaduct was restored. That is the crux of matters, of course. If you have a lot of good old stuff and you want to keep it, it will cost you. If you don't pay for it, you can't keep it. I believe I have just described modern Britain.

I drove on through lovely countryside on quiet lanes. Gradually the road climbed to higher ground and the landscape grew bleaker and rockier, but was still very beautiful. It is the contrast between the green valleys, with their herds of dairy cattle prettily dotting grassy fields, and the lonely uplands that makes this landscape so perpetually enchanting.

At Garsdale Head, a lonely pass miles from anywhere, I passed the famous Moorcock Inn (or Nymphomaniac's Plea, as I always think it), then descended to the busy, tourist-clogged village of Hawes, where I became the first person in history to drive through without stopping to look in shopwindows for an hour. Why people choose to go there when everywhere else in the world is not there is a mystery beyond answering. I drove on instead to Swaledale and Wensleydale, two of the loveliest of the dales. I stopped at Thwaite and walked to the village of Muker and back, on a path through fields of dairy cows, which mercifully failed to molest me. Then I drove to Askrigg, which once teemed with tourists and tour buses because it was the village of Darrowby in *All Creatures Great and Small*, but it seems pretty quiet now, which must make it a nicer place to live if not to sell souvenirs, cups of tea, and planks of wood with inspirational sentiments on them.

About five miles beyond Askrigg is Aysgarth Falls, a celebrated beauty spot. It isn't exactly Niagara, but rather a series of small falls, where the waters of the River Ure flow over limestone platforms, but what it lacks in drama it makes up for in comeliness, and there is always the pleasure of watching some idiot falling in the water while trying to cross the river on exposed rocks. Some noisy young oik splashed in while I was there to the delight of everyone present.

At length I arrived in Leyburn, a busy market town, full of cars. I stopped at a restaurant on the square called Penley's, where I had a spicy cajun wrap, and wondered what odds you would have gotten thirty years ago that one day people in Yorkshire country towns would be eating spicy cajun wraps.

May I take a moment to say a word in favor of British food? It's not that bad. In fact, it is often very good. The British are responsible for not only the two single finest foodstuffs ever invented (chocolate digestive biscuits and well-buttered crumpets), but also countless other wonderful and distinctive gustatory delights: Yorkshire pudding, hot cross buns, sherry trifle, shortbread, scones, mince pies, plum pudding, toasted teacakes, veal-and-ham pie, Lancashire hot pot, a galaxy of noble cheeses like Stilton, Wensleydale, and the obscure but delectable Dorset blue vinney, not to mention the ever reliable cheddar, red Leicester, and double Gloucester, and countless other scrumptious comestibles that have made me the indolent and contented lump I am.

To be sure, a lot of British foods don't sound very attractive—toad-in-the-hole, bubble and squeak, bangers and mash, faggots in gravy, gooseberry fool, clotted cream. No one, as far as I can tell, has ever satisfactorily explained why the British insist on endowing their foods with strange and unseductive names. I am convinced that if the British had given their foods pretentious names like "galantine of pork saucisson en croûte" or "julienne of vegetables Wellington," people would gobble them up and there would be no jokes about British cooking. But the fact is British food is pretty good and, more to the point, it is now accompanied everywhere by exotic foreign dishes like spicy cajun wraps. So let's hear no more about British food being crappy.

Except sometimes when it actually is, of course.

Leyburn is not the most attractive of places, but it is the starting point for a wonderful, secret walk. Behind the shops at the western edge of the marketplace is a wooded bluff called Leyburn Shawl, which runs for nearly two miles high above Wensleydale and provides the most magnificent views. According to legend, it got its name when Mary, Queen of Scots, dropped her shawl there while trying to escape from nearby Bolton Castle, where she was held prisoner for six months in 1568. The problem with this story is that "shawl" isn't first recorded in English until 1662, long after Mary had a neck to wrap anything around. The *Oxford English Dictionary* doesn't have an entry for "shawl" as a landscape feature, which is a curious oversight, but there you are. Life sometimes bitterly disappoints.

Beyond the Shawl—considerably beyond, as it turns out—is the village of Preston-under-Scar and then the striking, solitary upright known as Bolton Castle, which stands like a giant forgotten chess piece on a hillside. For reasons considerably beyond my knowledge, the castle is called Bolton Castle while the village beside it is Castle Bolton. Bolton Castle dates from the late fourteenth century and is impressive in an austere sort of way. Admission to view the castle was £8.50, which was more than I was willing to pay by a multiple of about four. Besides, I was running very late. It was much farther from Leyburn than I had remembered. It had taken me nearly two hours to get there, which meant that I wouldn't get back to my car till after 5 p.m., and I still had about an hour's drive after that. This little side trip, glorious as it was, was costing me my happy hour. So with a certain scoot in my stride, I bade farewell to

Bolton Castle Bolton and strode briskly back toward Leyburn and my trusty rental car.

I spent the night in Barnard Castle, a pleasant market town on the River Tees in County Durham. I arrived much too late to go to the famous Bowes Museum there, a disappointment. So instead I had a walk around the town as darkness fell, and found it entirely agreeable. C. Northcote Parkinson, I was interested to see, was born at No. 45 Galgate, a fact commemorated with a plaque on the house. Never has anyone milked a single thought more vigorously and successfully than he did. The line for which he is remembered was "Work expands to fill the time available for its completion," still known as Parkinson's Law. It was first elucidated in a comic essay he wrote for *The Economist* in 1955 while he was a professor at the University of Malaya in Singapore. Parkinson then expanded the essay into a thin book, called *Parkinson's Law,* which became a global bestseller and made him rich and more famous than anyone deserves to be for having one fairly obvious idea. He was given visiting professorships at Harvard and the University of California at Berkeley, and undertook many long, lucrative speaking tours. He wrote several other books, including some novels, though nothing he wrote enjoyed anything like the success of *Parkinson's Law.* Nonetheless he made so much money that he became a tax exile in Guernsey. He died in 1993, aged eighty-three, having done nothing of interest for thirty-five years. Even so, he gets about fifteen hundred words in the *Oxford Dictionary of National Biography,* while poor old Charles Sharland, forgotten father of the Settle-to-Carlisle railway, gets none. Go figure.

Barnard Castle has many pubs, most of them pretty promising-looking. I called in at the Old Well Inn for a predinner beverage and found it most congenial, I must say. Beside my table was a recent issue of a trade magazine called *Pub and Bar,* which I picked up and read with interest and then admiration, for it was not only engaging but literate—and how often can one say that these days? I was particularly taken with an article about a pub called the White Post on Rimpton Hill on the Dorset-Somerset border. The county boundary runs right through the middle of the bar. In former times when Dorset and Somerset had different licensing laws, people had to move from one side of the room to the other at 10 p.m. in order to continue drinking legally until 10:30. I don't know why but this made me feel a pang of nostalgia for the way things used to be.

Afterward, I went to an Indian restaurant and had a lavish, spicy meal and a not inconsiderable number of bottles of beer, then returned to my room and spent the next ten hours having pangs of quite another sort.

Chapter 25

Durham and the Northeast

I

Just outside Gloucester Road tube station in London is an open area that used to have a large planter in the middle of it. The planter contained some hardy shrubs and was enclosed by a low wall on which people could sit to eat a sandwich or wait for friends. It wasn't sensational but it was pleasant.

Then one day the council took the planter away, turning the open area into a kind of arid plaza. Soon afterward when I passed through, a couple of council officials in bright yellow vests were standing in the newly created emptiness making notes on clipboards. I asked them why they had taken away the planter, and they told me that the borough didn't have the resources to manage planters anymore. And I just thought: Is that really what we have come to now, in this cheap, shittily dispiriting age in which we permanently reside—that we can't even afford a few shrubs in a planter?

Now hold that thought just for a minute while we speed north to the fine old city of Durham and stand outside the majestic heap of stone that is Durham Cathedral. I once spent an enjoyable morning being shown around by the cathedral's architect, Christopher Downs. I was a little surprised, frankly, to discover that a cathedral requires a full-time architect, but it does. It is in the nature of old buildings to want to fall down, and they need constant attention to prevent that happening. Stone, for one thing, isn't nearly as eternal as you might think. Even hard stone tends to split and crumble after a couple of hundred years of facing into wind and rain. When that happens, Christopher told me, masons carefully chip out the old stone and slide in a new one. This puzzled me. Why, I asked, didn't they just pull out the existing stone and rotate it to a new face?

He looked at me, surprised at my architectural naivety. "Because the stones are only about six to nine inches thick," he explained. It turns out that the walls of Durham Cathedral are not solid stone, as I had always vaguely supposed, but consist rather of an outer skin six to nine inches thick and an inner skin of similar thickness and in between a cavity five and a half feet across, which the build-ers filled with rubble and hardcore held together with a kind of gloopy cement-like mortar.

So Durham Cathedral, like all great buildings of antiquity, is essentially just a giant pile of rubble held in place by two thin layers of dressed stone. But—and here is the truly remarkable thing—because that gloopy mortar was contained between two impermeable outer layers, air couldn't get to it, so it took a very long time—forty years to be precise—to dry out. As it dried, the whole structure gently settled, which meant that the cathedral masons had to build doorjambs, lintels, and the like at slightly acute angles so that they would ease over time into the correct alignments. And that's exactly what happened. After forty years of slow-motion sagging, the building settled into a position of impec-cable horizontality, which it has maintained ever since. To me, that is just amazing—the idea that people would have the foresight and dedication to ensure a perfection that they themselves might never live to see.

Now I am no expert on the matter, but I am pretty sure that

we are a lot richer today than we were in the eleventh century, and yet back then they could find the resources to build something as splendid and eternal as Durham Cathedral and today we can't afford to keep six shrubs in a planter. And there is really something seriously wrong with that, if you ask me.

I'm biased, but I believe Durham may be the nicest small city on the planet. It is friendly, brainy, carefully preserved, very beautiful. Its university is the third oldest in England, after Oxford and Cambridge, and one of the best. It is the only one in the world that is also a World Heritage Site. I said some complimentary things about Durham in *Notes from a Small Island* and the university gave me an honorary degree. When I came to accept the degree, I said some more nice things and they made me chancellor. This is my kind of town.

Being a university chancellor is a position that almost nobody outside the world of British academia understands. When my hero and friend Sir Kenneth Calman, who was then vice-chancellor at Durham, invited me to take on the role in 2005, my first question to him was: "What does a chancellor do?"

"Ah," he said in a tone of genial wisdom, "a chancellor is rather like a bidet. Everyone is pleased to have one, but no one knows quite what they are for."

A chancellor is nominally the head of a university, but in practice has no role, no power, no purpose. A university is really run by the vice-chancellor. "Your job," Ken told me, "is to be harmless and amiable, and to preside over graduation ceremonies twice a year." And so for six years that is what I did, and I loved it. It was, I discovered, a little like being Queen Mother and Santa Claus at the same time.

The British do a lot of things remarkably well and often seem hardly aware of it, and nowhere is that more true than in the provision of higher education. Compare the situation of British universities with that of American ones. As everyone knows, the amount of money American universities have at their disposal is staggering. Harvard University's endowment is $32 billion—that's more than the gross domestic products of most nations. Yale has an endowment of $20 billion, Princeton and Stanford are both at $18 billion, and so on through a very long list.

In Iowa, my own state, Grinnell, a nice, eminently respectable liberal arts college but one that not many people outside the Midwest have ever heard of, has 1,680 students and an endowment of $1.5 billion—or more than all British universities put together apart from Oxford and Cambridge. Altogether eighty-one universities in America have endowments of $1 billion or more.

That's just endowments. It doesn't touch on the huge sums they take in from tuition and sports programs and a good deal else. Do you know, Ohio State University earns $115 million a year from its sports programs, of which some $40 million—I am actually embarrassed to say this—comes in the form of donations. That's right. People give $40 million a year to the Ohio State University football team just so it can attract better players—and, for all I know, better cheerleaders. Forty million dollars is about equal to the total endowment of Exeter University in the UK. Only twenty-six British universities have total endowments greater than the amount given annually to the Ohio State University football team.

I first became interested in all this when I sat at a dinner next to a fund-raiser from the University of Virginia, who mentioned, as if it were the most natural thing in the world, that they had just embarked on a five-year campaign to raise $3 billion. To achieve this, the university employed a dedicated fund-raising staff of two hundred and fifty. The head of the department was paid $500,000 a year—more than anybody at the university except the football coach. The University of Virginia, in short, had turned itself into a mighty cash-raising machine.

It met its target, a remarkable accomplishment, but here's the thing. According to the 2014 *Times Higher Education* world rankings (which are generally held to be the most exacting of their type), the University of Virginia ranks 130th among the world's universities. Eighteen much more modestly funded British universities rank higher. On the world stage, according to the *Times Higher,* Virginia is about level with Britain's Lancaster University, which has an endowment fund one-thousandth the size of Virginia's. That is pretty extraordinary.

And it is all the more extraordinary when you reflect that despite perpetually modest funding Britain still has three of the world's top ten universities and eleven of the top one hundred. Put another way, Britain has 1 percent of the world's population, but 11 percent of its best universities, and accounts for nearly 12 percent of total academic citations and 16 percent of the most highly cited studies.

I very much doubt if there is any other realm of human endeavor in the country that produces more world-class benefit with less financial input than higher education. It is possibly the single most outstanding thing in Britain today.

One of the weirdest experiences I have ever had occurred on an ancient and noble span called Elvet Bridge in Durham, which I had forgotten all about but remembered now as I strolled across the bridge on my way to the cathedral. Elvet Bridge dates from the twelfth century and because of its great age and narrowness is closed to motorized traffic. I used it a lot when I was in Durham for Congregations, as graduation weeks are known, because it stood between my hotel and the cathedral, where the graduation ceremonies took place in an atmosphere of stirring pomp and glory.

One morning, as I was hurrying to the cathedral for the day's first ceremony, I felt an irresistible urge to look over the side of the bridge. I have no idea why; it wasn't something I normally did. Directly beneath me, thirty or forty feet below, two young mothers with strollers were chatting on a path beside the swift and rain-swollen River Wear. One of them had a toddler. As I looked down, the toddler, unnoticed, stepped onto a boat ramp beside them. It was a bigger step down than he could quite manage and he immediately unbalanced and tumbled into the water. He sank completely, then bobbed up on his back, still slightly submerged, with an exceedingly startled look on his face. I was directly in his line of sight. We made eye contact—shared this unexpected moment. The little boy was in an eddy sheltered by the ramp, and for a moment he lay becalmed, but then he began very gently to spin, and to move toward the open river, as if being tugged by a current.

All this happened in an instant, but to me, and I daresay to the toddler, it proceeded in a kind of paralyzing slow motion, in complete silence. I was watching a little boy go to his death, and mine was about to be the last face he would ever see. How's that for an image to spend the rest of your life with?

And then, abruptly and miraculously, real time reasserted itself and the world became noisy again. I shouted and his mother in the same instant looked over and, with a shriek, scrambled to the water's edge and snatched him out before he was swept away. The mother and her friend fussed over the little boy, but I could see he was OK. After a few moments, the friend looked up and signaled an all-clear to me and a kind of thanks. There was nothing more I could do and I was late anyway, so I waved back and continued on my way.

I am not a religious soul, but I must say it does seem a little uncanny that on that morning of all mornings I should have looked over the bridge at such a propitious moment. I mentioned the story at lunch to one of the members of the cathedral, and he nodded sagely and pointed a finger heavenward, as if to say, "It was God, of course."

I nodded and didn't say anything, but thought: "Then why did He push him in?"

Beyond Elvet Bridge, a cobbled street called the Bailey leads up to Palace Green, a giant lawned square with the cathedral rising like a mountain of shaped stone at one end and Durham Castle, now part of the university, standing sentinel at the other. I entered the cathedral through its massive oak doors and for about the two hundred and fiftieth time, I would guess, was staggered by its grandeur. It is unquestionably one of the great, humbling spaces of the world.

At the eastern end of the cathedral, in the Chapel of the Nine Altars, is a breathtakingly enormous rose window, ninety feet in circumference, a giant kaleidoscope of stained glass of an almost liquid intensity, held in place by the most delicate stone tracery. I was once told by a member of the cathedral staff that some years ago, while putting together a program of maintenance, a team of conservators comprehensively measured every facet of the window and sent the numbers off to an engineering firm to be crunched in a supercomputer. Soon afterward an urgent message came back saying: "Whatever you do, don't build that window!"

I asked Christopher Downs, the architect, about this when I met him and he smiled tolerantly. The story, he said, was apocryphal, but the substance was true. No one would dare to build such a window now. It is, he told me, at the very limit of engineering tolerances. "Somehow, without computers or other sophisticated tools, they knew precisely how far they could push things," he told me. "It is quite miraculous really."

I had a look around the cathedral now, then strolled through the exquisite cathedral close—known here as the College—then along the Bailey and down to a woodland path to another landmark, Prebends' Bridge. It is unquestionably one of the loveliest views in England, with the cathedral above and the river, tranquil and green, sliding along below. It is a prospect that has barely changed since it was memorialized in a well-known painting by J. M. W. Turner in 1817.

People come from all over to marvel at the cathedral and enjoy these views without appreciating that not one bit of what they see takes care of itself. Prebends' Bridge is part of the cathedral estate. A couple of years ago, it had to be assessed for structural wear. The dean of the cathedral, Michael Sadgrove, told me that the scaffolding alone would cost £100,000. I asked him how much cathedral visitors donated. The average visitor leaves 40p, he told me. More than half leave nothing at all.

I had to hasten on to Newcastle to attend a dinner and then take part in a charity walk for the Northern Institute for Cancer Research, a heroic organization that I first learned of through Jon Davidson, my old friend who force-marched me through the Lake District in 2010 as part of his coast-to-coast charity hike. The institute is run by Prof. H. Josef Vormoor, who is Sir James Spence Professor of Child Health at Newcastle University and one of the foremost child cancer specialists in Britain.

I was thinking about Josef because on the drive to Newcastle I listened to the news on the radio, and it contained an item about the prime minister, David Cameron, renewing his pledge to cut drastically the number of immigrants. Britain has become obsessed in recent years with immigrants, mostly because of an influx of people from Eastern Europe, who enjoy free movement within Europe once their countries join the European Union, as most have. Many Tories and others of a conservative temperament would like all these people to go home.

My ears always perk up at immigration stories because of course I am an immigrant myself. So, too, is Josef. He is from Germany. His wife, Britta, is from Germany, too. She is a physician in family practice. I wish she was my physician because she is smart and kind.

Now here's the thing that just drives me crazy. If Josef and Britta went home tomorrow, the British government would log it as a gain. Britain's immigration numbers would be reduced by two and therefore the nation would have moved a tiny bit closer toward some notional concept of perfection. The smartest person I know is Prof. Carlos Frenk of Durham University. He is one of the world's leading cosmologists. He attracts the best possible talent to his department. Carlos is from Mexico. He comes from a fabulously wealthy family; he isn't in Britain because it is making him wealthier. He could be at Harvard or Caltech or anywhere, but he likes Durham. If he went tomorrow, it would also be logged as a net gain to the country. Do I really have to point out how foolish that is?

I am not suggesting that Britain, or any country, shouldn't try to control its population numbers. I am just saying that the process ought to involve a little more than a body count. Jon Davidson's wife, Donna, comes from America. She is enormously lovely and very gifted. She helps design visitor centers all over the world for an American company, so she earns dollars for the British economy, and, not incidentally, in her spare time raises lots of money for the Northern Institute for Cancer Research. There are tons of people like us in the world—people who live in another country because of considerations of marriage or family or quiet affinity—and I would submit that if you think the only people you should have in your country are the people you produce yourselves, you are an idiot. In this respect (and one or two others, frankly) the Conservatives are idiots.

That evening I attended a most enjoyable fund-raising dinner for the NICR and then the following day went to the Blagdon Hall estate, north of Newcastle, which was hosting the charity hike.

Blagdon Hall is the ancestral home of the Viscounts Ridley. The present viscount is the author and kindly soul more widely known to the world as Matt Ridley. I have known Matt for years but for a very long time had no idea that he was a viscount–in-waiting. It was only when I visited him at his house for the first time and found him standing at the front door of a building about the size of my high school that I realized his background involved a certain measure of privilege.

In his younger years, Matt worked as a journalist on *The Economist* and for a time was based in America. He told me that once he went to Iowa for the political caucuses and was checking into a motel when he noticed that on the wall behind the check-in desk was a reproduction of a painting of an English country estate from the eighteenth century. The painting was awfully familiar to Matt since it was of Blagdon. The original hung in his house. He said to the young check-in clerk, "I don't suppose you'll believe this, but that's my house." She glanced at the print and then looked at him as if he had just told her that he lived in Tinker Bell's castle at Disneyland, and completed the check-in process without reference to his comment.

Matt's wife, Anya, who is also lovely and has a brain like a mainframe computer, is a leading neuroscientist based at Newcastle University. She's American, too. Their son, Matthew, a student at Cambridge, was one of the members of last year's winning team on *University Challenge*, a really hard quiz show for college students, so he is obviously tremendously smart, too, as is their daughter, Iris. The children are British, but half their brains and frankly about three-quarters of their looks are American.

That really is all I am going to say about this.

The walk was a great success, as it always is, and a lot of fun, but above all heartening because nearly everyone on it had been touched by childhood cancer as parent or sibling or victim. Afterward, Matt told me he had something he wanted me to see, and he took me in his car to some nearby parkland, now home to a giant piece of earthwork sculpture called Northumberlandia. It was designed by an artist named Charles Jencks and erected on land donated by the Ridleys, who also provided part of the funding. Matt is very proud of Northumberlandia and for good reason. It is just the most wonderful creation. It is an enormous figure of a recumbent woman, a quarter of a mile long and a hundred feet high, made of earth dug up during the course of mining for coal on Ridley's land, then lined with paths and planted over with grass.

The scale of it is staggering. "It is," Matt told me, "the largest representation of a woman in the world." It is beautiful to behold but also a pleasure to walk over. Paths lead to the top of her head, to the twin summits of her breasts, along her arms, down her grassy thighs. It was just splendid, the best thing I have seen in a long time.

I would love to have spent hours clambering over Northumberlandia now, but I had tracks of another sort to make. It was time to head to Scotland. My English adventure was coming to an end.

II

I stayed the night in North Berwick, ninety miles north of Blagdon Hall and comfortably inside Scotland. My plan was to drive to Edinburgh in the morning, then proceed north through the Cairngorm Mountains to Inverness and thence onward to Ullapool and Cape Wrath. I didn't have much time to linger—the Cape Wrath season, such as it is, was coming to an end—but I was looking forward very much to the experience of driving into the Highlands. It's a strange thing because nobody can say exactly where the Scottish Highlands begin and end, but there comes a moment when the world fills with clean, sparkling air and the mountains take on a kind of purply glory and you know you are there. That's what I was looking forward to.

North Berwick is sometimes confused with Berwick-upon-Tweed, a famous border town, but North Berwick is a different place entirely, forty miles farther up the coast on the broad inlet melodically known as the Firth of Forth. (I was aching for someone to ask me if this was my first visit to the Firth of Forth because I could honestly respond: "No, it's my fourth or fifth to the Firth of Forth." But no one asked me.) I knew nothing about it and ended up there simply because it was conveniently on the way to Edinburgh. Well, it is lovely—a prosperous and attractive coastal town with an oceanfront golf course strikingly similar to St. Andrew's. I liked it a lot.

I dropped my luggage at a hotel, then strolled into town. I went into the Ship Inn, which seemed a pleasant place, and read a day-old copy of the *East Lothian Courier* which I found lying on a table. The paper had an interesting report on a recent litter pick by an organization called the Forth Coastal Litter Campaign. The FCLC not only fastidiously picks up litter, bless it, but then apparently counts it all. Altogether it collected over fifty thousand pieces of litter on this recent sweep, including fifty-five party poppers, twenty-three traffic cones, twelve toothbrushes, forty-three surgical gloves, and fifteen colostomy bags. It was the colostomy bags that gave me pause. How do you account for that? Did one person drop colostomy bags on fifteen separate occasions or was it a party of colostomy bag users on perhaps an annual outing? If the latter, might this also explain the party poppers? Unfortunately, the *Courier* failed to specify.

The news pages of the paper were liberally sprinkled with articles about pub beatings—five on one page, just from this area—but everything else was about flower shows and fun runs and people shaving their heads for charity. I had never seen such a range of kindliness and violence coexisting in one locality. When I went for a second pint, I turned around and a guy was standing behind me waiting to take my place at the bar. We went through that little side-to-side dance where you keep inadvertently blocking the other person's way. I smiled helplessly, as you do, and he looked at me as if he was thinking about shoving my head through the wall. That is the problem with Scotland, I find. You never know whether the next person you meet is going to offer you his bone marrow or nut you with his forehead.

Afterward I dined at a Thai restaurant on the main street, then went down to the seafront and looked across to a scattering of islands just off the coast. One of them, called Fidra, is said to have been the inspiration for Robert Louis Stevenson's *Treasure Island*. He spent a lot of time in the town as a boy evidently. The view was lovely. I didn't see any colostomy bags.

As I stood there, I was severely startled to have my phone ring. It was my wife telling me that there was a problem at home. I can't tell you what it was. I was involved in litigation—I had begun action against someone in America—and part of the subsequent settlement of that case was that I agreed not to discuss it. But something big had come up and I had to go home. The Highlands would have to wait.

Chapter 26

To Cape Wrath
(and Considerably Beyond)

I

THERE ARE TWO HARD things about getting to Cape Wrath from the south of England. The first is getting to Cape Wrath from the south of England. It is a long way, you see—seven hundred miles from my back door, according to Google Maps—and involves at a minimum a train journey, a car journey, a ferry trip across the lonely Kyle of Durness, and a bouncy ride on a minibus through an uninhabited wilderness. So the logistics take some working out.

The second and even more unsettling part of the undertaking is determining whether you can get there at all. The Cape Wrath website stresses that ferry crossings are subject to the vagaries of tides and weather, which in this part of Scotland can be both disruptive and extreme. The whole of the Cape Wrath peninsula also closes from time to time, apparently without a great deal of notice, when the Ministry of Defense, which owns twenty-five thousand acres there, uses it to practice shooting and blowing up things. On top of all that, the ferry and minibus services shut for half the year. If you miss the last autumn ferry, you have to wait six months for the next one in the spring.

Hoping to introduce a little certainty into the process, my wife called to make a reservation for me.

"We don't take reservations," the man told her.

"But he's coming a long way," she said.

"Everybody who comes up here has come a long way," the man pointed out.

"Well, what are the chances of him getting on the boat if he just turns up?"

"Oh, he should be OK," the man said. "We're not that busy at the moment. Well, most days we're not. Sometimes we are."

"I don't know how to interpret that."

"If he gets here early, he should be OK."

"How early?"

"Earlier the better," the man said. "'Bye now." And he rang off.

Thus it was that I found myself on a rainy Sunday evening, in a mood of vague unease, with no certainty that I was going to get to where I ultimately wanted to go, walking along the imposing length of the famous Caledonian Sleeper train at Euston station in London and finding my way to carriage K and the little berth that was to be my home for the night and my conveyance to the distant north of Scotland.

The train, I have to say, was a little past its best. In fact, if I am completely honest, it was several miles past the point at which it was merely a little past its best, but it was clean and reasonably comfortable and the staff were friendly. According to a leaflet left on the bed, the company will be acquiring seventy-five new sleeper cars in 2018, but in the meanwhile is making some other small improvements. The leaflet noted with particular pride that all the bed linens had been "refreshed," which sounded to me like at least one whole level below laundering, but perhaps I was just misreading things.

I wandered down to the lounge car for a drink. Half a dozen people were there already. I had a look at a little menu that stood on my table. Everything on offer was robustly Scottish and not in the least appealing to someone from Iowa. (I believe I can speak for my entire state on this.) The dinner options featured a plate of haggis, neeps and tatties, and the snacks included Tunnock's teacake, haggis-flavored potato chips, and Mrs. Tilly's Scottish Tablet, which sounded to me not at all like a food but more like something you would put in a tub of warm water and immerse sore feet in. I would imagine it makes a fizzing sound and produces streams of ticklish bubbles. The drinks were all Scottish, too, even the water. I ordered a Tennent's lager.

It is perhaps dangerous to conclude too much about the character and intentions of a nation based on a snacks menu in a railway carriage, but I couldn't help wonder if Scottish nationalism hasn't gone a little too far now. I mean, these poor people are denying themselves simple comforts like Kit-Kats and Cornish pasties and instead are eating neeps and foot medications on grounds of patriotism. Seems a bit unnecessary to me.

Years ago—back in the early 1980s, I would guess—I was in Scotland when England had a big soccer match against Italy, which I watched in a hotel bar in Aberfeldy in Perthshire. Early in the match, England nearly scored, but I was the only person in the room to raise his arms in tentative joy. A few minutes later, Italy scored and everyone in the bar responded with great pleasure and took a big drink from their glasses, and I remember thinking: "These people are not part of Team UK." I was severely unsettled by this. I thought everyone cheered for their cousins. I always cheered for Scotland and Wales and even the Republic of Ireland on the grounds that we were all basically kin. I had no idea that the Scottish so loathed the English that their favorite team in the world is whichever one is presently playing England. Despite this, I try to be big about it and cheer for Scotland in neutral matches, though part of me frankly is also secretly thinking: "Fuck 'em. I hope they struggle to beat Malta." Amazingly often, I get my wish.

Anyway, I was glad when Scotland voted in a referendum in September 2014 to stay in the union. I like the Scots, especially the ones who don't look at me like they might in a minute have to shove my head through a wall.

I turned in early and slept like a baby and only awoke because the steward knocked on my door and presented me with a cooked breakfast on a tray, which I hadn't expected and appreciated very much.

"We're running two hours late," he told me cheerfully.

"Oh," I said.

I popped open the curtain. Outside it was the Highlands—mountains and glens and a narrow black road racing along beside us. How exciting it is to wake up in a new country. At length, we came to Kingussie station and stopped, and then stayed stopped so long that it began to feel permanent. The train took on that kind of silence that gives you perfect hearing. I could hear voices in other cabins and a fly in death throes by the window. I glanced out and saw three people I recognized from the bar standing on the platform smoking. I went out and found lots of people just standing around. Our steward passed and told me that a freight train had broken down farther up the line and that our engine had gone to save it.

I lost track of how long we stayed in Kingussie. All I can say is that we arrived in Inverness, our final destination, more than fifteen hours after boarding and several hours later than we should have. I walked out to a zone of light industry a mile or so from the station, where I collected a rental car and, with a light heart and good attitude, headed north and west for Ullapool.

Ullapool is a tidy village in a superlative setting on the shores of Loch Broom, some sixty miles from Inverness. I checked into my hotel, then went straight out for a walk, happy to get my legs in motion again. Ullapool was busy with tourists who looked uniformly relaxed and happy. It seemed an entirely agreeable place—prosperous, friendly, very clean. The harbor was dominated by a terminal for ferries to Stornoway on the Isle of Lewis, which lent the waterfront an air of purpose and enterprise, and there were some pleasant shops and galleries to nose about in. I liked it all.

It occurred to me that if you could just make all of Britain like this—if you could somehow infuse this comfortable orderliness and unshowy prosperity into places like Blackpool and Grimsby—you would have a nearly perfect nation. May I tell you what I would like to see? I would like to see a government that said: "We're going to stop this preposterous obsession with economic growth at the cost of all else. Great economic success doesn't produce national happiness. It produces Republicans and Switzerland. So we're going to concentrate on just being lovely and pleasant and civilized. We're going to have the best schools and hospitals, the most comfortable public transportation, the liveliest arts, the most useful and well-stocked libraries, the grandest parks, the cleanest streets, the most enlightened social policies. In short, we're going to be like Sweden, but with less herring and better jokes." Wouldn't that be delightful? But of course it will never happen.

I had a commendably early night and arose at five the next morning for the two-hour drive to Cape Wrath. The air was clear and promised a splendid day. I was beyond excited. The whole world was still abed as I headed north on the little A835. The rising sun set the mountaintops aglow, like the bars of an electric fire. The landscape was pure grandeur—mile upon mile of hills, lochs, open sea, tumbling rills, and massive glens, all continually reshuffled into new combinations of unsurpassable majesty. It wasn't nearly as remote in feeling as I had expected. All along the way there were crofters' cottages and rambling lochside hotels, even occasional small communities. At the village of Scourie, I passed a sign that said "Scourie Beach and Burial Ground," which seemed an enchanting combination. ("We're burying Grannie tomorrow. Don't forget to bring your swimsuits.") I was very happy.

I arrived at the ferry landing just after 7:30, the only person there, and staked my place at the water's edge. The setting was sensational—a backdrop of monumental hills overlooking the fjord-like Kyle of Durness. The Cape Wrath peninsula, bleak but beckoning, stood half a mile away at the far side of the strait. Birds swooped low over the water. On a distant sandbar, a log stirred to life—a seal!—and rippled across the beach to the water.

At about 8:20, someone across the loch maneuvered two mini-buses, one at a time, into positions at a landing stage, and then a whole bunch of people arrived all at once on my side. A minute later a man with an air of authority arrived also and everyone crowded around him at the top of the slipway, about twenty feet from me. People handed the man money and he issued them with tickets. No one paid any attention to me. I waddled up to the top of the ramp.

"Excuse me, I was here first," I protested to the man in charge.

"These people booked," he replied.

Now we need to pause just for a minute. I had risen at 5 a.m. and driven two hours to get here. I had been standing on this spot for an hour. Also, I was about three large cups of coffee short of total mental stability and on the brink of a dangerous medical condition known as caffeine tingle. This was not a good time to trifle with my equanimity.

"But I tried to book," I said. "My wife called and she was told you don't take bookings."

"You should have booked," he said again, and turned to transact business with another customer.

I looked hard at the back of his head. "I tried to book, you Pictish oaf!" I wailed in a little padded room in my brain that I keep for conversations like this. Outwardly and more calmly I said: "But I tried to book. The man told us you don't take bookings."

"Ah, you must have talked to Angus," he said. I don't remember what name he actually used, but he seemed to think that that was an adequate explanation for why I had just traveled all the way from Hampshire to remote Scotland to no purpose. I watched in dismay as he led his charges down the boat ramp and began loading them onto an open boat.

"I've come seven hundred miles," I said plaintively.

"*I've* come from Calgary," piped up a plumpish woman in a yellow rain slicker, pleased to outdo me.

"Oh, fuck off," I urged her from my padded room.

"There's a seat spare," the ferryman said to me.

"I beg your pardon?"

"You can have that seat if you want it."

He nodded at an empty seat.

Bewildered but overjoyed, I clambered aboard, lightly but intentionally hitting the Calgary woman in the back of the head with my pack, and took a seat. I paid the ferryman £6.50 for a ticket and we departed.

The journey across the loch took only about five minutes. At the other end, I climbed aboard a waiting minibus, paid the driver an additional £12 and a few minutes later, the bus loaded, we departed up a steep, bumpy track. Cape Wrath lay eleven miles away across a barren peninsula. I was going to get there after all. I was very happy again.

Cape Wrath isn't actually named for its violent nature. "Wrath" is an old Norse word for turning-place apparently—where Viking ships turned the corner to head for home—but it is plenty wild anyway. Winds in the winter can reach 140 miles an hour, we were told. The seas around northern Scotland, where the North Sea and

Atlantic crash together, are said to be the liveliest in the world. In one nineteenth-century storm, a little farther east along the coast, a wave struck the top of a lighthouse almost two hundred feet above the sea and tore a door off its hinges. That is pretty assertive weather.

Our driver was a cheery soul named Reg who kept up a line of patter as he hauled the vehicle around and through potholes. The road to Cape Wrath is technically a public highway, the U70, but it was last paved in 1956 and has more holes than asphalt. It crosses a great empty moorland, lightly scattered with old military trucks and half-tracks, put there as targets.

It took about an hour to traverse the eleven miles to the cape, where we were greeted by a big black-and-white lighthouse standing on a cliff high above a blowy sea. The lighthouse was built in 1828 by Robert Stevenson, grandfather of Robert Louis Stevenson. Today it is automated and doesn't need anyone to operate it. The site has a caretaker, named John Ure, who runs a café for visitors in one of the outbuildings. He is the peninsula's sole full-time inhabitant and must spend most of his life as just about the most isolated person in Britain.

There is nothing much to do at Cape Wrath. The lighthouse is closed to visitors, so all you can do is wander around and enjoy the views or go in the café. I stood on a grassy knoll and gazed for some time along the rugged, very beautiful sea cliffs stretching off toward faraway Dunnet Head. In the eastern distance, just offshore, was a large mass of land, which could only be Hoy, southernmost of the Orkney Islands. I looked later and found that it was eighty miles away. Is it actually possible to see that far?

I did a circuit of the lighthouse, then went and stood on the rocky precipice in front of it, and cautiously peered over the edge. It's a three-hundred-foot drop to sharp rocks and crashing waves. This really is the end of Britain. Ahead of me there was nothing but dancing seas all the way to the polar ice cap, to the left an equal emptiness to Newfoundland. I stood for a few minutes, reflecting with secret pride that I was the most northwesterly person in Great Britain. How often does anyone get to say that?

Now that I had reached the cape, I rather expected some feeling of finality and accomplishment to settle upon me. I was, of course, aware that I hadn't exactly pushed myself to my physical limits to get here, and that indeed most of my time traveling through Scotland so far had been spent fast asleep. Even so, this was a milestone moment. I might not be the first person in history to touch both ends of the Bryson Line, but I was certainly the first to do it and know he had done it.

So I stood, hands clasped at my back, staring into the wind, patiently waiting, but no special feeling came. At length, I abandoned that idea, and instead walked around the cliff top a little more, then went into the café in the hope that Mr. Ure could do something about my very serious need for caffeine. Happily, he could.

II

I spent a few more days touring around the Highlands. I went to Inverness and visited the battlefield at Culloden, where two thousand men lost their lives fighting the English, and then to Glencoe, where still more died when Campbells notoriously massacred Macdonalds, and I somberly reflected that the history of the Highlands is five hundred years of cruelty and bloodshed followed by two hundred years of way too much bagpipe music. I took a day ferry from Port Appin to the island of Lismore in the middle of Loch Linnhe and walked around there, too. It was splendid, though it rained a lot. My favorite experience was at Glenelg, on a little bay enjoying fine views across to the Isle of Skye. Just outside Glenelg, in a tranquil clearing that feels rarely visited, stand two of the most extraordinary structures you will find anywhere. They are called brochs and they are unique to Scotland.

Brochs are prehistoric stone towers, typically about thirty feet high and sixty feet or so around at the base, shaped roughly like the cooling towers of nuclear power stations, and made from carefully stacked stones in a complicated design involving two walls and a cavity between. There is no mortar in any of them, yet they were so well built that even after twenty-five hundred years many of them are still largely intact. The two at Glenelg are said to be the finest in mainland Scotland and they are simply, quietly, elegantly awesome. But what I particularly like about them is that they are completely mysterious. No one has any idea what they were for.

They would have been useless as dwellings or gathering places of any type because they were windowless and more or less completely dark inside. There is no sign that anyone was ever interred in them. It has been suggested that they might have been defensive bastions, but any people that crowded into them would effectively have been imprisoning themselves in a darkened space while leaving the invaders to help themselves to their crops and livestock. Doesn't seem entirely plausible. They might have been lookout towers, but many are in places where there was nothing in particular to look out upon. Usually they stand in isolation, but occasionally, as at Glenelg, they come in pairs. Their construction indicates that they were designed to be divided into multiple stories, but nearly all were built in places where there was too little wood to make floors. Every single thing about them, in short, is a bewilderment.

It occurred to me as I stood there that this was one of the things that I really, really like about Britain: it is unknowable. There is so much to it—more than any person can ever see or figure out or begin to know. There is so much stuff that no one can definitively say how much there actually is. Isn't that splendid? I had just by chance read an article in the journal *Current Archaeology* about a man named Olaf Swarbrick, a veterinarian by profession, who spent a good portion of his life tracking down all the ancient standing stones in Britain. It seems no one had done this before. Swarbrick found 1,502 stones at 1,068 locations. That is a much larger number than it sounds. If you decided to visit one standing stone a week, it would take you twenty years to see them all.

It is like that with every historic thing in Britain. If you tried to visit all the medieval churches in England—just England—at the rate of one a week, it would take you 308 years. You would need additional vastly daunting lengths of time to visit all the historic cemeteries, stately homes, castles, Bronze Age hill forts, giant figures carved in hillsides, and every other category of built structure. Brochs would take a decade to see. All the known archaeological sites in Britain would require no less than 11,500 years of your time.

You see what I am saying. Britain is infinite. There isn't anywhere in the world with more to look at in a smaller space—nowhere that has a greater record of interesting and worthwhile productivity over a longer period at a higher level. No wonder my trip didn't feel complete. I could never see it all.

I took that thought home with me and then on to America, where I had to go again for work. One day, not long after my Cape Wrath visit, I was in a very quiet department store in Indianapolis, just killing time, when a saleslady decided to be my new best friend and mentor. She followed me all around the menswear section and helpfully identified each type of clothing I touched.

"Those are our neckties," she would say. "We have more neckties over on this side of the table, too."

I would say thank you and she would say, "Uh-huh." She was about ninety-eight. Eventually she became interested in my accent. I told her that I had grown up in Iowa but had lived in England for years.

"England?" she said with unreserved amazement. "Why do you live in *England*?"

"Because it is nothing like Indianapolis" was my first and frankest thought, but of course I didn't say that. I just said something vague about marrying an English girl and liking it there.

"Uh-huh," she said. "And these are our shoes."

It occurred to me afterward, as I relaxed in a nearby food court (for I was living life to the full in Indianapolis), that her question was a reasonable one. Why would I choose to leave the most successful country in the world, where my taxes would always be lower, my house warmer, my portions of food larger, my gratifications more immediate and abundant, and decide instead to live on a rainy island adrift in a cold, gray sea?

As with most things in life that we take for granted, I didn't really have an answer to that. Not a considered one anyway. If someone said to me, "What are the five things you most like about the UK?" I would have to request time to think about it. I determined to make a list of my five reasons for choosing to live there. (Apart from family and friends, I should say for the record.) I already had my first reason thanks to my visit to the brochs of Glenelg: that Britain is delightfully and inexhaustibly distracting. But I wasn't at all sure what the other four ought to be.

I pulled out a notebook in the food court and began to list all the pleasing Britannic things I could think of, randomly, as they occurred to me:

Boxing Day
Country pubs
Saying "you're the dog's bollocks" as an expression of
    endearment or admiration
Jam roly-poly with custard
Ordnance Survey maps

I'm Sorry I Haven't a Clue (a popular and hilarious radio
   program)
Cream teas
The 20p piece
June evenings, about 8 p.m.
Smelling the sea before you see it
Villages with ridiculous names like Shellow Bowels and
   Nether Wallop

When I paused to review the list, I realized that it consisted
entirely of things I would never have encountered if I hadn't come
to England. That is the great thing about being a foreigner—that
you get to spend your life with a whole new set of cultural attach-
ments in addition to the ones you inherited at birth. Anybody who
has a second country is greatly favored, in my view, but if the second country is especially interesting and lively and diverse—if it
has cream teas, a noble history, and an extra day off at Christmas—
well, that's just the dog's bollocks, if you ask me. Anyway, that
became my second point: that Britain gave me a million good
things that I wouldn't otherwise have had.

Item three is that Britain is fundamentally sane. I appreciate that in
a country. I regret to say that this point also occurred to me while
traveling in my native land. Let me say at once that America is a
wonderful country. Think what the world would be like today if
the United States hadn't intervened in the Second World War and
led the reconstruction afterward. America has given us a pretty
decent modern world and doesn't always get enough thanks for
that. But for reasons that genuinely escape me, it has also become
spectacularly accommodating to stupidity.

Where this thought most recently occurred to me was in a hotel coffee shop in Baltimore, where I was reading the local paper, the *Sun,* and I saw a news item noting that Congress had passed a law prohibiting the U.S. Department of Health and Human Services from funding research that might lead, directly or indirectly, to the introduction of gun controls.

Let me repeat that but in slightly different words. The government of the United States refuses to let academics use federal money to study gun violence if there is a chance that they might find a way of reducing the violence. It isn't possible to be more stupid than that. If you took all the commentators from FOX News and put them together in a room and told them to come up with an idea even more pointlessly idiotic, they couldn't do it. Britain isn't like that, and thank goodness. On tricky and emotive issues like gun control, abortion, capital punishment, the teaching of evolution in schools, the use of stem cells for research, and how much flag waving you have to do in order to be considered acceptably patriotic, Britain is calm and measured and quite grown up, and for me that counts for a great deal.

Quality of life, I decided, is my fourth point. There is something in the pace and scale of British life—an appreciation of small pleasures, a kind of restraint with respect to greed, generally speaking—that makes life ineffably agreeable. The British really are the only people in the world who become genuinely excited when presented with a hot beverage and a small plain biscuit.

On international quality-of-life comparisons, Britain always does remarkably well. Some nations are happier and some are wealthier, but almost none are happier *and* wealthier. Britain also comes near the top in a category called "life satisfaction," which, I must say, surprised me. I've known the country pretty intimately for forty years and I don't recall ever meeting anyone you would really call satisfied, but then it occurred to me that that is the secret of it.

The British, you see, are always happy when they ought to be—when the sun is shining and they have a drink in their hands and that sort of thing—but they are also very good at remaining happy when others would falter. If, for instance, they are walking in the countryside and it starts to rain, they pull on their waterproofs and accept that that's just the way it sometimes is. Living in a British climate teaches patience and stoicism. I admire that.

But what really sets the British apart is that when things go very wrong and they have a legitimate reason to bitch deeply, bitterly, and at length, that is when they are the happiest of all. A Briton standing in a minefield with a leg blown off who can say, "I told you this would happen" is actually a happy man. I quite like that in a people.

My fifth reason is one I knew from the outset. I have put it last only because it is the most important to me. I don't suppose you will be surprised to hear that it is the beauty of the countryside. Goodness me, what an achievement.

Just after I returned home from America, I went to a place I had hoped to go while traveling for this book, but never quite managed to reach: the ancient White Horse of Uffington. This is a giant stylized chalk figure of a horse, nearly four hundred feet long, carved into a hillside in Oxfordshire. It is strikingly modern—it could have been designed by Picasso—and very beautiful. It stands just beneath the even more ancient track known as the Ridgeway.

This is where England gets really old. The Ridgeway has been a thoroughfare for at least ten thousand years. For a long time, nobody could say just how old the White Horse is, but now with a procedure called optical stimulated luminescence it is known that it has been there, galloping across its hillside, for three thousand years. So it is older than England, older than the English language. For all those centuries it has been continuously maintained. If people didn't climb up the hill and regularly tend it, grass would grow over the chalk and the White Horse would disappear. The White Horse is a magnificent creation but its preservation and continuous maintenance over three thousand years is perhaps more magnificent still.

You can't actually see the horse from the Ridgeway. You have to go partway down the hill to see it at all, and even then you can't tell what it is because of the contours of the landscape and the figure's immense size. But if you can't see the horse from White Horse Hill, you can see the countryside for miles around and that is awfully fine, too. I have said it many times before, but it really cannot be stated too often: there isn't a landscape in the world that is more artfully worked, more lovely to behold, more comfortable to be in than the countryside of Great Britain. It is the world's largest park, its most perfect accidental garden. I think it may be the British nation's most glorious achievement.

All Britain has to do now is look after it. I hope that's not too much to ask.

Afterword and Acknowledgments

In the interval between the events just described and the book's publication quite a lot happened in Britain.

In May 2015, the Conservative Party under David Cameron won a general election, which it interpreted as an endorsement of its strategy of perpetual austerity.

In July 2015, a panel called the Airports Commission under Sir Howard Davies recommended that a new runway be built at Heathrow rather than at Gatwick. The government's final decision on the matter will come after this book is published, but, if nothing else, it appears that Staines Moor and the lovely gravel ponds of Wraysbury are safe from development.

In the midst of all this, I became a citizen of the United Kingdom in a small ceremony in Winchester, and, most important of all, my daughter Felicity—last seen heavily pregnant in Chapter 4—had her baby (Daphne, exquisite, thank you).

As of this writing, I am still looking for Little Dribbling. I am sure it is out there somewhere.

As ever, I am immensely grateful to many people for encouragement and guidance in the preparation of this book. In particular, I wish to thank my saintly and patient editors and publishers Gerry Howard, Kristin Cochrane, Larry Finlay, and Marianne Velmans. I am also much in debt to my kind and sporting friends Aosaf Afzal, John Flinn, Andrew Orme, Daniel Wiles, Matt and Anya Ridley, Josef and Britta Vormoor, and the entire Davidson family—Jon, Donna, Max, and Daisy.

For additional help I am most grateful to Margaret Paren, chief executive of the South Downs National Park; Beth McHattie of English Heritage; Kate Davies and Lucy Barker of Stonehenge; and Edward J. Davis of Davis Wright Tremaine LLP in New York.

Thanks also to all my family, with special thanks to my daughter Catherine for devoted secretarial assistance, and to my son Sam for the author photograph. Above all, and as always, my most special thanks to my dear and saintly wife, Cynthia.

About the Author

Bill Bryson's bestselling books include *A Walk in the Woods, Notes from a Small Island, I'm a Stranger Here Myself, In a Sunburned Country, A Short History of Nearly Everything* (which earned him the 2004 Aventis Prize), *The Life and Times of the Thunderbolt Kid, At Home,* and *One Summer*. He lives in England with his wife.